What Adventures Shall We Have Today?

Travelling From More To Less In Search Of A Simpler Life

What Adventures Shall We Have Today?

written by Dan Colegate
edited by Esther Dingley

Copyright © 2020 Dan Colegate

www.estheranddan.com

www.instagram.com/estheranddan

www.facebook.com/estheranddan

To all of the wonderful people who have guided our steps

Thank you

Contents

Prologue

"Do you want to throw him?" I asked, gazing out over the cloister gardens of Wadham College and the ornate Oxford skyline beyond.

It was a perfect June evening in 2003. The early summer sun was lighting up the sky like a golden watercolour while the silhouettes of Oxford's many venerable rooftops, domes and battlements stood like timeless sentinels, apparently guarding against the rampant march of change. Yet in a city so full of youth, creativity and learning, change was always and inevitably in the air. Perhaps that's why Oxford captivates so many people, that beautiful balance of the new and the old perpetually dancing together. Not that my friend John and I had come up to the roof of the library to appreciate any of that. We were up here to make a sacrifice.

Initially, there had been nothing special about 'Pear Man'. He'd started out as a simple conference pear, not too big, not too small, not too green and with a fairly average length of stalk. But then, with just a few bits of molecular modelling kit and a little imagination, he'd become our mascot. With eyes of nitrogen (two bits of blue plastic), a nose of oxygen (white plastic) and electron-pair arms and legs (short plastic straws), a humble piece of fruit had been bought to life. For three months he'd sat astride the desk lamp John and I shared in the library, shrivelling and leaking slightly as we tried to cram as much chemistry knowledge into our brains as possible. But now it was time for him to go, a sacrifice to whatever Gods of exams might have been watching.

"No, you throw him" said John. So I did, tearing out his limbs and features before hurling the soggy fruit from six storeys up. We didn't even hear him land.

"Bar?" I asked.

1

"Bar" John agreed.

Tomorrow morning it would be our turn, along with almost two hundred other chemistry students scattered throughout the thirty-odd Oxford colleges, to join the other finalists sitting the exams that would determine their degree classification. We'd wake up, pull on our suits, clip on our white bow ties and shrug undergraduate gowns onto our young shoulders. We'd tuck a mortar board under our arms and pin a white carnation to our lapels, a flower that had been gifted to us by a friend, as per tradition. For later exams we'd wear a pink carnation until the very last paper when it would be a red one, a city-wide symbol of imminent freedom. We'd meet in the college entrance lodge with our friends, the same place we'd gathered for lectures together for the past three years, then walk slowly to the gilded Examination Schools building where we'd find out if we were ready. Or not.

For chemists, like us, it would be eight exam papers that would decide the issue. Twenty-four hours of examination time scattered across only four days. Three hours each morning, three in the afternoon. There had been no coursework. No modules. No credit already in the bank. Just four days and then the rest of our lives. Hence the light relief of 'Pear Man' and his silent fall from grace.

This time next week we'd be back in the bar with the others who'd already finished, watching the dwindling numbers still shackled to the library, still awaiting their turn. We'd have pinned on that red carnation, handed in our last answers and emerged to a crowd of shouting friends, confetti and cheap champagne. We'd probably have drunk ourselves into oblivion, nursed grateful hangovers and cried tears of joy or regret.

But then what? Adult life was waiting just on the other side of this long anticipated hurdle. In many ways university life had been simple. There'd been no worrying about what to do or where to be. No existential angst about

2

who I was or what it meant. It had all just made sense, even when it was hard. Especially when it was hard in fact! I'd relished the cerebral challenges and the minor victories over tricky questions, confident in the belief that it all meant something, even if I didn't know what.

For me, living in a college surrounded by hundreds of like-minded, kind and enthusiastic people while studying a subject that I found fundamentally interesting had been simply the happiest time of my life (so far). A whole world of experience had been opened up to me, experiences far removed from anything I could have imagined before coming to live in the city of dreaming spires.

I was the son of good, humble, hard-working parents. I'd spent my childhood helping dad on his milkround and watching mum working late nights in call centres. My own first job at sixteen had been the nightshift in a warehouse packing newspapers. I'd never encountered bow-ties, punts, rowing boats and the ridiculousness of cucumbers floating in Pimm's before. But I'd loved it. All of it. I'd thrown myself into Oxford life with the confidence and enthusiasm that came from having no idea how little I knew. Even surrounded by unnecessary cutlery, wood-panelled halls and faded portraits of severe-looking, long-dead dons, it had never crossed my mind to feel out of place. Quite the opposite. I'd felt a greater sense of belonging here than I had at school, where enthusiasm or ambition had been mostly ridiculed.

In fact, while I felt fairly ready for the exams in the morning, I didn't really want to face what came after them. I wanted to bottle this moment on the roof instead, right on the cusp of opportunity but without having to face the uncertainty of the future.

A Necessary Push

"There's no time for anaesthetic" are not words anybody would ever wish to hear, especially not from a tired young surgeon at midnight on a sleeting January evening. As he stood over me in the accident and emergency ward, staring at my bloated abdomen and hastily explaining why it was necessary to fetch a scalpel very quickly, part of me struggled to believe this was really happening. To say that this was an unwelcome development in the grand scheme of life would be to put it mildly. In less than four weeks Esther and I were supposed to be getting married.

In what should be a hopelessly romantic anecdote, but isn't, the very first words I ever said to Esther were "I love you". Unfortunately I shouted those words into a friend's mobile phone, a phone that I'd grabbed hold of shortly before staggering into an unfamiliar college bar and trying to convince a young female couple that I was a lesbian. It's not something I'm proud of. I wasn't a champion of the gender identity movement, just a drunk young fool with all the charisma of a wonky door handle.

Esther and I wouldn't actually meet in person for several more weeks and, when we did, I didn't exactly make the best second impression either. There's no need to dwell on the incident involving an oversized stone head, a sharp set of railings and a surprisingly heavy traffic-cone that left me with blood pouring down my best white shirt, except to say that it was the catalyst for the most important relationship of my life. "Oh, you're the idiot that spiked himself outside the Sheldonian" doesn't sound like a promising seed for romance, but somehow we turned it into one. I suppose I should be grateful that, even back then, I

4

was sometimes able to manage long intervals of near-normality between my frequent episodes of climbing things, falling off things, and putting my foot in my mouth.

To cut a long story short, that first unfortunate encounter left me with both an interesting scar and a meeting that would blossom into a love affair, one that's lasted eighteen years and counting so far. When I finished my degree I remained in Oxford for another year, taking up a job as a research assistant in the newly opened Chemistry Research Laboratory so that we could live together. Then, when Esther secured her own first-class degree in economics, I insisted we move to Durham where I had the offer to study for a PhD.

"Why rush?" Esther had questioned. "We have our whole lives to work and save. Why not postpone the start date? Let's adventure now while we can."

"It's too risky" I countered. "We're not students any more. It's time to get serious."

Throughout my childhood I'd been immersed in a work ethic so strong that you could break rocks on it. One or both of my parents always seemed to be working, no matter what time of day it was, and I'd always understood that they did so in order to take care of me and my two younger brothers. Likewise my maternal grandparents, who were just as important in our lives, instilled the same principles regarding jobs and responsibilities. Grandad had started at Boots sweeping floors and risen up over the decades to a managerial role. Every morning he caught a 5.30 a.m. bus so that he was never late and, as he told us, so that he could get ahead. Working 'just a bit harder than the rest' wasn't just a good idea, it was simply how things got done. It was what decent adults did.

"If it was fun son, they wouldn't call it work" my dad used to say, along with other classics such as "life's shit, then you die." These were the kinds of maxims I was raised to believe in and that I accepted as fact. Needless to

5

say, going off travelling after graduation didn't fit into this world view. Esther and I had travelled a little during the long summer holidays, bookending our weeks of Interrail adventures with various menial jobs. Thanks partly to some successful college grant applications, but mostly to Esther's imagination, an initially sceptical young Dan had experienced the joys of city-hopping by train and the happy simplicity of tent life.

We'd met the authentic Santa Claus on the Arctic circle in Finland (he's very tall), got stuck in a nudist campsite somewhere near Munich (I can't say where, we were lost), and mistook Genoa for Geneva in a hellish night-train saga that almost got someone killed (spoiler alert: it didn't). They'd been eventful weeks and I'd enjoyed them very much, but that had been student life, not adulthood. It was time to box up such childhood dreams and call them nice memories. Or at least that was my opinion.

At the same time, I'd been born with a birth defect that had left me totally bowel incontinent. While my parents had made the brave decision to send me to mainstream school, one side-effect of that choice was that even as an infant I became incredibly good at hiding my frequent accidents from the world. By the time I was a teenager even my parents thought I'd "grown out of them". Sadly the truth was quite the opposite. I still soiled myself dozens of times a day, but since I'd never known anything else I came to accept that as well. Stuffing my underwear with tissue, if anything, made me feel 'special' precisely because I could deal with it. I felt 'stronger' than everyone else.

A more positive consequence of spending so much of my childhood energy avoiding "bad attention" (from adults and classmates alike) was that doing well at school became a reliable source of "good attention". I've no doubt that my 'problem', as it was always known in the family, was part of the reason I ended up with a first-class degree, not quite top of the year but not far off it. Such things

6

mattered to me back then. By the time a PhD was put on the table Esther was pretty much the only person who knew I still had problems. Even then, she didn't know the full extent of them.

All of which perhaps explains why walking away or even postponing a PhD just didn't seem like a valid option to me at the time. I was so determined that I even threw down an ultimatum. I was going to Durham and Esther could come with me or not. It was up to her. That she did stay with me, going on to complete a master's degree in Durham herself, was a huge relief. I thought I'd saved her from herself.

So we bought our first home together and began making a life 'up north'. After almost four years of lab work in Durham we moved again, this time to Cambridge, where I'd landed a job as a postdoctoral research assistant in the Department of Engineering. Esther, as able and qualified as always, secured a fixed-term fellowship at Wolfson College.

In a sense this entire story could well have ended there. If both of us had chosen to continue climbing the academic career ladder at that point then we might still be on it now. Esther even had the offer of a prestigious PhD scholarship of her own on the table in Cambridge, a huge achievement in her specific field of study.

Except life is never so simple, or at least it never seemed to be back then. As two young, ambitious, driven high-achievers always looking for an extra edge, during our final year in Durham we'd entered (and won) a business planning competition. 'Student entrepreneurship' was becoming a big buzzword at the time and our idea for a networking website specifically designed for early career researchers was a genuinely novel idea back then. We'd even launched a proof-of-concept website, with me teaching myself database and web programming alongside my PhD and Esther marketing the result. After a few months we had

7

over twenty thousand members signed up and using the site from more than eighty countries. Initially we'd felt like champions of the world.

Now, running this website alongside demanding day jobs had been tough to say the least. Various people kept advising us to pick one focus and run with it. Business types said we should knock academia on the head and secure some major investment. Academic types said "well done, but get back to your research." In the end we did neither and kept trying to juggle too many balls at once.

Torn between the life I'd long worked to create, but which I was finding unexpectedly hollow now that I'd got it, and the promise of life-changing successes in the totally unfamiliar business world, we spent the next year working twenty-hour days to fit everything in. Living in a tiny studio flat close to the Cambridge ring road, a weekend treat became a pack of doughnuts and a 'day out' in the bland conference room of the engineering building, working side-by-side on business plans and site code. "Life's shit, then you die" indeed!

It was around this time that any last traces of romance slipped away from us. We clung onto the belief that we still loved each other, beneath all of the animosity, but it was hard. "We'll get through this" was like the motto to our life.

It seemed ludicrous to think that we'd only entered that initial business planning competition because we had a dream of spending more time together. Now, about a year later, I dreaded coming home because it just meant more work, more stress and more problems. I even stopped enjoying the academic stuff, viewing it mostly as the 'easy' part of my day, which isn't something you're supposed to say about research work at Cambridge.

But that's precisely why we couldn't give up either. The more pain and arguments we battled through, the more trapped we felt. All we had to do, we told ourselves, was secure some investment, then it would all be worth it. Of course, when we did eventually secure some investment it didn't really solve anything, it just changed the problems and made them bigger.

I won't even try and explain the complex and overlapping chaos of income streams that came next. Like the good little capitalists that we'd become, we chased every opportunity that came our way, never saying no and never considering if our bodies or our relationship could bear the strain.

Four years after moving to Cambridge, by the summer of 2013, we were looking back on a life trajectory that had left us both shell-shocked. We had a dormant business, a dried up consultancy, three rental houses, correspondingly enormous debt, lapsed academic careers, love handles and matching diagnoses of depression. I was on a phased return-to-work scheme in a mid-level administrative job at Newcastle University. Esther had retrained completely and become a self-employed personal trainer, though she now had her own additional diagnosis of ME to contend with as well.

As mad it might sound, life had actually improved a lot since the business had failed. We'd got more free time back in our lives for one thing, time we often used to spend our weekends walking in the Lake District, a new discovery for us. Or we'd just sit and be together. Then again, something was still deeply wrong. Neither of us seemed able to enjoy the many comforts and gifts in our lives and that bothered us deeply. We hated ourselves for our own ingratitude when there were billions of people with much bigger problems than us. Why couldn't we just be happy? In my case I largely felt either numb or angry, there was nothing in between, as though my settings had been frazzled by the previous half-decade.

The reason I was on a phased return-to-work was because somewhere among the mess of investors, broken promises and spreadsheets overtaking tenderness in our relationship, I'd finally sought medical help for that lifelong bowel incontinence I mentioned. There aren't many positive things that can be said about anorectal physiology tests, most of which had left me feeling like the pocket on a pole-vaulter's runway, but it had been the gateway to a world of support I'd always insisted (to myself and Esther) didn't even exist.

After a year of tests that needed lubricant and various subsequent surgeries, I now faced a choice. I could continue with the do-it-myself home enema kit I'd already been prescribed, a solution that had instantly eliminated 95% of my accidents but was proving troublesome for my work routine. Or I could wear a permanent colostomy bag.

The latter is what my employers seemed to want. At the time my enema routine required a high degree of flexible working that hadn't been part of the job description, issues a colostomy would almost certainly overcome. On the other hand, the enemas were basically working for me.

'Quality of life' and 'self-care' obviously weren't phrases that had played much of a role in my life to this point, but it was this particular decision that would eventually bring them to the fore. When I got a call one Friday afternoon from the hospital saying "we've had a cancellation, can you come in on Monday for the colostomy surgery the next day?" we looked at each other and just knew we weren't making good decisions any more. More than anything else, we just needed a rest.

Buoyed up by the certainty that somewhere inside of us were still two starry-eyed, loved-up teenagers who viewed the world with optimism instead of cynicism and regret, we resolved pretty much there and then to take a career break. We'd sell all but one of the houses, clear most of our debts and take off for a while. Six months was the original plan, long enough to have some adventures and relax but not so long that we couldn't slip back into a more peaceful version of the life we'd be leaving behind temporarily.

We might have been depressed but we weren't stupid, or so we thought at least. We couldn't, and wouldn't, walk away from everything we'd achieved. Having been raised to define 'success' as the ability to pay the bills each month, it never occurred to us that we'd been 'wrong' or that we hadn't succeeded in a material sense. We still believed that we'd done well thanks to our work ethic, intellect and willingness to act. Walking away completely would have been madness to us back then.

No, a career break and a bit of streamlining was all that we needed, a chance to recharge and be together for a while. So we began making preparations to do just that. Naturally, we also managed to turn that into a 'project' as well.

By the time Christmas 2013 arrived we were less than two months away from a February wedding (travel-themed, naturally), which would then be followed by a six-month-long trekking expedition as a honeymoon inspired by our walks in the Lake District. Not quite the restful 'break' we'd first daydreamed of, but it would be an impressive accomplishment nonetheless. Hell, we'd probably be even more employable when we got back.

As you might expect, introducing a layer of bickering about wedding decorations, seating plans, route choices and resupply boxes did rather suck the joy out of our planned escape. What was supposed to be a chance to rediscover our love for one another did, at times, seem to have transformed into a festering pit of mutual loathing out of which we now had to climb. To be honest, when one of the old surgery wounds on my belly tore slightly and left me with a hernia, I was slightly relieved. At least it gave us something else to focus on.

A mercifully swift referral to see a surgeon combined with a last-minute cancellation seemed, at first, to put our plans back on track.

"No carrying anyone over the threshold" he told me, "but you should be able to carry a pack by mid-March as long as you take it easy."

Happy to agree to such a mild restriction, I went under the knife the very next morning. Unfortunately, seven days later I had red and yellow discolouration spreading from my belly button to my spine. Having proved myself determined to ignore the fever and the swelling, it was Esther who, on the advice of a friend, insisted on taking me to the out-of-hours doctor at Durham's University Hospital. The doctor stared in silence at the wobbly bulge for a few seconds, said "well, I'll just call the surgeon then", and personally took me over to accident and emergency. These were the first stages in the process that lead to those fateful words "there's no time for anaesthetic".

The cut was excruciating but it was what came next that nearly finished me off, a seemingly endless splurge of putrid slime that gushed out of me and began pooling under my back, soaking into my clothes and filling the air with the scent of long-rotten meat (which is precisely what it was). That's also when Esther walked back into the room.

When it had become obvious that I wasn't going home that evening, but was still waiting for the on-call surgeon to come out of theatre, she'd popped home to collect a few essentials for me. When she'd left I'd been dozing slightly on a gurney, a saline drip in my arm and a small amount of codeine giving me a slight buzz. But now, returning with some clean pyjamas and a toothbrush, she found me covered in my own blood and guts with a strange gentleman's fingers probing about beneath my skin.

Now, I'd never actually seen anybody faint before, not in real life. Thankfully the surgeon had and, without removing a single finger from my innards, he used his clean hand to catch Esther and deposit her on a nearby chair. What a guy!

Twenty minutes of scraping, prodding and a second opinion from a senior colleague later, the surgeon gave us the lowdown.

"I've done as much as I can for now" he said "but the inside of your wound doesn't look good. It's black and that could mean necrotising fasciitis. My colleagues agree it probably is, so we need to cut it out urgently. I can't do that while you're awake."

"How much will you need to cut?"

"Until I get in there I just can't say. The external colouring is almost the whole way around. If it's spread too far we'll have to keep you in an induced coma in intensive care so that we can monitor and return you to surgery as required. It's bad Dan. This is serious."

What I didn't get told at the time, because the surgeon only said it to Esther after I'd been wheeled up to a ward, was just how close I'd already come to death.

"Well done" he told her. "If you hadn't bought him in tonight I'm almost certain he wouldn't have woken up tomorrow. When that abscess had burst internally he would have gone straight into toxic shock and died. Make sure you say a proper goodbye though, just in case."

It was three in the morning when they came to wheel me to theatre. I'd been placed in a room alone on the ward and I was grateful that the night staff had let Esther sit with me. I can't really remember what we talked about but I do know that I said 'sorry' a lot.

Hours earlier we'd been cutting out wedding decorations, bickering about dehydrated soup pouches and wondering how far we'd get on our hike. Now a cloud of uncertainty hung over the question of whether we even had a shared future. One thing was certain though. Never mind putting our lives on pause and leaving the door open to return. If we came through this then life would never be the same again. We were going to make sure of it.

Finding Homer

While I was saying hello (and goodnight) to an armful of general anaesthetic, Esther got the rough end of the deal, returning home to a silent flat littered with half-made wedding decorations and yet-to-be-packed hiking gear. Not knowing when, or even if, we'd speak again, she embarked on a one-woman-war against every speck of dust in sight. By the time our good friend Ali arrived at seven a.m., she was on her hands and knees scrubbing the kitchen floor.

That was when the good news arrived. I was out of surgery and it looked like the necrotising fasciitis hadn't spread as far as it might have done. I'd had a big slice of belly taken out but, provided the antibiotic cocktail I was now receiving did the business, it looked like I'd be climbing things, falling off them and pestering Esther for a while longer yet.

To be honest, I was too stoned on morphine to realise any of that at the time. By the time I came down from my happy place and started getting acquainted with the melon-sized chunk of myself that was missing, the news was increasingly positive. I still stayed in hospital for almost a fortnight though, during which time we made the tough decision to cancel our wedding and put our previous career-break-cum-honeymoon plans on ice. Instead, we stayed home, with me riding the sofa and Esther doing her best to stop me wandering around. I never was an easy-going patient. Our days were punctuated by nurse visits and the Sochi Winter Olympics, . Who knew ice dancing could spark so much controversy!

Slowly but surely my health returned, aided in no small part by my live-in nutritionist and full-time carer. Walks to the end of the street soon became walks around the block. Esther was a total and utter champion throughout, dealing with my frustration and frequent lack of gratitude in addition to soiled dressings and every other aspect of home life. It would be mid-April by the time the consultant responsible for my care gave me a tentative 'all clear'. I still had a surface wound but hospital-level attention was no longer required. It was time to get on with our lives. The only question now was 'how?'

In a cruel irony, the infected hernia repair had also been removed along with my pound of flesh, leaving me with the same hole in my abdominal wall that had started the whole affair. For the time being the hole was apparently being plugged by a mass of dense scar tissue, but we'd been told explicitly that I would need months of gentle exercise, slowly building up before I could even consider something as strenuous as carrying a fully-laden rucksack across the planet.

Likewise, formal unemployment was imminent. Newcastle University had bent over backwards to support us, extending my notice period for an extra two months so that I could continue working from home during my recovery, including for several weeks after my replacement had started work. By the time the all clear arrived I had a few weeks of paid employment left and my boss seemed fairly happy to ignore me now that I was somewhat surplus to requirements. But the reality remained that, since Esther had already handed over all of her clients as well, there would soon be no more income. We needed a new plan, and quickly. Fortunately, one solution stood out above all the rest.

Motorhomes were not something that had ever been on my radar before. The Colegate Clan had briefly dabbled in summer caravan holidays but after one particularly eventful fortnight in Cornwall, during which our awning was torn away by a storm, our campsite was cut off by flooding, and I burnt all of the skin off my right foot by dropping a boiling kettle on it, we stopped. I'm still not sure why. Even now I can fondly recall my brother Chris sympathetically asking if "he's going to cry like this all night?"

That made Esther, relatively speaking at least, an old hand. Her parents had once owned an American Winnebago RV, nicknamed 'Winnie', who had taken them across the channel every July for wandering tours around the coastal idylls of Brittany and Normandy. Her dad would drive while her mum made sandwiches, they'd sing songs, soak up the sun, dine out on moules marinière in petite family bistros, and dance the night away at summer fetes in the villages where they stayed. Esther still gets misty-eyed talking about those times now.

Of course, deciding to buy a motorhome and actually doing so are two different things. I've always found the physics and chemistry of combustion much more engaging than the mechanics of cylinders and fuel injectors. I didn't even pass my driving test until I was twenty-six, so I've never had more than the slightest awareness of vehicles, their value and the pitfalls of buying them.

Then again, I reckon this is an angst many people feel when standing face-to-face with a used car salesman, and the salesman knows it. We go around kicking tyres, staring knowingly at rusty bits and looking at oily plastic parts, all the time fighting the inner voice that says "I don't know what I'm doing". Short of a missing engine and a family of badgers living under the bonnet, I really couldn't say if a vehicle is going to get me beyond the car park or not.

Gluing a living room to the back of a builder's van only makes matters worse. All of a sudden it isn't just spark plugs and brake lines that can go wrong, but toilet seats and 12 volt fridge-freezers. Plus they can be frighteningly expensive. A new motorhome can easily cost over fifty thousand pounds and they hold their value pretty well. Trying to work out what a fair price is for a second-hand motorhome is nigh on impossible. Objectively assessing a near-infinite range of combinations of mileage, layout, length, engine size, service history, solar panels, refillable gas systems, number of owners, bike racks....etc. is like trying to read with your eyes shut. You stare and stare and stare, but you still can't be sure what you're looking at.

After several interminable afternoons lost on Auto Trader, eBay and the Caravan Club website, we at least agreed on a budget. Fifteen thousand pounds, we reckoned, would get us something more than a battered van with a mattress and a bucket in the back but without totally wiping out the travel fund we had.

We felt very lucky that, whatever we might have experienced in the preceding decade, it had put us in a position where we owned both a mortgaged house and flat plus had some cash in the bank. As long as there were no major, unexpected repairs and provided we could rent both out to reliable tenants, we'd have enough income to cover about half of our 'guesstimated' expenses on the road. The rest would be coming from our remaining savings.

That said, we still felt very precious about the impending outlay. Like almost everyone else, our savings represented years of hard work, foregone holidays, arguments and, in our case, illnesses. We didn't want to throw that away because some smooth-talking shyster dazzled us with his sales pitch.

Over the course of the next week we drove a lot of miles and had a few false starts, most of them involving despicably inaccurate descriptions and palpably slimy dealers, one of whom arranged for three potential buyers to arrive simultaneously to try and drive his price up. But it was on a damp Harrogate driveway that we eventually fell in love. For a man who'd long considered all cars to be nothing more than moving boxes, to step inside a vehicle and suddenly feel so much connection was an unexpected, and slightly worrying, experience.

Homer just felt right. She (because obviously she was female) was five-and-a-half metres long, two-and-a-bit metres wide and despite being ten years' old, she was still in almost mint condition. Her interior was nothing like any of the newer, space-age designs we'd seen online. Instead, with her plump yellow and red upholstery, brown carpets, beech effect cabinets, two-bottle wine rack and full-sized oven/grill/hob combination in a natty shade of beige, she was more like a rolling living room from the eighties. Instantly we loved her for it. She even had two double beds, one in the bulbous over-the-cab construction that made her look like an enormous white mushroom from the front, and another we could build downstairs if we wanted to spoil ourselves.

As luck would have it, we were the first to view Homer and we were too in love to walk away. We knew it and evidently so did the seller. The asking price was seventeen-and-a-half thousand and although we tried to haggle, we might as well have haggled with a bollard. Still, at least the Yorkshireman in question agreed to leave in a thimbleful of diesel, just enough to get us to the nearest petrol station (as long as we chose the one at the bottom of the hill). Later on we discovered an overlooked tin of baked beans in a cupboard which further sweetened our sense of victory.

We paid a deposit and arranged a day to collect Homer the following week, giving time for a very minor fault that we'd noticed to be repaired (once we'd agreed the deal, the seller really was very helpful about it all). In the meantime, the other activities required to put our old life in stasis gathered pace. In fact, the speed of change now that we'd made a commitment truly astonished us.

Everything that wasn't coming on tour was jammed unceremoniously into boxes and vacuum bags, ferried across Durham and manhandled into our friend Barry's attic. Our flat went up for rent and was taken the very next morning at the full asking price, the only condition being that the tenant wanted to move in just a few days later. And we asked around for friends who could look after our house rabbits for a year, with people coming forwards within twenty-four hours.

It all happened so fast that by the time we were driving back from Harrogate to Durham in Homer, celebrating glamorously with a flask of tea and a sandwich at Wetherby Service Station, it was already our full-time home. I still had a week of formal employment left and only a nearby friend's driveway to do it from.

Whether any other neighbours noticed that our lights were on at night, or that I emerged each morning freshly shaved and suited from what was essentially a Tupperware on wheels, we never knew. I certainly didn't tell anyone at the office that their soon-to-be-leaving colleague was living out of a van.

One of my final acts at work was to be present at a potentially very lucrative license negotiation, seated alongside a dozen university heavyweights facing off against an army of expensive corporate lawyers. It was mostly pleasant enough as the various sub-sub-sub-clauses were hammered out, yet I found my mind regularly drifting to the fact that Doctor Daniel M. Colegate, Research & Enterprise Team, would soon be going home to his five metre house, emptying his toilet cassette and driving south into the sunset.

My final day in the office was both joyous and sad. I'd already been a peripheral presence for at least a fortnight, watching my more-than-capable replacement listen politely and then find her own, better ways of doing things anyway. It had been fun, but it was also bittersweet. In a sense, I'd already left long before my last day, though it was nice to be presented with a pair of insulated Thermos mugs and a small portable kettle from my colleagues over a final shared lunch. And then, as is the way of these things, everyone went back to their desks.

As I sat twiddling my thumbs in a corner, watching the clock and wondering if it would be inappropriate to leave at two-thirty, I reflected on what a bizarre few months it had been. It was now the end of April and just four months earlier we'd been planning a wedding-cum-trekking-project. Since then, I'd had two surgeries, almost died, managed not to, put our entire material life into boxes and bought a portable sofa with an engine attached to it.

Life, it seemed, was a funny old thing. And so, with a final goodbye and a spring in my step, I walked out into the early afternoon sunshine for my final commute.

Due South

There's an art to squeezing one's life into a small space. During the time we'd spent squatting on a driveway we'd been gradually refining our routines and packing as we adapted to life in a compact living-room-cum-kitchen-cum-bedroom. I suppose most people pack their motorhomes and then move in, but we simply hadn't had the time. Instead, for the first week, we'd gotten used to having 'stuff' covering pretty much all of the surfaces, stuff that had to be moved around if we wanted to accomplish anything complicated, like boiling water or using the toilet.

Homer, as with most motorhomes of her age, had no storage spaces accessible from the outside. Everything we took with us had to be packed and available from inside of our living space, one way or another. Bike helmets went under the bench seat, our juicer was in the wardrobe, hiking boots got stacked behind the driving seats and everything loose got packed in with a thick wedge of socks and underwear. Thanks largely to Esther's efforts while I was daydreaming and clock-watching at the office, everything had found a place in the end. She'd even managed to make space for the thirty kilograms of homemade dehydrated soup we'd been stockpiling for our cancelled trekking expedition.

We'd made the soups using more than a dozen different recipes, all of which came out tasting of just two flavours once they were rehydrated: red or brown. We couldn't live with the idea of wasting so much usable food (or invested time). That's why we had sandwich bags of powder jammed into all sorts of nooks and crannies, regardless of whether my underpants would smell like korma or my hiking boots of pizza by the time I next used them.

Rattling south on the A1(M) from Durham, with Little Lion Man by Mumford and Sons booming out of the cab speakers, holding hands and singing along with our modified lyrics (..."we really fucked it up this time, didn't we my dear...."), was a moment of pure exhilaration and total liberation. It was as though we'd just shed a heavy burden and were standing tall for the first time in months. Our hasty preparations had been exciting but this was a whole new level of thrill. I couldn't remember feeling this much hope and optimism for years, almost like that distant evening on the roof of Wadham's library.

A month later we rolled into the furnace of Besançon in eastern France, about halfway down the country and not too far from Switzerland. Four weeks seemed to have vanished in a puff of farewell visits and hazy late-spring happiness. I don't think there was a family member who hadn't sat and smiled from one of Homer's plump cushions. Parents, siblings, grandparents and family pets, all had boarded our new home and gotten the always-brief tour.

"So, this is the living room / bedroom / kitchen, and this is the bathroom. Ta-da!"

My nana had been a little unsettled when we first announced our plans to take off in a motorhome, responding with an uncertain "Oh" before leaving the room with the words "I'll just go and put the kettle on then". But by the time she met Homer 'in person' we could see that the idea had now become accepted. It was 'only for a year' after all.

I could also understand her initial reticence. In my grandparents' own words, I'd always been the grandson that they "didn't have to worry about". The sensible one. The Oxford one. The reliable one. Now I was the unemployed one. The lost one. The "we don't know where he is" one. Still, weighed down by a bagful of homegrown cucumbers and tomatoes, we'd been hugged and kissed on our way with all the love and care that grandparents offer.

23

Parting had been even more emotional for Esther, whose 96-year-old Oma (the Dutch word for grandma) had recently moved into an assisted living apartment complex. She remained, as usual, in robust health with a mischievous twinkle in her eye. Having lived in occupied Holland during the Second World War, this was a lady who had once waded into flooded shell craters searching for allied food parcels, doing so barefoot so that tins and packets could be found with toes sunk into the dangerously sucking mud. Some of her friends had drowned doing the same thing, just one of many tragedies and atrocities she'd been exposed to during the occupation. She'd never lost her enthusiasm for life though.

While a nomadic existence was a universe away from my own upbringing, Esther's mother had come to the UK with a suitcase in the sixties, so travelling was more in her blood than mine. Oma even treated us to our very first Satnav, an entry-level device that we called Goma and who directed us down a three-foot-wide cycle track within ninety seconds of switching her on. Six years later and she's still playing the same tricks on us. I think we only keep her nowadays because it's fun to watch several hours vanish from the remaining journey time whenever we ignore her.

Anyway, back in summer 2014, with a still-semi-trusted Satnav and a truckload of good wishes at our back, we eventually drove away from family and friends towards whatever unplanned and unknown events awaited us. Lots of people had asked us in the preceding weeks what we wanted to see and where we wanted to go? These were both excellent questions, especially for two people setting off in a travelling home. We hadn't spent a lot of time seeking advice online, but the few motorhome bloggers we'd looked at back then seemed to have done things like visiting every capital city in Europe, for example, or driven from Paris to Moscow. Yet each time people had asked us where we were going, we'd been unable to come up with a solid answer.

The best we'd managed was that "it's not a particular place we're looking for, but a feeling".

Personally I still think that's a reasonable objective, it just doesn't do much good when you're driving past the industrial chimneys of Rotterdam with an unprogrammed Satnav looking at you accusingly. We did, for a fleeting moment, consider driving to the place where the borders of Holland, Belgium and Germany all come together, just for something to do. There's a special marker there, apparently, and a maze. Fortunately we then realised that it would be totally and utterly dull, so instead we just drove south hopefully, pausing in Luxembourg primarily to fill up on miraculously cheap fuel. We did take a stroll into Luxembourg city, but it was a Sunday and there are only so many closed banks you can look at.

On reflection, I think we already had a vague idea that we wanted to go to 'the mountains' but there was still nothing fixed in our minds by the time we arrived in Besançon, eight driving hours south of Holland. Also, although Besançon itself is really quite lovely, positioned in a horseshoe bend on the River Doubs with an extensive walled citadel and a stunning cathedral, we didn't know any of that when we pulled up. All we knew was that we were allowed to park a motorhome there. That really had been our sole reason for coming this way.

Motorhome aires, also known as camperstops or stellplatzen depending on where you are and who you're talking to, are essentially places where motorhomes are formally allowed to park overnight. Sometimes they're free; sometimes they charge; sometimes you can only stay for a certain length of time; some have water and waste emptying facilities while others are just for parking. No two aires are ever quite the same, either in terms of services or local amenities, but for weary travellers who don't want to risk falling foul of any unknown local rules, the key point is that they exist.

In fact, in most European countries they exist in huge numbers, especially France. Since this was in the Dark Ages of 2014 and years before we got ourselves a smartphone, we were using a good old fashioned book to find places to sleep. In the front of the book was a generic map showing different parts of Europe, each with red dots and page numbers to direct the reader to the relevant details and GPS coordinates. Many of these maps were so smothered in red dots it looked like the continent had developed a rash. Not so in the UK, unfortunately, which had the guidebook equivalent of a near-perfect complexion.

During our farewell tour of Britain we'd always felt highly conspicuous pulling up near to friends' houses in our big white box and had, several times, been asked to move on before we'd even turned off the engine. People had come dashing out of their houses in their dressing gowns as though we were about to set up a permanent pitch on their driveway, shit on their lawn and tether a horse to their fenceposts. Thankfully for us these were the exceptions. Generally speaking, we just got funny looks or our friends got a polite knock to ask if their "visitors" were staying for long?

Quite why the idea that people might park for a night in a quiet spot, make no noise and leave without a trace the next morning is basically tolerated in France, for example, but not the UK remains unclear to me. Perhaps there's more of a perception that people would abuse such privileges in Britain? That it would lead to subsequent falls in house prices? That the world would come crashing down as traveller kingdoms arose on every unguarded street corner? Or maybe people are just nosier?

Either way, from what we've seen countless times across Europe, providing a dedicated place for motorhomes to park for free usually does little more than ensuring a steady flow of extra customers for local shops and restaurants. Certainly the Besançon motorhome aire was full with smart white boxes when we arrived late on that Sunday evening.

By ten o'clock the next morning, with a hot sun climbing quickly into the clear blue sky, Homer's insides were rapidly becoming like a greenhouse. By the end of the day it would get so hot that a couple of interior light fittings even started to melt. It was only early June and as a mini-heatwave swept through, we were just starting to get into the swing of our still novel and exciting motorhome lifestyle. Looking out of our window, deck chairs were being produced by various neighbours of all nationalities, as were pastries and full cafetières. Evidently the pace of motorhome life on the outskirts of this riverside town was happily sedate.

For us, after a few pleasantries, we set off for a short jog along the river followed by a stroll up to visit the old town and cathedral. Unplanned ambling had long been our preferred mode of sightseeing.

During our summer travels as students, after forking out for the Interrail pass and plane fare, we were left with a daily budget of around five pounds each per day, so our activities were mostly limited to 'strolling aimlessly about'. We'd roll into a new city, walk around in search of a campsite or tourist office (whichever came first), ditch our heaviest possessions and go for a wander. This was in the era of expensive internet cafes, so we rarely knew what we'd find. Our destinations were chosen based on a vague combination of things people said to us, convenient train connections, and a crumpled stack of pages we'd torn out of travel brochures on our way to the airport.

Destinations such as Salzburg, Vienna, Venice, Geneva and Copenhagen were just names and photographs to us before we arrived, but through our independent and unguided explorations they'd gradually and beautifully yielded up countless scenic treasures. The gardens at the Mirabell Palace, the columns of St Stephen's Cathedral, the hectic surface of the Grand Canal and the colourful jumble of masts along Nyhavn, all had opened their arms to our impoverished student selves. And, as a result, we'd learned that there was nothing like walking to really understand and appreciate a city, getting utterly and wonderfully lost in its intricacies rather than hopping between landmarks via underground metro trains and crowded tourist buses.

That's why we've never seen walking through an unfamiliar town as a poor alternative but rather as our activity of choice. In Besançon we strolled hand-in-hand along the picturesque Vauban Quay, looking out on the sedate waters of the Doubs to our left and the bustle of French city life humming around us. Bakeries were busy, cafes were setting out their chairs and there was even a mime artist putting on his make-up. It was all so overwhelmingly tranquil.

It may have been a Monday morning but in our own world we were now a lifetime away from offices, train station platforms and progress meetings. It felt marvellous to be alive and together in that moment, as though nothing could ever go wrong again. Or that, even if it did, it wouldn't matter at all now that we'd experienced this binding and ethereal sense of contentment. It was good to be here, but it was thousands of times better to be here together, just as we hoped it would be.

By the time we returned back to the aire, hot and sleepy after a couple of hours of haphazard exploration, we found that Homer had sprung a leak and was 'having a wee' all over the car park floor.

Without wanting to be too specific, motorhomes generally generate two types of waste, politely referred to as 'grey' and 'black'. Grey waste is the used freshwater that swills down the plugholes after washing up and showers, collecting in a large tank that should emptied out over dedicated service points. It can get a bit whiffy after a few days, with soap, toothpaste and aging washing-up water all sloshing about together, but it's nothing too unwholesome.

'Black' waste is the stuff that collects in the sealed cassette beneath the toilet and needs no further explanation. Again, this is correctly disposed of at service points, where a clearly marked drain and a dedicated tap for rinsing is usually available. Or at least that's how it should be. We've seen some shocking things done with waste over the years, none of which I'll go into.

Anyway, our initial fears were that Homer was leaking waste and that's why she'd drawn such a crowd. Thankfully, she wasn't. It was fresh water. However, that didn't mean our neighbours were too pleased that we'd made a shallow paddling pool around everybody's motorhome.

Stepping into our sweltering plastic box, we could hear Homer's pump whining mournfully and switched it off. Something unknown had broken and we didn't really know where to start. Although we now felt very comfortable living in Homer, it's fair to say that she was still pretty much a mystery when it came to asking how the magic happened? There was a very basic control panic which, as far as we knew, controlled a network of hidden pipes and wires buried in the floor, but tinkering with such dark arts was still a little out of my comfort zone.

I'd spent a lot of my PhD dismantling and reassembling expensive bits and pieces, but in that case I never owned any of them. Homer was by far and away the most expensive item we'd ever bought outright and I was still terrified of breaking anything.

Thankfully (I think), our next door neighbour Jan and his mate Willem didn't share my reservations. With only the mildest hint of invitation, they came aboard with a hefty toolbox and quickly set about removing drawers, unscrewing fixings and moving panels to get at the boiler, from where it seemed the leak had sprung. They then began talking very quickly about severing certain pipes and splicing them together to bypass the apparently malfunctioning valve. I could have said "stop" I suppose, but it's hard to refuse help when it's being given so enthusiastically, even when you begin to question if it still counts as help.

Mercifully their wives then called them home for dinner before they did anything permanent, otherwise I swear they would have carried on taking bits out just for fun and left us with a DIY motorhome kit laid out in the car park. But they had at least identified the issue and revealed that the motorhome was a far less complex beast than we'd initially supposed. Essentially, beneath all of the decorative bits, was a hodgepodge of off-the-shelf parts, screws and bolts that could be bought fairly inexpensively.

More importantly, and this is why I'm even telling this story, it was our first real taste of the overwhelming kindness and unity of the traveller community. Everywhere we've been, in every country and from all sorts of different people, we've rarely encountered anything except welcome, friendliness and help if we've needed it.

We, in turn, have always done our best to pass that on. Because, while the modern world is so often portrayed as a selfish one, where the most sensible course of action is to 'look after number one' and treat strangers with suspicion, that's not at all what we've found on the road. Quite the opposite. As far as we can tell, kindness and openness are far more likely to produce the same result in return.

The next day we found a motorhome dealership who sold us the necessary valve, fitted it for us 'tout suite' and sent us merrily on our way with Homer restored to full health.

The real adventure was just beginning.

Mountain Magic

"So, basically, he was an old man who liked looking at nude young women then" I surmised, rather expertly as it happens.

It was our third day in Martigny and we'd decided to sample a little high culture by visiting the Pierre Giannada Foundation, a combined art gallery and museum that was hosting a large exhibition of work by the impressionist painter Auguste Renoir. Most of them, as I'd already discerned, were of naked ladies, especially the ones from late in his career.

As you might have guessed, art was not something that had played an important role in my life before this moment. My main interests had largely fallen into the categories of sport and science, which I saw as complementary. Music, painting and languages, for instance, had all fallen by the wayside. The only exception was reading where, because Grandad had been a bookbinder for most of his career, I'd always enjoyed a steady supply of books. From Austen to Tolkien, I'd read whatever I could lay my hands on, stalking the halls of Pemberley or roaming across Middle Earth every night from my box room at home.

Even at Oxford I'd failed to take advantage of having free and easy access to some of Britain's' most renowned museums, not even visiting the Ashmolean which was practically on my doorstep for almost five years. For many years, to my shame, if anyone had asked then I might even have queried the underlying purpose of art when compared to other more practical matters, such as engineering, medicine and physics. The fact that I liked reading and listening to music wouldn't have struck me as hypocrisy, or the fact that I had occasionally chanced upon a picture that had stopped me in my tracks. William

Turner's 'The Fighting Temeraire' is one example. I saw a print of it when I was a teenager and the spectral impression of a boat on its final journey had moved me in ways I couldn't even begin to understand. Still, such experiences were sufficiently rare that I'd never felt moved to think about such experiences, or take a deeper interest in either art or artists.

Perhaps it was the humility of falling into depression in recent years, being faced with my own mortality, or simply the onset of something resembling maturity, but by the time we hit the road in Homer I'd already started to broaden my opinions on what life was all about slightly. Like a steak being tenderised by a hammer, recent life events had finally softened me to the possibility that I didn't have a monopoly on good sense after all. And that my worldview was no more valid than anybody else's.

From what little I've seen in more recent years, such insight usually comes from encounters with adversity. Those who are fated to float through life, never confronting a challenge that highlights their frailty and fallibility, are more easily tempted into believing that they 'know better' (or worse, 'are better'), an illusion I hoped I was starting to see through. I might have lived with bowel incontinence for nearly thirty years, but my coping mechanism had been to close myself off from doubt and harden up against the world. It was only recent events that had finally cracked my shell of certainty and (often misplaced) confidence.

That said, the modern art installations at the Pierre Giannada Foundation still left me rather bemused. I tried to feel something, I really did, but the six-foot-wide brass breast protruding perkily from the lawn left me cold, as did the bulbous multicoloured figurines that stood over five metres tall, the twelve-foot-tall thumb and the giant ladybirds. Renoir's naked ladies, on the other hand, I could at least understand.

Likewise, the extensive Roman artefacts displayed in the museum section were genuinely fascinating, complementing the extensive open-air ruins that are dotted around modern-day Martigny.

Martigny was an important trading hub during the Roman period and was, for a time, the capital of the Pennine Alps under the name of Claudii Vallensium. Of the huge number of excavations that are scattered about, some are covered by plexiglass but many others are left open to explore. On the south-west tip of the town is a complete amphitheatre, seventy-five metres across, that was built in the 2nd century A.D and can be strolled through like a Roman noble inspecting his gladiators. There are more exposed ancient brickworks in parks, in private gardens, next to the pavement and, in one bizarre case, beneath a car park constructed on concrete stilts. To think that we were looking at the remains of floors that were walked upon over two thousand years earlier was hugely captivating to me.

"Who laid that stone? What was their life like? What did they do next?" are the sorts of questions I've always caught myself pondering on when confronted with the physical remains of human history. I did it as a child and it's not just the ancient world either, it might be an abandoned farmhouse from the last century, a rusting tractor circa 1970, or even an old spade worn smooth by years of use. "Who made it and what did it mean to them?" Perhaps, on reflection, I wasn't so clueless about the purposes of art after all. I just didn't know what to call my infant musings on meaning.

Anyway, we hadn't come to Switzerland solely to look at man-made art. Nature is a far more patient sculptor and had crafted a monumental gallery of treasures that we could no longer resist exploring. Martigny sits in the broad, flat bottom of the long Rhone valley that runs generally east to west, following the path carved by now vanished glaciers and hemmed in to the north and south by tall and rugged

33

peaks that disappear towards the clouds. It was to those peaks that we now turned our attention.

We'd only been in Switzerland for a few days and didn't even have a map of the country as a whole, never mind a guide to the nearby peaks and valleys. However, consulting our magic book of sleeping spots, we located a nearby red dot that seemed to be buried among the hills and started driving excitedly east along the valley floor.

At first the going was smooth and effortless, carrying us swiftly along the E62 motorway alongside large pastures, apple orchards and green slopes lined with agricultural terraces. We cruised past Sion, the capital of the Canton of Valais (one of twenty-six administrative cantons in a country of highly devolved government), gazing up at the imposing ruins of Tourbillon Castle on a rocky outcrop and continued on towards the district capital of Sierre. So far, so easy. And then the nature of our route changed drastically and dramatically.

As the motorway continued ploughing up the valley in an unbroken string of smooth, straight tarmac, we found ourselves directed onto a small roundabout and upwards along a vanishing thread of road that seemed to heading into space. Bearing in mind that we were still relative newcomers to the task of driving a 3.5 tonne vehicle and that our experiences so far were limited almost exclusively to motorways, the sudden narrowing and steepening of the way ahead was an immediate and non-trivial matter.

Of course, if we'd given the matter any thought in advance we should have expected this. This was the mountains after all. Roads would need to go uphill and they probably wouldn't all be motorways. However, we hadn't given the matter any thought. We were in drifting mode, flitting from whim to whim like butterflies on the breeze. Advanced thought and planning were not only absent from our minds, they were pillars of a life we were actively trying to forget, at least for a while. And besides, this was

Switzerland, not the jungles of Bolivia. Surely there could be no such thing as a 'bad' road here?

Fortunately, as became clear just a few minutes into the climb, it wasn't so much a 'bad' road as it was a much more challenging one with occasional moments of terror. With cliffside sections that pinched down to just one lane (with barrier-enclosed passing places), we were basically ascending a series of steep hairpin switchbacks towards the gaping mouth of the Val d'Anniviers, one of many glacial valleys that cascade elegantly away from the 4000 metre-plus summits that separate Switzerland and Italy.

All along the lush and fertile Rhone valley, smaller (but still enormous) valleys like this feed in from both the north and south. To the north they cut upwards through the bedrock towards the Bernese Alps, home to the famous peaks of the Jungfrau, Eiger and Mönch. To the south and the Italian border lies the Matterhorn, Weisshorn, Dent Blanche and Monte Rosa, the second highest peak in Europe at 4634 metres. Famous ski resorts such as Zermatt and Saas-Fee are also here, hidden among the deep valley clefts beneath their respective slopes and ski lifts, while their less developed but no less beautiful neighbours line up side-by-side, separated by monumental 3000-metre ridgelines and forbidding glacier tongues.

Although we'd selected our destination based solely on the existence of a dot in a guidebook, as we climbed we found ourselves plunging ever deeper into this natural spectacle. As the agricultural sprawl and industrial landmarks of the Rhone valley vanished from sight behind us, the initial horror we'd experienced at the sudden pinch-points, damp tunnels and the high-pitched complaining of Homer's overworked engine began to fade. Sadly, it was soon replaced by the whooshing menace of oncoming traffic. Trucks and buses appeared around corners, hurtling along with the confidence that can only come from over-familiarity. With myself in the right-handed driver's seat, I was mostly looking down at trees and sudden drops while Esther sat tense in the 'suicide seat', inches from the onrushing vehicles but with no control over events.

It took us an hour of mostly-second-gear chugging to reach the coordinates we'd input into Goma, whose occasional advice to leave the road and take a dive down a rutted dirt track had provided some light relief. We'd also pulled over at every available opportunity to let our ever-growing 'fan club' overtake us. In hindsight, having driven hundreds of other mountain roads since this first experience, we were absolutely over-reacting. At the time, however, we didn't know that. We hadn't a clue what was coming next or even if Homer's little 2.0 litre engine could take the punishment.

But we got through it, together, stepping out into the crisp, sweet mountain air of the village of Grimentz, 1553 metres above sea level and more than a vertical kilometre higher than we'd woken up that morning. As Homer's engine fans continued to whine in the background, we stared in wide-eyed wonder at a scene that instantly dissolved any pent up tension and stress from the drive.

It's no surprise that Grimentz is a regular feature in lists of most beautiful Swiss destinations. It's appears as a blissful blend of nature and urban life, a place where sun-blackened wooden houses with window-boxes overflowing with red geraniums lean against mountain slopes thick with green pine trees. The sound of rivers and waterfalls is in the air while near-vertical rock faces stretch up out of the forests, rising so fast towards the sky that their steepness and height mask the glaciers and snow-packed monuments that lie just beyond the foreshortened horizon.

We left Homer to cool down as we enjoyed our usual meander, soon finding ourselves lost among enchanting cobbled streets with traditional grain stores built on impossibly slender stilts. We'd only arrived a few minutes earlier and already we felt totally at home. It was the twenty-first of June, the sun was warm in the clear sky and yet, despite the stunning location and obvious charm of this picturesque village, everywhere was absolutely quiet. We'd seen a few people inside of little shops but were yet to see another soul outdoors yet.

Chancing upon a little wooden tourist office hiding between two taller and rather magnificent chalets, we struck up a conversation with the kindly lady behind the counter, Chantelle, who began working through the standard procedure of passing us brochures and drawing on a little map.

"And of course, you now pay the tax" she stated in her heavy French accent. Evidently something must have changed on my face because she quickly added, "but it is a good thing."

Now, we may have been in Switzerland for less than a week at this point, but even I was sceptical that the Swiss were fans of doorstep taxation. To be honest, I'd always been under the impression that they were famously tax averse, although that attitude comes mostly from James Bond movies so I can't claim to be an expert.

"Tax?" I queried. "Tax!"

Perhaps I hoped that by saying it over and over again it would go away. Or maybe I was just annoyed. The 't-word' has that effect on me. I can still remember watching my parents struggling to pay the Poll Tax in the early nineties and, while I personally have no issue paying higher taxes if they support health, safety and support services, for instance, I do have a sceptical streak regarding government actions. Fortunately, I have a much more level-headed partner who tempers my infrequent but knee-jerk emotional moments.

In a nutshell, it was technically a tax because it was mandatory for anyone staying in the area overnight to pay it. However, in return for the paltry daily sum of just 2.50 CHF (equivalent to about £1.50), visitors were supplied with a pass that gave free use of all local buses, most cable cars, two swimming pools and a number of other local attraction and activities. Better still, that cash went directly towards supporting local businesses and environmental protection schemes, which is my kind of tax.

We explained that we planned to be staying at the motorhome aire for a couple of days, which was otherwise free at the time, and so handed over two days' worth of 'tax'. With an armful of leaflets, a paper pass and no idea what treasures had just been gifted to us, our inherent sense that we were 'travellers' now told our brains that we wouldn't be staying too long.

We left the Val d'Anniviers more than two unimaginably good weeks later. We'd ridden every cable car, sampled every bus service, swam in both swimming pools (several times), stargazed at the highest public observatory in Europe, and walked up loftier mountain trails than any we had ever before visited, all despite me still being technically in recovery mode.

Thanks to the cable cars that could deliver us to above 2500 metres with just a lightweight day-pack on, and little else to do but rest in the evening, what we'd imagined as a quick jaunt into the hills turned into something more like a natural spa break. With clean air, clean water and good food, our bodies felt infused with a new energy that woke us up every morning feeling stronger than the previous day.

We'd sat in the shadow of monumental glaciers, gazed up at dazzling snowfields and lost ourselves on trails so remote that we might as well have been the only people left on Earth. In other words, we had fallen in head over heels in love with the Val d'Anniviers. And, if it hadn't been for that lovely tax, we might never have known. 'Never a judge a book by its cover' and all that!

In future years we'd return several more times, occasionally trying new trails and at others repeating our favourites from previous visits. We've since come to think of it as our 'energetic home', a place where, for no single, isolated reason, we always feel at peace. It's like a green, brown and white oasis of calm in an otherwise hectic world, a land where the rock and the ice and the forests invariably soothe away the cares of life for a blessed while.

As if to underline the point, after leaving the Val d'Anniviers we hopped a couple of valleys further east, visiting the resort towns of both Zermatt and Saas-Fee in quick succession. After the almost-empty trails and villages we'd just left behind, these places were literally heaving with people. More than two million tourists a year visit Zermatt, for example, and it seemed they were all there at once, charging between the boutique high street stores and the busy ski-lifts in their droves.

We still enjoyed ourselves, hiking up onto the lower slopes of the Matterhorn itself and reaching over 3200 metres, standing in the shadow of the iconic needle-like summit framed by a perfectly azure sky. The trails might have been busier but there was a reason for that. This was a landscape so vast it almost absorbed the numbers. Sitting alone behind a tall snowdrift, with the Matterhorn rising another vertical mile behind us as we looked out over the sweeping enormity of the Gorner Glacier and the even larger bulk of the Monte Rosa massif, we couldn't help but wonder if we'd peaked too soon (no pun intended).

"How can it get better than this?" we asked each other aloud, genuinely concerned that we'd somehow cloud our eyes to whatever came next if we kept encountering such majesty. It was a foolish notion of course, essentially worrying about varying degrees of 'wonderful' and that we'd get numb to it all. In reality, we simply couldn't get used to it. The Aletsch Glacier underlined that for us just a short time later.

In a country studded with world-famous summits and natural monuments, the Aletsch Glacier will always remain a stand-out marvel. At more than 20 kilometres long, three kilometres wide and almost a kilometre deep at its thickest point, this phenomenal ice flow contains enough water to give every human being on earth a litre every day for a couple of years. That's over six billion tonnes of ice.

We got our first view of the Aletsch Glacier's grey and white vastness just after sunrise, cresting the ridge above the Moosfluh lift station and staring down into the smooth-sided valley it'd carved for itself just as the yellow light of dawn began to light up the ice that filled it. No words were needed, we just held each other tight and watched as the golden hue crept silently across the world.

Later that same day, as we trekked down along the aptly named Panorama Way, the lofty perspective we'd first enjoyed gave way to a more intimate inspection. Minor ripples in the giant expanse morphed into towering frozen waves that could swallow tower blocks, while light blue patches that we'd noticed from above focused themselves into enormous lakes of glacial meltwater. By the time we reached the very edge of the ice, about halfway along the flow (where a slight curve in the valley reveals a wedge of the glacier's side), we were looking up at three storeys of concrete-hard, blue-white power. Lightly touching the rough surface I felt instantly drawn in, closing my eyes to imagine how long ago the water molecules now melting gently against my fingertips had first fallen as snow.

It takes ten metres of compressed powder snow to form a single centimetre of glacial ice, and with a velocity of just 200 metres a year at its fastest flowing point, it would have taken at least 100 years for this particular ice to flow so far. I was touching history.

Which is how our Swiss voyage continued, constantly transporting us into a world of vast physical scale and geological time. Homer battled bravely up and across the 2164 metre Grimselpass, one of numerous high altitude passes in Switzerland. From there we took the opportunity to hike even higher in order to look out over the mighty Rhone Glacier, the source of the River Rhone that discharges into the distant Mediterranean Sea. Nearby were the beginnings of three other major European rivers. Within just a few tens of kilometres of each other the Rhine, Reuss, Ticino and Rhone rivers all start out as tiny trickles across dark Alpine rocks.

The Grimselpass itself actually sits directly on the European watershed, a drainage divide that cuts right across the continent. Rain that falls south of the pass will ultimately finds its way south towards the Mediterranean or Adriatic Sea, while rain that falls to the north will reach the North Sea. It felt like a metaphor for life as we stood there, reflecting on the buffeting but invisible winds that could determine the fate of each individual raindrop as it fell towards the space we were parked in. A little gust north or south at a defining moment and the whole course of that droplet's future would change.

After Grimsel we looped north and west around the Bernese Alps, pausing in the shadow of the Eiger to admire its permanently frozen north face. Since 1935 at least sixty-four climbers have perished attempting this climb, earning it nicknames such as the 'Mordwand', or murder wall. Even many decades after the climb was first completed in 1938, it still felt darkly voyeuristic to stare at the crags and drops that had claimed so many young lives.

We ended up staying in Switzerland for almost a month on this first visit, moving between places of outstanding natural beauty. It was both humbling and hypnotic to lose ourselves in this engaging vertical world, cut off from almost every aspect of our old lives entirely. Apart from a handful of tourist offices, we had no internet access and only poor phone signal for much of the time.

It was just as we wanted it to be, a deliberate choice to isolate ourselves not only from what our own lives had been, but also from the rhythms of the world in which we'd lived those lives. Whether it was Monday, Friday or Sunday no longer had any bearing on us, just the rising and setting of the sun, the gradient of the path and the colour of the sky. It all felt so much more immediate and vivid, invigorating to a degree we couldn't recall ever experiencing while chasing pay checks or prestige. We didn't know if it would last but, while it did, we didn't want to miss a moment.

Beside The Seaside

It was pitch black when Homer's skylight snapped off, torn away by the powerful wind buffeting us from side-to-side. Cupboards were shaking, pots were clanging and the sound was near deafening. The confusing part was that we were neither driving too fast or sheltering from a violent storm.

After so much Swiss solitude and tranquillity, we'd made the knee-jerk decision to switch countries and hop across the border into Italy. Returning to Brig in the Rhone valley, we'd been faced with two options. We could drive up the two thousand metre Simplon pass that appeared on the map we'd bought as a winding red snake ascending a mountain, or we could pay fifteen euros for a twenty minute train ride directly through the mountain itself. It wasn't much of a decision really. The idea of taking a train ride through a mountain was too much fun to miss.

Sadly the reality proved to be rather dull, just a long, noisy and invisible passage beneath billions of tons of solid rock. The idea was intriguing, but the experience was uneventful, at least until part of Homer was broken by the raging wind. One moment we were chugging along, staring into the darkness and wobbling side-to-side in unspeaking unison, the next moment the cab was filled with gale force gusts and a terrifying roaring sound. I spent the rest of the tunnel journey lying on our overcab bed, clinging tightly to the remaining parts.

When we emerged into the light, I pulled what pieces I could back into the van, taped it closed as best I could and hopped back down into the driving seat. When we'd shuttled into the blackness we'd left behind the stately buildings of Brig, sitting on the open plain of the valley floor and surrounded by rolling crags that built gradually towards a blue and cloud-free sky. Now we were in Iselle,

Italy, rolling off the train onto a small road that was baking beneath an inexplicably hotter sun, closely hemmed in by pine-trees and sharp rocky buttresses.

By evening we'd made our way down the winding SS33 highway to reach the gently lapping shores Lake Maggiore. As the second largest of the Italian Lakes after Garda, Maggiore is actually the longer of the two at almost 65 kilometres end-to-end. It also straddles the Swiss-Italian border at its northern tip making it simultaneously the largest lake in southern Switzerland.

It was undeniably beautiful but, more importantly for us at least, it was here on a peaceful campsite that we met two of the most inspirational people we'd ever meet. One of the great joys of travel are these apparently random, fortune-driven encounters that seem to occur so frequently that they defy coincidence. I read once that coincidences mean you're on the right path, which is not just a lovely little aphorism but also an excellent summary of how the meetings that have meant the most to us seem to have come about during our wanderings.

Paul & Elaine were a British couple in their early-fifties. After emigrating to Australia for work in their mid-thirties, they'd returned to the UK in 2012 because Elaine had been diagnosed with ovarian cancer. Making their new life on a narrowboat, they toured the waterways of Britain while Elaine received treatment and then, when she went into remission, they'd switched their boat for a motorhome and set out to tour Europe, just as we had.

What was most inspiring about Paul and Elaine, even more than their obviously adventurous spirit, was their indomitable positivity. It's rare to meet two people who are so unwilling to let a single day slip by unmarked by happiness, no matter what challenges life happens to lay down in the way.

We stayed in touch with Paul and Elaine for years afterwards. Elaine's cancer returned in 2016 and she passed away that same year. Paul continued to live with passion and kindness until he too was diagnosed with a brain tumour in late 2017, dying eighteen months later. Right until the end neither of them showed anything but eagerness to embrace the gift of life. "The future" they reminded us "is a gift, not a right. All we have is this moment right now." We'd experienced that ourselves as you know, at the sharp end of a scalpel, but it's incredible how easy it is to forget that message when the wounds heal and the scars begin to fade.

We pottered around the Italian lakes for a while, revelling in the Mediterranean feel of the region and the novelty of being in a country where we understood so little of the language. "Si", "Buongiorno" and "Ciao" were the only words we felt confident using, though it was remarkable how far you can get on them: Say hello, agree to whatever is said next, then say goodbye and walk away. To this day I have little idea what I agreed to in those early days. I might even be married given the number of flaking chapels we visited.

Lake Orta was particularly lovely, a delightfully small and quiet patch of blue that has been described in some publications as "the Italian Lake tourists haven't discovered". Tucked within a green, tree-lined bowl and with the small but picturesque San Giulio island drawing the eye, we found a renewed sense of peace there. There was a magical calm that seemed to hover over the area, soothing all who entered, including us. After parting with the wondrously quiet Swiss Alps and finding ourselves on the well-monied shores of the larger tourist-trap lakes, Orta was a welcome departure from the hustle and bustle we'd encountered during our initial time in Italy.

The roads were markedly quieter too. I'm not normally one to generalise, especially as there are plenty of bad drivers in every country on Earth. However, purely in terms of our own experiences, it's a fact that we've encountered more near-death experiences on the roads of Italy than anywhere else in Europe.

After the various mountain roads we'd encountered in Switzerland, we were feeling like fairly accomplished handlers of our unwieldy vehicle by the time we reached Maggiore. Then we'd tackled the winding lakeside roads. Italian drivers seemed to have Jedi-like senses when it came to knowing where the exact edges of their vehicles were, skimming down our flanks at such close range we could have easily exchanged bodily fluids.

We'd been encountering "the motorhome effect" ever since we'd collected Homer, the bizarre urge that consumes some drivers and pushes them to overtake a motorhome no matter the cost, even if the motorhome ahead of them is already driving at the speed limit. Yet there had been nothing to compare with the Italian drivers' wanton lust to get past us. It didn't matter what the road was doing or who was coming, they'd fly around blind corners on the wrong side of the road, horns blaring and tyres screeching.

Perhaps that's why so many Italian-plated motorhomes look battered and bruised. It became a running joke with us. Every time we saw van or motorhome with panels being held together by duct-tape, or pieces wired on with old coat-hangers, it almost always had Italian plates.

Sadly, such busyness and crowding resumed abruptly the moment we left Lake Orta, moving away from the Alpine foothills to drop south towards the Italian Riviera at Sanremo.

Extending for some 300 kilometres eastwards from the border with France, the Italian Riviera is a narrow strip of coastline that curves gently around the Gulf of Genoa, named for the foremost city on its shores. Synonymous with money, glamour and natural beauty, we found ourselves pulled up short when we arrived one night in the dark to find quite the opposite. After driving for four hours along chaotically busy roads, the promising coastal red dot that

46

we'd been heading towards turned out to be a disappointingly noisy and dirty mass of motorhomes parked haphazardly on uneven terraces. There were hundreds of them, with music, barbecues and parties taking place in the spaces in between.

In the darkness and confusion we handed over the ten euro fee to a young man on a moped who shepherded us quickly through the revellers, depositing us in a rutted corner. We slept at a strange angle that night, overlooking a smelly drainage ditch and waking to find ourselves on the edge of what was apparently a more established campsite. On one side of the fence was order and clean facilities while on our side was chaos. Not that anyone looked unhappy about the situation. Hundreds of Italian families were up and about already, relighting their barbecues to make breakfast in the morning sun, cracking open their first beers of the day and calling out to their neighbours. It basically felt like we'd crashed a mass family picnic.

Aiming to get our bearings we strolled towards the coast, finding the narrowest sliver of grey sand hemmed in tightly by the calm sea on one side and tall buildings lining the promenade on the other. Tables, chairs and fast moving waiters were everywhere, including on the sand which seemed to be totally claimed by private diners. If you wanted to get on the beach then you had to purchase a drink it seemed.

In the distance we could see the outlines of countless bright white boats bobbing on the swell, so we began walking towards them. In places the promenade opened up, with vivid green palm fronds swaying and swishing in the breeze. But bloody hell it was busy. We expected it by now of course. It was the middle of high summer season after all, and while summer in many parts of the Swiss Alps is still technically 'low season', the same is definitely not the case on the shores of the Mediterranean Sea.

We lasted just half a day in the end. I expect if we'd stayed longer we would have found another side to Sanremo, or that if we'd flitted further east along the Riviera we'd have felt its charm elsewhere. But we didn't. Instead we drove west beyond Monaco and crossed into France, entering the adjacent French Riviera instead.

Strangely, we enjoyed this far more. With destinations such Cannes, Nice, Monaco and St Tropez, mention of the French Riviera conjures up rich images of James Bond, fast cars and yachts just as much its Italian cousin does. However, that simply wasn't our experience, which just goes to show how important first impressions and one's immediate surroundings are.

It was simple chance (and another red dot) that took us to St Laurent du Var, a relatively quiet town around 8 kilometres west of Nice with a long beach of golden sand. Parking on a basic but quiet aire about a kilometre inland from the sea, we donned our beach gear and set out walking. In all of our years together we'd never once taken a sunny beach holiday, preferring moderately active trips on our bikes or wandering in the Lake District instead. But with temperatures in St Laurent well in excess of thirty degrees and an intoxicating holiday atmosphere floating through the air, even we couldn't resist the allure of the waves.

Kicking off our flip-flops and burying our toes in the hot yellow sand, we paddled out into the crystal clear water and burst into laughter. From the tops of mountains to the shores of lakes and now this. We were still counting the length of our escape in weeks and the variety continued to astound and delight us.

Over the next fortnight we stayed by the coast, exploring mostly by bicycle as we visited the decorative streets of Nice, the hot seafront at Cannes and the well-heeled tarmac of Monaco. Walking the famous Formula 1 circuit, watching builders vans and tourist buses chug along the tarmac that I'd seen in so many news clips, was surreal. I'd known that the Monaco circuit is a series of otherwise regular roads, but until I saw it myself it was hard to understand how overwhelmingly conventional it looks for fifty-one weeks of the year. Relieved of colourful crash barriers and whining engines spinning at over ten thousand rpm, it could almost be another location entirely. Then again, the scale of the transformation is so severe that I suppose it basically is.

The boats are still there though, super-yachts and liners floating in the harbour as a mobile testament to wealth and flamboyance, as is the Casino de Monte-Carlo, the architecture of which inspired the setting for Ian Fleming's first bond novel, Casino Royale.

Yet for all of this glitz and bewitching colour, the attraction that we fell in love with the most was the Aquasplash waterpark in Antibes. Spending a belated thirty-second birthday celebration whizzing down over two-thousand metres worth of slides seemed the ideal way to underline the shift in our lifestyle that had occurred over the past three months. Wedged together in dinghies and rubber rings, flying downhill in spray-soaked tandem, we were children again, free of any residual thoughts of cancelled weddings and hospital nightmares.

We also spent part of the afternoon in the sister park of Marine Land, watching in delighted amazement as teams of dolphins and orcas waved and leapt for the crowds. Like millions of other visitors before us, we sat in the tiers of seats feeling astounded but also utterly unaware of the immeasurable suffering experienced by these intelligent and sentient ocean creatures. It would only be later, with hard-hitting documentaries like Blackfish, that we became aware of the dark underbelly of this industry and the way in which welfare (and safety) are compromised for profit.

I like to believe that everyone does the best they can with the information that they have available to them, and while I could have left out our visit to Marine Land from this book (out of embarrassment that I was so unaware of such issues at the time), to do so would have been a missed opportunity to mention what we've since learned.

Several decades ago the world was a different place and perhaps zoos and such played a genuinely unique role in education and conservation, but the world has changed and so should our behaviours. It's not a black and white issue, but with more and more research underlining the genuine suffering of captive animals combined with media and technology offering new and wonderful ways for children to learn about the natural world, I do think people should look more closely into how the parks they visit justify their existence. I expect some parks still do valuable and vital work, but not all. Not any more.

Our time on the French Riviera also marked a watershed in my own health journey. With all of the gentle cycling, the walking and the careful hikes in Switzerland, it appeared that I was well on the mend. A little over six months after we were advised to say a 'proper goodbye' just in case, as we gazed northward at the distant silhouettes of the French Alps, we began to consider the next stage of our journey.

Tour de Fun

The first time we cycled up a mountain it wasn't so much an accident as an afterthought. Moving north from the Mediterranean coast, aiming vaguely towards the rising outlines that so captivated us, it wasn't long before the world of long, flat beaches had vanished and we'd returned to a stage composed of angled scenery, trees and distant crags. Unlike the Swiss Alps that we'd been visiting just a few weeks earlier, this far south there were no glaciers or snow patches to break up the massive waves of undulating stone, static to our eyes but dynamic nonetheless.

The whole Alpine range runs for over 1200 kilometres and is basically a crumple-zone formed by Italy crashing into the rest of the continent. That's an oversimplification of course, but it helps to understand why France, Switzerland, Austria, Italy, Slovenia, Germany, Monaco and Lichtenstein are all home to portions of the most extensive mountain range that sits entirely within Europe's boundaries.

That said, while it might look like a single mountain range to NASA's finest as they look down from the International Space Station, on the ground the Alps are composed of thousands of distinct and unique mountain landscapes. We'd already visited some of the Swiss giants before visiting the sun-soaked Italian lakes, but now we'd arrived in the so-called Maritime Alps, a much lower-altitude but no less charming region dominated by tree-encrusted flattened peaks and characteristic brown-grey cliffs. It still snows in winter, just enough for several small ski resorts to attract visitors, but it doesn't hang around much longer than spring.

The first place we washed up after saying farewell to the sea was Puget-Théniers, a genteel little village about 50 kilometres north of Nice that seemed to mark the boundary between large hills and small mountains.

Pulling into the car-park of the municipal swimming pool, where motorhomes were welcomed, on our very first night in town we managed to stumble into the annual summer fete. These ubiquitous festivals seem to take place in every village and town throughout France during the summer months, varying widely in size and exuberance but never wavering in their sense of welcoming hospitality. Even in some of the smallest, most remote villages that we've passed through, we've been warmly invited towards a vast picnic bench and encouraged to join with the handful of locals sharing a seasonal meal.

In Puget-Théniers, as it happened, we'd missed the meal phase and most of the 'spectacles' (open air shows put on during the day), but we had arrived just in time for the fireworks and street dancing. With the brightest stars just visible above the subdued street lighting, we stood like children gaping up at the colourful explosions and then sat foot-tapping as accordions and guitars erupted with folksy music that had most of the crowd singing within seconds.

Personally, I've always hated dancing on account of the fact that I'm terrible at it. During my university years it took at least two bottles of cheap wine to get me on a dance floor, a quantity of booze alarmingly close to the amount required to knock me out cold. I expect that's why my preferred dance style looked a lot like someone trying not to fall over. I'm told that I did once play air-guitar on my knees but I have no recollection of the event so I don't reckon it counts. Thank goodness I was a student before smartphones happened.

Esther, on the other hand, has always loved a good boogie. During our eighteen years together this has led to some inevitable friction, especially on the occasions that I've started picking out other men she might dance with in my desperation to avoid doing so. However, on that romantically star-crossed night in Puget-Théniers, even I was willing to sway in awkward but totally sober tandem while the enthusiastic accordions did their work.

The following morning, feeling like honorary locals, we decided to explore a little further afield. Having gotten into the habit of gentle cycling during our time at the coast, going out for a pootle on our bikes seemed the obvious choice. And so, armed with a tourist office leaflet and the reassurance that the road was basically flat, we set out on our bikes in the mid-morning sun, heading towards the mediaeval town of Entrevaux just eight kilometres away.

Set atop a teardrop-shaped pinnacle of rock that rises above a curve in the River Var, this mountaintop citadel is a marvel to behold. Founded over a thousand years ago, this fortified outcrop has survived centuries of siege, betrayal and war, and still stands today with its battlements and thick town walls as a relic of a more violent age.

That's why we were heading there, of course, but so were thousands of other people. By the time we got close enough to be staring straight up at the highest towers we could also see dozens of coaches offloading their human cargoes close to the main drawbridge. Even from outside the walls we could see the place was packed, with hundreds of people going in and out of the town. That's when we made the snap decision to just keep pedalling.

It wasn't that we would have minded the crowds too much but the sun was shining, the banks of the river were green and we were already revelling in the companionable joy of sharing the wind on our cheeks. When we'd left the UK it hadn't been at all clear what my body would be capable of safely doing in the year ahead, so being on a saddle in the mountains at all, even just in the foothills, was better than we could have hoped for. So we carried on.

Cycling together was a habit we'd acquired more than a decade earlier when, for another one of our student travels, we'd booked two borrowed bikes and some tatty paniers onto a Ryanair flight to Norway. Armed with a tent that cost £9.99 and some rubber ponchos that made us look like sea-going cowboys, we'd ended up cycling a thousand kilometre loop around the southern bulge of the fjord-lands. It had been an epic, unplanned adventure, like all of our student ones had been, but with the added bonus of being a physical challenge that appealed to us.

At the time we'd both still harboured sporting aspirations. I grew up playing ice hockey for a successful Nottingham club, the same sport I ended up earning my Oxford Blue for after facing off against the Cambridge team in front of thousands of screaming students. I also took up college rowing. Despite my stocky five-foot-seven frame being almost totally unsuitable for the sport, I reasoned that rowing was simply what you did at Oxford. I certainly didn't imagine I'd get another chance to try it. It helped that I'd been raised in a family of three boys and that my young adult self would rather vomit, pass out or die than admit defeat. In the macho world of college rowing this often seemed far more important than height, strength, or technical ability.

Esther, by contrast, was really rather excellent at rowing. She'd rowed for Great Britain as a junior and in our first years together was still winning national championship titles.

Sadly, when adult life started getting its claws into us, we'd both allowed ourselves to drift away from competitive sport. Never appreciating what a crucial factor the challenge and release of competition had been for our health and mental wellbeing, we surrendered it to the same perceived necessities that had filled our days with deadlines and debts.

We still did exercise, when we could. I bought a road bike, as so many young men do, and after a year or so persuaded Esther to give it a try with me. Predictably, she was a lot better at it than I was, winning local events within weeks of buying her first bike. And, for a time, we did feel reinvigorated by our Tuesday night escapes to the local 10-mile time trial.

Yet by the time we were running a business and growing love handles, our road bikes had also been put out to pasture, hanging on the hallway wall gathering dust. We didn't even bother bringing them with us when we left Durham in Homer. In fact, we almost didn't bring bikes at all. It was only on our way to the ferry terminal at Harwich that we stopped in a Halfords store and bought a pair of the cheapest adult bikes they sold, just in case they'd be useful around towns and villages. We never planned to tackle Alpine passes on them.

Lance Armstrong once famously wrote a book entitled "It's Not About The Bike", which was true since he subsequently admitted to using performance-enhancing drugs. However, the sentiment still stands. Three hours after bypassing the crowds at Entrevaux and more than 1200 vertical metres later, we leaned our heavy and unsuitable town bikes against a sign that said "Col de Valberg – Alt: 1672 m".

If the route hadn't been so beautiful I've no doubt whatsoever that we would have stopped sooner, but when we stumbled into a stunning gash in the landscape known as the Gorges de Daluis, it was simply too pretty not to explore. The first we knew about the gorge's existence was a small, brown tourist road sign that we followed hopefully. Then, when we found ourselves confronted with towering cliffs of red rock that plunged vertically down into a sliver of water far below us, with the rest of the gorge vanishing into the distance as it snaked away, we were instantly entranced. Our legs were practically turning themselves.

"Just one more corner" we'd say out loud as we passed beneath overhangs, alongside tall spires and through natural rock tunnels, the tarmac weaving with the contours of the earth. Here and there were scatterings of pine trees, lending an attractive green contrast to the red and weather-smooth surfaces of the gorge. Before we knew it we'd cycled up more than twenty kilometres of gentle incline, arriving in the tiny village of Guillames at 800 metres above sea level.

Our exploits for the day could have ended there. Perhaps they should have done, but a teasing white and yellow bollard covered in numbers egged us on. You find signs like this next to most long, uphill roads throughout the Alps. The style varies between regions but the purpose is always the same, informing passers-by (usually cyclists) how much further it is to the top, how much higher, and how steep the next kilometre is going to be. In the case of Guillames and the Col de Valberg, the playful little bollard told us we were 12 kilometres from the top and that the average gradient was 7.3%.

To be honest, that figure didn't mean very much to us at the time. It certainly didn't sound like a lot. Besides, our cheap and heavy bikes had twenty-seven gears, some of which we hadn't yet used. High on the view injection we'd just received and elated that we'd already come so far, to find ourselves at the foot of an actual Alpine cycle climb graced with distance and altitude markers was a temptation we obviously couldn't resist.

The mystery and allure that combines gears and gradients is well-established, though for anyone who hasn't experienced it it's hard to explain. The Tour de France has certainly done its part. Put the words France, cycling and Alps into the same sentence and even people who have never worn Lycra in earnest will probably think of the world's most famous bike race.

The first Tour de France in 1903 was a publicity stunt for a newspaper, l'Auto, the main French sports daily at the time. Sixty riders set out to tackle just six stages totalling almost 2500 kilometres. It took the winner, Maurice Garin, over 94 hours in the saddle to complete the course. It was an instant sensation, capturing French hearts with tales of courage and determination, turning the competitors into heroes and, as intended, tripling circulation of the paper.

Today France's annual festival of cycling is a global spectacle of carbon fibre and leg muscles so chiselled that Michelangelo would weep. Pulses rise, and not just for those racing along with their bums balanced on an inch of curved plastic. From armchair riders to weekend warriors, the sight of mountains adorned with majestic hairpin bends glinting in the July sun stirs the imagination. "How would it feel to do that?" people wonder. I'd certainly wondered it during the couple of years that we'd paid a little attention to professional cycling. Well, now we had a chance to find out.

As we'd discover that day, there's a hypnotic rhythm to cycling up a mountain, or at least there can be. Settling into a just-hard-enough-to-ache gearing and pushing our feet down metronomically, side-by-side we began to rise up the hillside. The Col de Valberg isn't the most scenic of climbs and has only featured once in the Tour de France (in 1973, I checked), but with each passing kilometre we felt like explorers that day, venturing into unknown realms of both the mountains and our own bodies. Pretty much all of the competitive sporting experiences in my life, on the ice or in a boat, had been about sharp pain, about tolerating intense hurt for long seconds, but you can't do that for thousands of slow, relentless metres. With each bollard we passed the remaining distance shrank while our sense of achievement grew. By the time we leaned our bikes against the sign at the top we felt awesome.

It took us a few minutes to notice how tired we were, which is also when we started thinking about the fact that we'd gotten ourselves more than forty kilometres away from Homer and that the sky wasn't looking very friendly any more. The increasingly humid warmth of the day was quickly building into a frightening stack of thunderclouds that didn't fill us with much enthusiasm. Flying downhill in a gravity-charged thrill-ride, we made it just halfway back along the gorge before the deluge began.

I've never seen rain like it, not before or since, a near solid wall of water that left the road almost six inches deep in places as the drains failed to handle the sudden torrent. Yet because the tarmac had been so hot beforehand, the water was instantly warm. It was like cycling through a shallow bath.

On the final run-in to Puget-Théniers, with visibility becoming laughable (and dangerous), a Good Samaritan pulled over, waved his arms at us to get off and then tossed our bikes into the back of his truck. We climbed in after them, completing our 'little pootle' in a small metal swimming pool complete with floating timbers and building rubble. A short while later, as we leaned against Homer in our sodden clothes, there was just one question on our minds: "When can we do that again?"

'Two days' was the answer. The Col de la Cayolle from Guillames involved another 32 kilometres of uphill cycling, rising over 1500 metres towards the 2326 metre pass. A week after that we did the Col d'Allos (2250 metres), then the Col de la Cayolle again but from the other side.

We did other activities in between, of course, like visiting markets and continuing to amble around old village churches, but all of a sudden cycling up mountains had become our shared joy. Dressed in old cycling Lycra that didn't at all match with our cumbersome choice of bicycles, we began seeking out as many natural monuments to scale as the remaining summer sun would allow. Without regular access to the internet, we relied mostly on road signs and occasional tourist office leaflets to guide our way. This was no pre-planned cycling holiday with a tick-list of famous passes to tackle; we were more like dandelion seeds caught on the wind, moving slowly north and getting excited every time we stumbled upon a stretch of rising asphalt.

In geographic terms we didn't actually get very far through the Alps that summer, and we hardly scratched the surface when it came to the better known cycling passes. Those would have to wait for another year. One thing we did manage, however, was to pedal our way right to the top of Cime de la Bonette at 2802 metres, the highest road loop in Europe and the highest point ever reached by the Tour de France.

As far as I can tell, tourist office staff worldwide are always looking for creative ways to lay claim to a superlative or two. Highest, longest, tallest, shortest, smallest or deepest status is a highly prized possession when it comes to leaflet production. It doesn't matter how many descriptive refinements it takes, if a puddle can become the 'greenest puddle within a stone's throw from a bakery selling lemon meringues for less than a euro', then a brochure author will probably take it.

The makers of the Cime de la Bonette went one step further, actually building extra road specifically to get their hands on 'highest' status. The Cime de la Bonette is essentially a pointless circuit of road that both starts and ends at the 2715 metre Col de la Bonette. You reach the col and then keep on going uphill for another kilometre before looping around the grey 2860 metre conical summit and going back down the other side to return to the col. At the top is a small monument and a footpath that goes to the very top of the peak. It's quite lovely, with stunning views that stretch for hundreds of kilometres on a clear day, but as a road it's basically surplus to requirements. A decent footpath directly from the col to the summit would have probably been cheaper to build.

However, while there are three paved roads in Europe that still go even higher than the Cime de la Bonette, they're are all dead ends, while the next one down the list is the Col de l'Iseran at 2770 metres, a genuinely useful road pass but one that just so happens to be 30 metres lower than the Cime! A cynic might be tempted to think they built the road loop with this in mind.

None of which changes how challenging and marvellous it is to cycle up. In the height of summer, being overtaken continuously by leaner, well-tanned athletes riding sleek high-performance bikes, we struggled uphill for twenty-four slow kilometres, rising 1589 metres closer to the sky. When we were almost at the top we started passing apparently suicidal thrill-seekers shooting downhill on skateboards and then, closer still, we passed a tow-truck hoisting a car on to its flatbed. Talk about rubbish places to break down. But we made it, arriving at the summit sweaty and rather pleased with ourselves. Propping our bikes up against the shale flanks of the mountain, we wobbled towards the rock monolith that marks the top of the road and jostled with several dozen other cyclists and tourists keen to get an unhindered snap.

It's a scene that repeats throughout the mountains and is generally good natured. Keeping a polite distance, each new arrival steps up when the coast is clear and waves their camera at a stranger, the universal sign for 'will you take a photo of me please?' They always say yes. Whether it will be a good photo or not is just a chance that has to be taken. All of our best travel and mountaintop photos have been taken by complete strangers. We also have a lot of close-ups of our faces, shoulders, belly-buttons and even feet taken in some of the most magnificent landscapes in the world. You win some, you lose some.

Up on the Cime de la Bonette we got our photo and we also got some unexpected approval.

"You got up here on these!" exclaimed Geert and Hugo as we returned to find them holding our bikes with some amusement. "Bravo. Can we try?"

As the two Dutch chaps with leather-like skin and matching team Lycra vanished back down the final kilometre of the ascent, which also happened to be the steepest part (11%), we found ourselves twiddling our thumbs next to their own carbon fibre steeds. They returned ten minutes later grinning like kids in a sweet shop.

Geert and Hugo were Dutch and filled with all of the effusive jollity that Dutch folk usually acquire on holiday or whenever there's an excuse for a party. Visit Holland when there's a World Cup happening and the streets turn orange with bunting, streamers and whatever football-themed paraphernalia the supermarkets are giving away at the time. Even we had a dozen two-inch-tall 'Hup Holland Hamsters' stuck to Homer's dashboard after visiting Oma a couple of months earlier, courtesy of the supermarket chain Albert Heijn. It only lasts for three weeks, of course, until the Dutch team get knocked out in the group stages, but for those brief, hopeful weeks the Orange nation is high on community spirit, orange food colouring and Oranjeboom beer.

After wishing Geert and Hugo a safe descent, we ascended the final sixty metres to the summit and looked out in awe at the Alps unfolding away from us. In the years ahead we'd come to know and identify the various standout peaks, such as the 4102 metre Barre des Écrins, Europe's southernmost 4000-metre summit. But back then it was just a giant, unknown canvas that hid countless future adventures.

We rode up a couple more hills in the Alps after that, but it wasn't long before the rain and cold nights of early autumn forced us to move further south. So we drove down to the French side of the Pyrenees and cycled up some of the hills there. Picking a handful of valleys at random we found ourselves at the foot of several climbs we'd heard of and many that we hadn't. Not that it really mattered, it was the shared adventure of grinding uphill into the unknown that we craved, following the tarmac snake wherever it might take us, from forested slopes to exposed plateaus.

The Col d'Aubisque, Hautacam, Col du Tourmalet, Luz Ardiden, Col d'Aspin, Col de Peyresourde and other lesser known challenges kept our excitement levels high. We honestly hoped it would never end.

But it had to, eventually. Pushing on into October and even early November, we began taking a pannier with us stuffed with down jackets, waterproofs and extra layers, but we knew we were fighting a losing battle. Arriving back at Homer shivering and on the verge of hypothermia after an almost intolerable descent of the 1250 metre Col de Port in the Ariege, we knew our days in the mountains were numbered. We'd clung on for as long as we could and our hearts were heavy. We'd discovered so much shared joy, passion and fitness again on our heavy, out-of-place bikes. There didn't seem to be anywhere they couldn't take us. But now it was time to try something new. We had to, because winter was coming.

Seeking Purpose

It's pitch dark in the Niaux Caves, the sort of total blackness that lets the imagination run wild. It would be easy to get lost in this complicated maze of underground passages and chambers, devoid of torchlight and dependent on echoes and fingertips to find the way. Not that such a challenge was expected of us. We were wearing headlamps and, any moment now, the tour guide would ask us all to switch them back on so that we might once again enjoy the geological intricacies of this underground palace. That said, we weren't really here to gape at the swirls and spires crafted by the efforts of water and time. We were here for a completely different sort of artistry.

Incredibly, long before the advent of artificial light, sturdy hiking boots or even organised agriculture, between 17,000 and 11,000 years ago the people scraping out their hard lives in this region explored deep into this labyrinth and left a special message behind. Scattered throughout the various chambers of the Niaux cave system are dozens of vivid wall paintings, executed in the black-outlined style typical of the period with occasional splashes of red. Some drawings exist alone though most are clustered together in specific chambers. Flora and fauna dominate the walls, with bison, horse, ibex, deer and fish depicted. There is even a single weasel, a simple line drawing unique among all the various cave-art sites in France.

As the tour guide confessed, nobody will ever know for sure why people ventured so deep into the darkness (more than 800 metres) to create these drawings. No domestic remains have ever been found in the cave and it's thought that those who drew the images actually lived on the opposite side of the valley. Were the drawings the focus of a group celebration? A ritual? Did they sing in these chambers? Or were they the work of holy people visiting alone? Standing in the half-light of our guide's headlamp, staring at these ancient stylised depictions of nature, we could only imagine what it must have meant to those crouched in the dark beside a flaming torch. These paintings were done in the last part of the Ice Age. So even here in the Pyrenees the weather was distinctly colder than now, with the glaciers larger and longer, but just beginning to melt 11,000 years ago"

Halfway back to the exit our guide stopped for a final time to point out one more drawing, the outline of a single hand. There were no other pictures nearby, just this simple impression created by someone placing their hand on the wall and daubing paint around it. It was a small hand, probably that of a child. "I exist" it seemed to say. "I was here".

Blinking back into the November daylight it was impossible not to be moved by what we'd just seen. We climbed silently onto our bikes and cycled the chilly few kilometres back to Tarascon-sur-Ariege, the small town in the Pyrenean foothills where Homer was parked on a campsite. The next day we visited the nearby 'Parc Prehistorique', revisiting the drawings in the comfort of a museum (courtesy of a life-sized reconstruction). Other exhibits included a scale model revealing the full complexity of the cave system, the maze-like tangle that people had once navigated by firelight alone, plus another full-sized reconstruction, this time of human footprints found on the cave floor. Again, some of the footprints were made by children.

By the time we left the park, having also thrown spears at wooden bison, poked paint onto a plastic wall with our fingers, and squatted in the dirt watching a craftsman chip flints, we could almost picture the harsh, unforgiving lifestyle once shared by those living on the precise spot where we now stood. The world had spun many thousands of times since those drawings were first imagined, many prestigious civilisations had risen and fallen, but in essence we as people were no different. We still asked the same fundamental question, what the bloody hell are we doing here?

For most of my life I'd either ignored such concerns or dismissed them. I'd been happy to accept that life was simply a random accident of physics and chemistry, the result of the law of large numbers which demands that if you have enough universe to play with, life will pop up somewhere in the end. And, if there's anything that can be said with certainty about the universe, it's that it's unfathomably large. So large that if you think you've got your head around what a tiny part of it we are, you've probably misunderstood something. There's simply no single analogy that does it justice.

A more interesting question for me had always been, "since I am here, what should I do next?" As it happened, it was pretty much this same question that Esther and I had been deliberating for the past fortnight.

On the surface the only question we really had to answer was "where are we going next?" As summer's last traces had faded into the damp and cold throes of a mountainous autumn, we'd increasingly found ourselves sat inside of Homer's comfy (but chilly) interior watching rain hit the windows. Spain, sand and warmth remained just a short hop away, directly south, through the mountains and across the border, but we still felt reluctant to take the leap. Instead, we'd continued waiting, hoping for just one more nice day that we might take advantage of before saying farewell to the mountains we'd enjoyed so deeply and contentedly.

The damp weather wouldn't have been such a problem if we'd had access to unlimited power and gas to run our heater, but we didn't have a solar panel and, for reasons far too dull and technical to describe, changing our propane bottle was a massive hassle. As a result, whenever the temperature dropped we tended to treat Homer like an overly large tent. We'd pull on our biggest coats, put blankets over our knees and think warm thoughts. Sometimes we permitted ourselves a candle.

A reluctance to leave the mountains, however, was only part of our inertia. We were also slightly scared. Advice is a commodity where supply always outstrips demand and, all summer long, whenever fellow motorhome travellers had found out we were just starting out they'd share their 'top tips'. Mostly this had involved telling us where the cheapest supermarket was nearby, but a chunk of the advice was also made up of warnings. Some of the stories we'd heard over and over again sounded like urban myths, but a common theme was how watchful we'd need to be in the economically struggling regions of Europe such as Spain and Southern Italy. "Watch out if you go there" people would say, "they'll flag you down by pretending there's something wrong with your motorhome. Don't stop!"

As wide-eyed novices we'd absorbed all of this advice. The fact that a lot of it was coming from people several decades older than us also made us respectful of it. At the time the safety of our perceived 'valuables', such as passports, a camera, an old laptop and our mobile phones, was of paramount importance to us. We'd done our best to leave our financial affairs stable 'back home', but a break-in or act of vandalism terrified us. Even parked in the middle of nowhere, we'd never left Homer without hiding everything in pre-planned cubby holes. Sometimes we even took Homer's steering wheel, which happened to detach, with us. Mostly we'd felt very safe in France and Switzerland but even after seven months of unmolested adventures, we were feeling a low-level but genuine amount of concern about crossing the border into Spain.

On a deeper level, we were increasingly aware of an uncomfortable restlessness regarding our life choices and our future, a shadow that had grown seemingly out of nowhere and now cast a veil across our previously carefree mindset. For some reason, as the adventures of summer ebbed away, we began to feel like we needed to 'do more' somehow. I supposed you could call it an identity crisis, our modern day equivalent of "what the bloody hell are 'we' doing here?"

"What are two Oxford graduates like you doing bumming around Europe at your age?" one guy had recently asked us and, although it was the most direct version of the question we'd heard, it wasn't the first time we'd been asked. Nor were we oblivious to the fact that most of the other motorhome travellers we'd met were officially retired while we were still in our early thirties, financially comfortable (for now) but definitely not even close to being set up for life. What exactly were we doing?

It seemed a valid question but one that we didn't have a satisfying answer to, at least not to ourselves. Having fun and recharging made sense within the limited boundaries of a defined career break, but we both knew that what we were doing was more than that by now. Our entire lifestyle and worldview was evolving in ways we'd never imagined possible before and, while that was a beautiful thing, it was also unsettling.

Then again, perhaps we were just overthinking things as a result of spending too long stuck together in a small box because the weather was bad. Which is why, in early December, no longer able to ignore the golf-ball-sized hailstones threatening to punch a hole in Homer's repaired skylight, we gathered up our courage and fled further south, heading directly towards a large campsite just outside of Barcelona. Just as we hoped, the instant newness immediately overrode any niggling existential nonsense.

"Ah English" the prim receptionist had said to us within seconds of us opening our mouths, "we'll put you in the English corner".

We hadn't thought much about it at the time, but after a few hours it dawned on us that there was a peculiar national segregation in operation. Dutch, Germans, French and British number plates were all in abundance and, almost exclusively, parked next to a matching country. We had, quite literally, arrived in Little Britain, which was next door to Little Germany, Little France and Little Holland.

As we'd soon come to realise, there are two basic types of traveller who spend their winters in Spain. Both come for the weather, but while one group moves around, the other stays in one place. Long-stay campsite deals can make it incredibly inexpensive to spend a winter in Spain, much cheaper than paying heating bills back home anyway. We were part of a handful of transient visitors to this particular mega-site, but the vast majority of people around us seemed to be settled in for the long term. So much so that we now had a small army of garden gnomes glaring suspiciously at us whenever we stepped outside. Most of the gnomes were loitering innocently enough around a host of pot plants, one was fishing in an obviously empty bucket, but one was slouching angrily right outside of our door, staring at us with a pissed off look on his face. Honestly, who brings their gnomes on a winter break?

We began touring again forty-eight hours later, right after a fast and hectic walk around Barcelona itself. Three months of cycling up winding mountain roads and returning to secluded parking areas had left us unprepared for the mania of a big city visit. We'd wanted to see inside the Sagrada Familia, but the thousands already queuing to get inside had put us off. Instead we'd raced along Las Ramblas, Barcelona's most famous street, stood next to the magic fountain of Montjuïc, and sat on the steps of the nearby National Museum of Art of Catalunya. It was enough for us. Barcelona seemed like a lovely city, but the tube trains, exhaust fumes and crowds overwhelmed us.

Which is probably why we soon found ourselves avoiding urban sprawls and hopping between free beachside parking areas instead. As we relaxed into Spanish touring life and spoke to some of the many thousands doing the same thing, our previous overblown fears of imminent and inevitable mugging at the hands of roadside bandits quickly subsided into a more sensible level of background watchfulness.

Mostly we divided our time between walking hand-in-hand on quiet sands, relaxing with a shared book, or taking our bikes on rare trips into medium-sized towns for supplies and sightseeing. Valencia, surprisingly, was a delight to visit. With a large green space at its heart constructed in the dried up bed of a former river, the graceful curves of modern buildings and bridges meshed nicely with the ornate old town in a way that Barcelona simply hadn't, at least to our eyes.

With our days predominantly bookended by extravagant sunrises over the sea and night skies peppered with twinkling stars, we soon began to lose ourselves in an entirely different form of nature, an environment characterised not by summits and snow, but by mile upon mile of unbroken sand, wading birds and battered driftwood. Just a fortnight after driving nervously over the border we were feeling much more at home in a country where we'd gone back to linguistic infanthood, where almost every conversation began with a querying "Ingles?"

Spain was indeed a beautiful country. Sure, the embankments of major roads were strewn with litter, urban sprawls were sullied by enormous and garish advertising billboards, and vast plastic grow tents covered huge areas of earth in the pursuit of cheap tomatoes, but between all of that was a desolate charm. Sun-baked orange groves and cactus studded terraces covered the lower slopes of the many small mountains while stretches of undeveloped coastline could still be found in abundance.

Naturally we soon began to pick up other basic words, like "playa", "agua" and "¿Cuánto cuesta?", plus a smattering of numbers, but while we agreed that a basic vocabulary was a common courtesy we had little motivation to go further. There's a naïve innocence that comes from not being able to understand most of what's said and written around you. Some might think of it as a vulnerability or wilful ignorance, but we found it freeing. Apart from when we heard English, French or Dutch spoken, we heard no complaining, no worrying and no incessant marketing. Christmas would come and go that year and we'd hardly notice. We marked the occasion simply by making each other a card, taking a long walk on a beach and building a 'sandman' complete with woolly hat and scarf.

"Even if we won the lottery tomorrow, I wouldn't change a thing about our lives right now" Esther said to me that day.

She was right. Despite our short-term sadness about the end of summer, life had effortlessly taken care of things, especially when we stumbled into the Cabo de Gata Natural Park. That really was like winning the lottery.

Positioned right on the south-east tip of Spain, Cabo de Gata is a small and startlingly gorgeous oasis of peace amid a stretch of often concrete coastline. To the north are resort towns like Mojácar and Garrucha, popular destinations for the expats of Europe, while to the west is the famously busy Costa del Sol, home to high-rise apartments and theme pubs. But no such places exist inside the Cabo de Gata Natural Park. No gigantic tomato tents are allowed here. Or tower blocks. Or enormous shopping centres. The handful of villages that do exist within the park boundaries are mostly tiny fishing communities that remain a vision of what they would have been like hundreds of years ago.

Separating these small collections of white houses with blue shutters are famously golden beaches and jagged volcanic cliffs that hang precariously over the crystal clear waters. Hidden coves, tiny offshore islands and coral reefs abound with colourful marine life thanks to the coast's protected status, while on land the region has the driest climate in the whole of Europe and is officially classed as a desert.

The moment Homer crossed the park boundary it was as though we'd cruised back into a low-altitude version of summer. Looking around at the arid, red and undulating landscape, we felt that same surge of excitement that we'd experienced approaching the Alps, daydreaming of what adventures might lay hidden in front of us.

Wild camping isn't allowed inside the park boundaries so we checked into a small, simple campsite at Los Escullos, just five minutes' walk from the sea (and without a garden gnome in sight). We were right at the foot of the highest mountain in the park, El Fraile, which rises straight out of the waves up to 493 metres above sea level. On a clear day it's possible to see right across the Alboran Sea to Africa from the top.

Initially we checked in for just a fortnight, which already reduced the daily rate by some margin, but that fortnight soon turned into a month and then two months. It was a story we heard time and again from the other medium-term residents on the campsite.

"We were touring around, got here and, well, we're still here...."

When our initial fortnight was coming to an end we'd gotten out our map of Spain, weighed up our options, and decided to stay. Evidently we'd already been charmed by our initial explorations to the flamingo peppered salt flats of El Cabo de Gata, the idyllic sands of Playa de los Genoveses and the vibrant red sunsets above the western cliffs, to name just a handful of the park's many charms.

Perhaps if we'd been strictly limited to twelve months on the road we'd have pushed on across the Costa del Sol and into Portugal. However, ever since setting off Esther had religiously kept a record of every euro cent we'd spent and on what. We had a food budget, diesel budget, campsite budget, 'fun' budget and a whole range of other divisions of our outgoings. Whether or not we visited a paid museum, used a laundrette or did handwashing, or paid for water on a service station versus running back and forth from a mountain stream with bottles was all factored into her calculations.

Wonderfully, as 2014 ticked over to 2015, it seemed we were basically living within our means. Our savings had gone down, but not worryingly so, while our tenants had carried on paying the rent which covered our fixed overheads back home and left some extra for spending money. In short, nomadic motorhome life was proving a lot cheaper than we'd imagined from our Durham sofa, or at least it was the way we were doing it. Faced with the fact that we could afford to keep going, if we wanted to, it wasn't a difficult decision to make.

That said, we had realised that we had to come out of 'holiday mode' at some point if we wanted to keep going. After ten months of moving every few days, or faster, part of the reason we chose to stay longer in Cabo was also to regroup and rest while we waited for spring to return. We even moved out of Homer for six weeks, taking up residence in a so-called 'bungalow'.

If you can imagine a large, white, wobbly garden shed with internal walls then you have some idea of what we were living in. There was a reason it cost the same amount as parking a motorhome.

They say a 'change is as good as a rest', but two adults probably shouldn't be as excited as we were about moving into a flimsy shed. There were several available so we'd borrowed all of the keys, visiting each one in turn to critically inspect the identical layouts and utilities as though we were buying our first home all over again. Eventually we settled on 'number six' and in a busy couple of hours had moved the sum total of our lives from a small box on wheels to a marginally larger box on wooden stilts. It did have a ceramic toilet though.

The first shower in our own private bathroom was sublime. Due to the aforementioned gas problems in Homer, we'd had cold showers for most of the year. Returning sweat-stained and encrusted with streaks of suncream from the top of an Alpine giant, we'd strip off and jump around frantically beneath our icy shower for twenty seconds to get wet. Then we'd lather up before spending another twenty seconds rinsing off. Not only did this save gas it also meant we spent less time refilling our water tank.

Life had gotten slightly better since we'd arrived in Spain and discovered that the free showers next to beaches were usually warmer than Homer's. Nobody ever commented on us going for a twilight walk wearing only towels, flip-flops and carrying soap, but while everyone else was gathering in deck chairs and chugging cheap wine, we'd wander to a quiet shower and strip off.

"It's amazing" I said to Esther as I emerged steaming from the bathroom after fifteen minutes of self-indulgent bliss. "You're going to enjoy it so much". What I didn't realise was that I'd used up all but an eggcup-full of the warm water. Thankfully, for Esther, it only took twelve hours for the tank to warm back up again.

We also acquired a temporary cat. Various scraggy-looking moggies lived around the site, scratching a living in the dustbins or by charming visitors out of their breakfast, but one grey-and-white ball of attention-seeking selfishness seemed to adopt us from the moment we moved into shed six. Every morning we'd wake up and open our wobbly door to find 'Felix', who we named before noticing she was female, sunning herself just outside and waiting for us. Needless to say, she did quite well out of the deal.

While settling back into domestic comfort for a few weeks was sensually luxurious, it was also remarkable how much time was suddenly freed up. We'd never minded the practical compromises of motorhome living, not for an instant, but to be abruptly relieved of some of the daily necessities such as bed construction, waste emptying and 'stuff' rearranging was a welcome novelty.

Most mornings (after satisfying Felix) we'd set out from the shed to explore, rambling up various long-extinct volcano slopes, paddling on sparkling golden beaches, or cycling along wild clifftop paths, but whenever evening fell we began to find ourselves at a bit of a loss once more. We loved Cabo and we'd made friends with some fantastic other guests. Yet although we'd made a very conscious decision to take a break from touring before starting a second year, the ability to just sit still and enjoy having nothing to do eluded us again, just as it had briefly in the rain-drenched Pyrenees. The days were shorter and the scenery had changed but the nagging sense that we could (and should) be doing something 'more' was the same. What was going on? And, more importantly, how could we make it go away?

It might seem obvious to you what the problem was since you read our back story in previous chapters, but it's so often easier to see the truths that other people hide from themselves than it is to see our own idiosyncrasies.

The truth was, as a fully-employed PhD chemist, businessman or desk-jockey in university administration, I'd never seriously questioned my purpose in life, I'd just taken it for granted that I was living it. I might have gotten angry and depressed from time to time as a result of constantly pushing for a better, more financially secure existence, but I still fundamentally accepted that the struggle was part of modern life. The struggle *was* my identity. It relieved me of the need to ask why I did it, or if it was worth it. I did it because everyone else did it and that's the way it was.

Douglas Coupland, author of Generation X, once said that "Too much free time is certainly a monkey's paw in disguise. Most people can't handle a structureless life." The 'monkey's paw' is a reference to the classic horror story about a paw that grants three wishes but always at a (hidden) personal cost. The idea is that while many people wish for total freedom and unlimited free time, most would struggle to adjust to it if it came true.

Although we didn't realise it at the time, at least not so succinctly, that was us in a nutshell. We were struggling to adjust to a life without the regimented demands of day-jobs and the administrative necessities of the suburban existence we'd left behind. Instead, we were a pair of overly thoughtful, highly-educated, previously high-achievers sat in a shed in Spain feeling insecure about how we might justify our life choices to the world. Or, even if not to the world, then to ourselves and our own illusions of what the world might be thinking.

That's when we decided to become travel bloggers, creating a mobile, work-based persona that meshed with our newly acquired traveller identity. It made sense at the time anyway.

With regular access to the internet for the first time all year, we reasoned that our experience running an online business combined with our love for the outdoors would make a great basis for a popular travel blog, one that could attract advertising revenue and sponsorship. Not only would this give us a compact answer to the question "what are you two Oxford graduates doing to contribute to the world?", it would be a welcome return to the self-made success personas we'd once enjoyed and potentially solve any future money worries too. It seemed like a triple win.

The fact that we were almost living within our means already, or that we much preferred having adventures to talking about them, didn't occur to us. We had time on our hands and so dived right in, sexing up a blog template with our best photos and ploughing through lists of post titles that we saw other people writing about. "How we fund our travels" and "how much does it cost to tour Europe" were the big ones, alongside "top five places for a motorhome in Spain" and things like that.

We didn't actually enjoy it very much, but we 'pushed on', exactly as we always had. We also created Twitter, Pinterest and Google Plus accounts (remember that?), and started sharing things on them. That seemed to be the recipe that other successful bloggers used and we saw no reason we couldn't reproduce that formula. Pretty soon our wonky little shed had become a home office while our routine, so peaceful, relaxed and loving until just a few weeks earlier, had started to look uncomfortably like a previous incarnation of our lives.

It was an intense few weeks and, for the first time since leaving the UK, we found ourselves arguing with each other. There were a lot of suppressed emotions and bad memories bubbling to the surface and, while I'd love to say it was at least cathartic, it was mostly just uncomfortable. Somehow, through our insecurity, arrogance and a latent need to still have a conventional purpose in the world, we'd turned paradise back into day jobs. It takes a special kind of stupid to achieve that, one that comes with a lot of degree certificates.

Thankfully it didn't last too long. By the time we moved back into Homer in late February, our dabbling in the sexy world of travel blogging had given us several very important insights. Firstly, we had absolutely no interest in becoming travel bloggers, at least not the way we'd gone about it. Rushing to reproduce what others had done made everything feel artificial, as though we suddenly needed to explain our life through the lens of what other people wanted to hear. One day we might indeed have something to say, but not now and not like this. It just didn't feel right. When we did share our stories we wanted it to be done our way, with the intention of 'giving' joy to others, not trying to 'get' followers.

Secondly, we'd started to realise that the only source of our urgency to 'do something public' in the first place were our own insecurities combined with a sense of social guilt. All our lives we'd achieved things publicly, via grades, medals and money. Apparently, having chosen to remove such things for a time, that same urge had crept in through a back door. Our lives had changed drastically, but there were still two scared children buried within us, both seeking the approval of the world.

Finally, most important of all, our relationship was far more valuable to us than a slice of Instafame. Ultimately it was the return of tiredness, pain and the arguments that had opened our eyes to the lunacy we were inviting back into our days. What was the point of anything if it drove a wedge between us?

Blowing In The Wind

In any other setting, the appearance of a two-foot-tall technicolour frog riding a bicycle would be cause for concern. A sign that it was time to put the bottle down, place the corkscrew back in the drawer and go to bed, especially considering the luminous rabbits, dancing polar bears and the tiny blue whale swimming through the air nearby. But no, this wasn't some drunken nightmare or the result of a dodgy mushroom, it was the 2015 edition of Ceillac's annual festival of everything that flies "in the air and in the wind" (it sounds catchier in French).

Quite how frogs, flamingos, turtles and assorted sea creatures had made the cut I wasn't sure, but as we stood on the fringe of a huge field full of magnificently crafted banners, kites and streamers, the overall effect was astounding. After a rough few weeks, today felt like a fresh start, a good day to be alive.

We'd been living at 1640 metres altitude in this remote Alpine village for the past three weeks. With a permanent population of less than 300 people, Ceillac was the very epitome of a French mountain settlement. Simple stone houses clustered together on the smooth plateau left behind by the grinding work of a long-vanished glacier. A tall-spired church rose above the rooftops and sounded its bells throughout the day, while down among the cobbled streets no less than two artisan patisseries sold their wares in addition to a small a shop that also sold fresh bread. Everywhere we went in France the ratio of bakeries to people was always pleasingly high.

Then again, while that would indeed be a lot of cake for 300 people to eat, now that high summer had arrived the number of camping guests and day visitors swelled numbers well into the thousands. With lush green slopes rising steeply towards craggy natural spires and summits that stood over 3000 metres tall, Ceillac in July was a thronging hub of outdoor activity. From cyclists to paragliders to hikers, by mid-morning every day the valley was teeming with ant-like trails of people heading off to bask in the sun-kissed glory of the Alpine summer.

Not that we'd known any of that when we decided to drive up here, as usual. Initially we'd intended simply to show up, park up and sod off, trekking into those blessed hills for an attempt at a week-long walking tour. It was all part of our plan to inject some extra excitement into our second year on the road. That we'd ended up staying so long had mostly been down to a combination of inertia, inexplicable lethargy and (unfortunately) explosive diarrhoea.

Although we'd eventually seen that we were chasing something unnecessary when we'd gotten worked up and restless in Cabo de Gata, we'd never fully shaken off the cloud we'd invited into our lives during those computer-bound days in the shed. We'd driven pretty much straight back to the UK after Spain in order to get Homer's MOT check done, deal with a few bits of paperwork, see some family and friends and then quickly truck off again into the great unknown (or at least those parts of it we could drive to).

Eastern Europe would be next, perhaps, or possibly Scandinavia? Our first year had been unquestionably fantastic, especially the summer months. Now that we'd committed to at least one more year on the road (and hopefully more than that), it felt like it was time to up the ante a little. If some is good, then more is better is what the accepted dogma of our time preaches. Having resolved to park all of the existential silliness regarding justifying our choices to the universe and just dive head first back into the unknown, it seemed natural and exciting that we'd go one step further than last year for our own sake.

Chugging north back towards the UK, our minds had been filled with lofty imaginings of glacier fields, fjords, inaccessible villages and base-jumping-style dreams. It didn't matter that we weren't Instafamous, or that nobody was even watching. We just wanted to be out there again, losing ourselves on the limits of human endurance, pushing ourselves once more so that we could feel the edge and dissolve into the bliss of the moment.

But then, when Esther was diagnosed with appendicitis back in Britain, it was as though an earthquake split the ground in two. On one side were the lofty dreams and aspirations we'd been creating, on the other was the cold reality of more surgery, recovery and waiting. When she received the diagnosis Esther instantly passed out cold, folding up like a concertina that had lost its wind.

"I don't want surgery" said Esther shakily as she came back around. "After what happened to Dan last year I just don't want it unless it's totally necessary. There must be something else I can try?"

And so our stay in the UK had been drawn out into an open-ended lingering. Esther began to experiment with intermittent fasting and juice-only diets while we continued to hop between countless driveways and occasional spare rooms.

At first it was no big deal. We were grateful that Esther might not need surgery and with such a lovely spring unfolding around us, we were content to sit back and wait, at least for a while. As familiar faces had thrown open their homes to us, we had more offers of hospitality than we could have used in a lifetime. Whatever we needed was offered up to us without a second thought, reminding us after a year of fleeting acquaintances the deep and meaningful value of lifelong friends. We were loved and cared for wherever we went.

Additionally, the fasting and dietary changes were clearly working. We'd already switched to a plant-based.

whole foods lifestyle years earlier, for other health reasons, so a couple of months being extra careful about portion sizes and identifying possible trigger ingredients wasn't exactly a huge hardship.

Yet by the time we rolled back up to the Harwich ferry terminal, ready to repeat the same journey we'd taken almost exactly a year earlier, something was absent. The first time around we'd been infused with an overflowing enthusiasm and love that transformed the otherwise industrial setting into a place of opportunity. This time around the magic didn't quite as intense. We could both feel that something had changed and we even talked about what it might be. But no matter how much we hugged and told each other we were "back on our way", we just weren't able to switch the same level of excitement back on. I'm not saying we were unhappy, just confused as to why we weren't *happier*.

Another restful month in Holland had followed, a month of sedate beach walks, slow bike rides and daily visits to Esther's grandma. Our cycle route from Homer to her sheltered accommodation took us through a park where a dozen moorhen nests were busy with newly-hatched chicks. Every day we'd hop from nest to nest, watching as the tiny birds with their scraggy down and bald heads grew and chased around. "Morning Mr Moorhen, morning Mrs Moorhen" we'd call out to each set of proud parents.

It was all so delightfully cute, safe and necessary. Esther's pains had cleared up but we knew we had to be careful for a while yet. It's ultimately why we'd ended shelving our plans to go somewhere new, choosing the more familiar setting of the French Alps instead. Our French still wasn't perfect, but we knew how the system worked and we felt more secure there, just in case.

The surgeon had told Esther that if she experienced no pain for three months then her 'grumbling appendix' had probably settled down safely. So we waited, phasing in

81

adventures slowly by repeating the same basic pattern as the previous year. Rolling cycle rides along valley bottoms gradually became more challenging attempts up long Alpine roads while gentle walks beside rivers became jogs along rough forest tracks.

And again, all of this should have been no big deal. We were young, alive and surrounded by some of the most beautiful scenery in Europe. We should have been elated, grateful and overjoyed, but that was the problem. We weren't. It just didn't feel quite as special as our first year and that bugged us. It bugged us slightly because we wanted to be happier, but it mostly bugged us because we were angry at ourselves. If we couldn't be truly happy here then what was wrong with us? We had an expectation and it wasn't quite being met.

In working life it's easy to find targets for dissatisfaction. Late trains, deadlines, noisy neighbours, weeds in the garden, queue-jumping in the supermarket etc. If you're feeling pissed off and don't know why, all you have to do is turn on the news and the reasons are rolled out across the screen. Frankly, if you watch a news bulletin nowadays and don't feel unsettled, it's probably because you've zoned out from the reality of the planet.

What happens though when you remove ninety-nine percent of all those triggers and box yourself up in the mountains with just one other person, and you still feel something's not quite right? What else is there to blame but the person right in front of you, or yourself?

We tried our best to make our discussions productive. We agreed we weren't really irritated at each other, just feeling a little stale. And so, when the three months passed without the need for Esther to go under the knife, we'd driven up to Ceillac in the Queyras Regional Natural Park and attempted to set out on a multi-day walking tour. It was a route we'd found online (the GR58) and, although we hadn't done anything like it for years, we both agreed it was precisely the spark we needed. Just the two of us armed with a tent, a stove, sleeping bags and a hundred-and-thirty kilometres of almost-empty trail. We spent three days packing our gear, preparing food and studying the route. It was going to be perfect, a slice of the honeymoon that never happened.

We walked for about eight hours on the first day, ascending and descending well over a thousand metres with fully-laden packs beneath a roasting July sun. Our calf muscles burned, our backs screamed and our shoulders rapidly bruised with the weight of it all. Staggering into Saint-Véran, the first village after Ceillac, we'd wolfed down watermelons and fresh fruit with a lust driven by extreme dehydration and fatigue. But it had felt so good.

We pitched our tent that night alongside a bubbling stream in the shade of larch trees, listening as the birds sang to the sunset. When the last rays of light eventually vanished behind the peaks that we'd just spent the whole day crossing, the temperature fell and we slipped into our sleeping bags. Kissing each other goodnight and chuckling at our mutual aches and pains, it was indeed perfect, just as we'd imagined.

The trouble started at midnight and, by the time the sun rose, the ground around our tent had become a veritable minefield of filthy horror. Being forced to wash our feet in an icy stream at 3 a.m. after our bottoms became fire hoses of unspeakable ferocity was not what we'd imagined. Nor was wrestling each other to get the tent zip undone before matters became even worse.

And so, sleep-deprived and with insides that felt like year-old birthday balloons, we caught a bus back to Homer. We laughed about it, a little, but mostly we just felt we were missing summer. Everything we planned, everything we hoped for, seemed to keep going wrong. A few months earlier we'd imagined unparalleled excitement. What we'd gotten was sore bottoms. Then a book hit Esther on the head, literally.

It was called "The Power Of Now" by Eckhart Tolle, and it contained everything we needed to hear at that precise moment in our lives. Somebody had mentioned this same book to us in Cabo while we'd been working in our shed, but we'd ignored the suggestion. Then, when we'd been in Britain helping at a jumble sale for a rabbit charity that we used to volunteer at, Esther had spotted an old copy of the book for just 50 pence. She'd bought it but, with everything else going on, hadn't opened it. Instead, it had been jammed in the 'book cupboard' and quickly forgotten. There it had remained, still unopened, ever since. That it chose the exact morning after our ignominious return to dive into Esther's face was remarkable.

"We need to read this" said Esther as I stepped shivering out of Homer's bathroom following a cold shower.

"Spiritual psycho-bollocks? No thanks" I replied after glancing at the cover.

So Esther began alone, reading excerpts to me every now and then as we licked our wounds and waited for food to stop shooting through us like greased duck poo. Slowly but surely, I accepted the sense in what I was hearing, so I read it myself. It was only a small book after all.

In a world saturated with snappy slogans, uplifting memes and self-declared life-coaches, it's easy to dismiss phrases such as "the past has no power over the present" as just another hollow collection of words designed to go viral. It also doesn't help that a lot of so-called spiritual teachings sound a lot like narcissism in disguise, an extension of the 'me-culture', declaring that you can manifest anything and everything you desire based on what you focus your energy and attention on, as though it's a simple causal chain from desire to delivery. Everything has a dark side (not just Luke Skywalker).

I mean, I'm all for positive thinking which can lead to confidence and ultimately help good things to happen, but I don't believe for a second that visualising an expensive car will make me rich. In fact, I'll go as far as to say that I find the idea that someone is poor because they subconsciously want to be poor to be repulsive. It's just not that simple. I'm far more on board with the idea that it's only our response to events that we have any control over, and even then that's limited. 'Stuff happens' and you can choose to accept it, ignore it, change it or rage against it. And that's essentially what Eckhart Tolle has to say.

Among all of the different books and speakers on mindfulness that we'd go on to listen to over the next few years, Tolle always remained as the simplest voice with the simplest message, namely that stress is caused by being 'here' but wanting to be 'there'.

It's hardly a complex idea and you've probably heard it before. It's essentially the basic principle of Buddhism, that desire is the root cause of suffering. At the time, however, we'd never heard anything like it! It was the first time such a concept had ever entered our lives and it was revolutionary to us.

The mere suggestion that our niggling dissatisfaction had nothing to do with each other, our environment, the world, or anything else except the thoughts in our head was genuinely mind-blowing for us back then. Of course, Tolle then elaborates on the idea and suggests practical ways to overcome the mind's relentless roving through the past or planning the future, always wishing to be somewhere else. Accepting our circumstances, we began to learn, didn't mean that we couldn't change things or have hopes and dreams. It didn't mean we had to become victims of fate, simply that it was possible to work towards our dreams calmly and greet unexpected roadblocks with equanimity.

Now, I'm not going to garble on about this too much here. I'm hardly an expert and this is, after all, a travel story. But as the days passed in Ceillac and we recovered from whatever nastiness had crawled into our insides we began, just a little, to understand why we'd so rarely felt at peace with ourselves before. We finished reading the concise and powerful pages of 'The Power Of Now' and followed up with some other recommended authors, all of whom shared the same simple message in different words.

Did it give us a permanent Zen-like calm? No. Did it make us into gurus? Definitely not. We certainly couldn't levitate, no matter how hard I tried. But it was a first step. It gave us the greatest gift possible, hope and reassurance that we didn't really have a problem after all. This was it, the glimmer of the feeling we'd been seeking when we'd first set out from Durham. Not the exciting distractions of the first year (which had been undoubtedly fantastic while they lasted), but deep-down joy and lasting calm. It was going to take a lot of work and we'd fall back into old thought patterns every day, but it was a new point of reference. A fresh start.

Which is why, after a brilliant day of colourful extravaganzas, kite displays, birds of prey demonstrations, music and fireworks, the final event in Ceillac's festival of everything that flies "in the air and in the wind" felt so symbolic for us.

To be honest, I've always thought of sky-lanterns as decorative littering and I still do, even apparently bio-degradable, organic ones such as they handed out in Ceillac that evening. Yet as we lit our own tiny candle together and watched the hundreds of glimmering lights ascend into the pitch dark Alpine sky, it really was like we'd turned a corner, not just in our travels but in our lives.

Farmers

The first time I saw Stephan, slouching against a pasting table covered in muddy courgettes, he reminded me of a Disney cartoon villain. With his dirt-stained jeans, baggy hoody, tanned skin and scruffy stubble hovering around the wonky stub of a roll-up cigarette, he certainly didn't look like the kind of person I expected to be selling organic vegetables at 8 a.m. on an August morning. Stolen watches perhaps, misshapen gourds no.

But, as we all know, appearances can be deceiving. We'd later discover that this skinny apparition lingering on the edge of Ceillac's Saturday market was the owner of a successful designer clothes boutique in Lille, a major city in the north of France. The fact that he was choosing to manage his shop remotely while spending the summer as a manual labourer was the reason he appeared to us as he did.

"I'm a woofer" he explained in his heavy French accent.

"A wuffair?" we repeated, confusion etched on our faces.

"Non. A woooofer" he tried again, emphasising the 'ooo' so much that his roll-up dropped to the floor.

"Oh, a roofer" I said as the penny dropped, albeit in the wrong direction. "You repair roofs".

"Nononon. I am working on an organic farm. Woofing is for World Wide Opportunities on Organic Farms. We work on the land in return for a place to sleep, food and learning how to farm organically and sustainably."

Clearly we'd never heard of such a scheme, but we were intrigued. During my time at Newcastle University, the Dean of Business Development had been a Professor of Organic Agriculture. As a result I'd sat through many lectures about the different yields and nutrient densities of crops grown to organic and non-organic standards. As far as the data suggested, the answer was clear. That was part of the reason we always tried to buy organic when we could, even though it cost a little more and we were on a limited budget. It's a topic a lot of people are sceptical about, understandably so since the official line from food standards authorities continues to declare that there are no personal benefits to choosing organic.

Part of the problem is that diet, health and environmental degradation are incredibly complex topics, while individual scientists necessarily have to focus on specific measurements that then get sensationalised and overblown by the media. A research group can do a meticulous study comparing vitamin C levels in tomatoes, leading to an academic article reporting a 17% increase using organic methods, but if the media then choose to report that as "Scientists Discover Organic Tomatoes Help You Live Longer!" then it does diminish the actual findings because it's so easy to rebut the headline claim. Especially when another research group does an apparently similar study and gets a different number a few months later.

The old adage that "they'll only change their minds tomorrow" appears all too true, making all such research appear unreliable. This is a perception that can then be exploited by certain food or ingredient manufacturers who want to imply that no consensus exists in nutritional research, even to the point of funding studies that are so limited in scope that they appear to suggest unhealthy food is good for you. Cigarette manufacturers did the same thing, relying on the fact that the intricacies of experimental design and statistical analysis are far too boring for most people to bother with. If you can't beat them, confuse everyone instead!

At the same time, how we feed ourselves remains a highly personal and highly emotional choice. Advice and guidelines can sound a lot like criticism or an attack on personal freedom, no matter how well meant they might be.

As I said before, I like to believe that everyone is doing the best they can with the information they have available to them. In our case, that means we now prefer to buy organic for both health and environmental reasons. If a particular food is just too expensive in a store, we simply buy something else. It's very rare that we're attached to buying a specific item. We much prefer cooking whatever food is seasonal and, therefore, fresh and inexpensive.

That's also partly why we love local markets so much. They mostly sell food fresh from the fields, the prices are lower and we can meet the person who oversaw the near-magical process of turning tiny seeds into edible produce. I mean, honestly, have you ever stopped to look at a tomato seed? It's so small that you could lose it under your fingernail and hardly notice, yet from it can grow dozens of kilograms more tomatoes. Think about that. It's awesome.

Anyway, that little diversion into food politics aside, our encounter with Stephan in Ceillac was soon to turn into much more than a couple of kilos of firm courgettes. It was about to show us a window into a whole new world.

It would be the end of August by the time we took up Stephan's invitation to visit the farm. For the preceding three weeks, having discovered mindfulness and shaken off the malaise that had slightly overshadowed us since Britain, we'd dived back into our mountain adventures with gusto. Our attempt at hiking the Tour de Queyras might have ended in smelly defeat, but with our spirits renewed we set out to discover what treasures we'd missed.

Centred on the river Guil that flows down from the high Alps close to the French-Italian border, the Queyras Regional Natural Park is 650 square kilometres of magnificence incarnate. Unlike the ten national parks in France, which are protected areas closed to any form of human industry (though open to responsible walkers), the Regional Natural Parks are larger, inhabited rural areas recognised for their heritage, landscape and fragility. Such parks use sustainable development plans to protect their resources for the future. There are more than fifty spread throughout France, dispersed across the entire nation from the North Sea to the Pyrenees.

Bearing in mind that the Queyras park is ringed by three of France's most stunning national parks, the Vanoise, Écrins and Mercantour, if it weren't for the existing roads and villages it could easily be one itself in terms of sheer natural grandeur. With vertically-side gorges that open onto pebble-strewn plateaus, petite and historic villages at the base of tree-lined mountainsides, a postcard-perfect castle atop a rocky pinnacle at Chateau Queyras, and some of the finest hiking and cycling terrain in the country, we couldn't have asked for a better environment to have rediscovered our mojo in.

We got back on our bikes and cycled up two of the most fearsome Tour de France climbs in the form of the Col d'Agnel (2744 metres, the third highest paved road pass in the Alps) and the Col d'Izoard (2360 metres), went trail running along the line of the national border, and went white-water rafting along the river in addition to a host of other mini-adventures. We got to experience several summer festivals, including one that involved a troop of fire jugglers, no safety barriers and what looked like six bottles of water as a minor nod in the direction of a risk assessment. Never before have flaming sparks landing in the hair of toddlers produced such delight. And we also met another inspirational family making their way through the world.

The Tomes family were travelling in a white VW pop-top campervan at the time, with mum, dad and two children all squeezed into the tiny space. But that wasn't what made it so joyful to meet them. That came from their effusive happiness and love for each other. In recent years they'd faced various personal and heart-rending challenges, but not for one instant did we detect anything other than optimism and genuine gratitude for what they had in the moment.

This was their summer adventure, a month-long family odyssey full of smiles, cycles, wild swimming and evening barbecues. Seeing them so happy and connected put our own recent dip into selfish self-pity into stark perspective. How had we ever imagined for a moment that we needed 'more'? Or considered our tiny, trivial little problems to be so important.

The farm itself, as we discovered when we arrived, lay just beyond the western boundary of the Queyras, right on the outskirts of the town of Guillestre. It's here that the river Guil feeds into the larger Durance River as flows out of the mountains, following the line of the Durance valley as it curves between Briançon (the highest city in France) and Gap.

Just above Guillestre is the historic fortified plateau of Mont Dauphin, overlooking the broad sweep of the tree-lined Durance valley as it swings towards the south-west. To the east are the rising cliffs of the Queyras, accessed through a winding, rocky gorge, while on the northern horizon the nearby summits of the wondrous Écrins national park rise high into the sky. It's a heart-stirring combination of landscapes and one that the farm we'd just arrived at happened to be facing.

"What an amazing place to live" we thought when we rolled up in Homer one late afternoon, bumping along a rugged dirt-track towards a worrying-looking slope. Homer's engine had never been the most responsive, but the instant we began to nose uphill through the overhanging branches of a huge willow tree we knew instantly we'd made a mistake. Just beyond the branches the track swung sharply to the left and, as Homer gave up her momentum, we immediately began sliding backwards on the rubble towards a jagged low wall. With wheels spinning we braced for the inevitable crunch of shattered lights and fibreglass when sudden hands appeared, pushing against our retreating backside and giving it just enough of a lurch to send us round the bend. We'd made it. The English had arrived.

Stepping out to meet Homer's rescuers we were confronted with beaming smiles, stubble and quite a lot of dreadlocks. Stephan was there alongside Cyrille, the owner of the land who spoke reasonable English and welcomed us with a warmth that belied the fact we'd never met before. It was hugs and kisses all around as we were invited to park up, explore the farm and join them for their weekly barbecue that same evening. It was to be the last gathering of summer and friends from all around the region were coming. We were welcome to stay for as long as we liked.

Doing our best to level Homer out on the bone-hard, churned earth, we began to take in our surroundings. The field next to us sloped gradually upwards for a hundred metres or so, and was perhaps just a couple of hundred metres wide with a dozen large planting areas cut out of the patchy grass. Tomato plants occupied about half of them, with courgettes, peppers and aubergines that we could see in some of the others. We'd later learn that a few other crops, like strawberries, raspberries, potatoes, herbs, beans and pumpkins were being grown in other random plots scattered around the fringes of the farm, but we didn't see any of those right away.

An open chicken coop sat to one side of the sloping field, its residents pecking randomly around the place, while at the top of the field was a ramshackle hut with a long table outside covered by a weather-beaten gazebo. Beyond the hut was a tall stone house where we assumed, wrongly, that Cyrille lived. In fact he leased the house out and lived in a converted railway carriage to one side of the plantations. Next to the house was a sturdy stable that played home to four working horses. No machinery was used here to work the land at ploughing time, it was all done by the muscles of horse and man. For the rest of the year the horses were used sparingly to tow a 'caleche' (a sort of carriage) around Mont Dauphin on market days, earning a few extra euros in tourist rides.

As a small farm there were just a handful of permanent occupants. There was Cyrille, of course, and Stephan the Woofer. Sonia, who lived in a tiny apartment on the side of the stables and mostly worked with the horses. Sandra, who worked in the organic supermarket in town and lived in a yurt buried in the nearby woods. And Thomas, a shop owner who lived part-time in a caravan close to where we'd parked but who had once been a professional jockey and helped out with whatever needed doing. Oh, and us, for as long as we chose to stay.

Our first night on the farm was like something out of a storybook camping trip. Stoking up an enormous fire in a deep and well-charred pit, an iron plate hanging from chains was swung out over the flames laden with home-grown vegetables and thick cuts of meat. Guests arrived from all walks of life, from tie-dyed, grey-haired hippies to besuited youngsters, scruffy teenagers and middle-aged librarians and everything in between. Some, we discovered, were here for the very first time like we were. Others were clearly more regular visitors, but everyone mingled, laughed and talked as though they were lifelong friends come together in this fireside Bohemia.

We did our best to join in, sitting close to the flames and mingling our halting French with a smattering of arm-waving, relying mostly on the excellent English of the people we met. One theme seemed to rise out above all the rest, that of 'escape'. We met so many people that evening (mostly of our own age) that had come to live in the mountains specifically to escape the rat-race.

For some it was a return to their family's roots while for others it was simply a place to run to, away from tower blocks, open-plan offices and hellish commutes. Lucie, who had swapped her lucrative architect's job for part-time work in a shop told us she had no regrets. "I can live here. I wasn't living before" she said. It was the same story we kept hearing, from Juliette the former lawyer, Arnaud who'd worked in insurance and Yannick who'd given up some sort of management job we couldn't understand in order to become a respected handyman. Everyone was different but there was a mutual understanding among the crowd that it was togetherness and community that mattered the most, not bank balances and pensions.

And so the evening drifted by, illuminated by dying embers and the thousands of stars in the clear sky. At some point a guitar appeared, strummed by a bespectacled youngster who played Eric Clapton songs like a professional as the audience sang the words in a mix of interesting accents. It was surreal. It was beautiful. It was perfect.

When the sun rose the next morning we volunteered ourselves for a little farm work as a means of thanking our host for such a special evening. Cyrille only smiled, an impish look that lit up his lean features framed by blonde dreadlocks, reiterating that we could stay for as long as we liked and do what we pleased. It was Stephan who stepped in, suggesting we weed the strawberry patch so that they might fruit again before winter arrived.

Now, I didn't really have a clue about gardening, and I still don't have much idea. There are some green-fingered souls in my family but the closest I'd been to the business-end of food creation at this point was standing in my grandad's greenhouse watching him whisper lovingly to his seedlings. Every year it seems that half the population of Beeston gets a tomato or cucumber plant pricked out in his fertile glass-enclosed kingdom.

Still, we enthusiastically set about the tangle of creepers and unknown bits of green that crowded the fragile strawberry plants, working methodically along the four rows of crop. It took us four hours of non-stop toil to clear the patch, shuffling forward side-by-side on our hands and knees, leaving enormous piles of torn out weeds and immaculately tidy rows of strawberry plants in our wake.

"Wow, it looks like when we first planted them" said Sandra as she left for her afternoon shift. Job done, we went back to Homer, scrubbed as much dirt as we could from under our fingernails and then went for a bike ride up a nearby hill, a 14 kilometre, 1000 metre tussle to a Tour de France summit finish (Ski Station Risoul) with a fantastic view towards the Écrins.

It was a routine that soon began to repeat. We had no fixed plans or intention to stay at the farm for a long time, but after more than a year of mostly nomadic life it was nice to get our hands in the soil and feel we were contributing something tangible, not sitting behind computers.

Often, at lunchtimes, we'd join the rest of the farm inhabitants and whoever else had shown up for a communal lunch under the gazebo. We chipped in the nominal ten euros a week for the kitty, which was used to buy staples like rice and oats for general consumption. This, along with the food from the farm and whatever Sandra bought home from work (because it was being discarded), basically accounted for everything the farm needed to eat.

Within just a few days we were walking the farm each morning to harvest ripe tomatoes, courgettes and peppers to be taken to market. Our weeding skills had graduated from fussy smartness to practically-minded utility, and we were increasingly coming to appreciate the effort and time Cyrille and his friends had put into creating this hub of the local community. All of the constant weeding, for instance, could have been eliminated overnight with weed killers and pesticides.

Getting our hands in the dirt gave us a renewed appreciation for the increased shop prices of organic

95

produce, the direct result of choices made at soil level to preserve the land for future generations instead of turning a higher profit margin for the immediate crop in the ground.

That was how Cyrille saw it, as he'd explained to us one lunchtime. When he was a boy his family had owned the campsite just across the road, but sold it when his father got ill. They'd retained this patch of land and, after travelling the world himself (including driving a truck through Africa with his former-wife and baby son), he'd returned specifically intending to create a place where everyone would be welcome.

He never said as much, but it seemed clear that he didn't really need the few euros he could make each week at the various markets in the Queyras. It was enough for him to live off his own land and give shelter to whoever needed it. That's why there always seemed to be friends showing up, helping themselves to a handful of food or just relaxing in the sun.

On one especially fine afternoon we joined the group as they made their weekly pilgrimage up to the top of the Mont Dauphin plateau for the market. Riding up the narrow switchbacks below the fortress walls in an open-topped carriage towed by the horses, it was as though we had stepped back into another era. The lush greenery of the valley hid most of the modern infrastructure from view, with the rooftops of Guillestre's old town standing out against the scenic brilliance behind it. It was 2015 but it could just as well have been 1815 as we made our jolting way upwards towards the keep.

Arriving in the historic streets of the village beyond the walls, we noticed a host of familiar faces plying their trade at various other market stalls. Regis, the beekeeper (and former Parisian journalist) was selling honey while Magelie the herbalist (a former accountant) stood nearby with bags of home-dried herbs. Although it was relatively late in the season the trade remained brisk and the crowds swelled even further when the evening's 'spectacle' began. In this case it was two clowns who got a lot of laughs by doing magic so badly it was obvious they were really quite good at it.

Two weeks after arriving at the farm we celebrated Esther's 32nd birthday. Sitting together under the gazebo in the twilight, a cake and home-made gifts appeared as some of the friends we'd spent a little time with arrived to surprise us. We both had tears in our eyes. It was, in every way that mattered, a temporary family.

Towards the end of September Stephan announced that he had to go back to his shop for a couple of weeks. For the most part we'd continued to help around the farm in the morning, tidying up and harvesting, before wandering off in the afternoon to jog, cycle or just walk along the river. Now, with Stephan leaving, we began to play a marginally more active role as the land was prepared for winter. The remaining tomatoes needed to be harvested and turned into sauce, for example. The best specimens also had to be set aside for next year's seeds. The same was true with the beans and some of the courgettes that had been left to go to marrow.

With an industrial sized cooking pot and under the tutelage of Cyrille's 85-year-old mother we blanched, peeled and simmered countless tomatoes. Cyrille's farm was part of a nationwide initiative to protect ancient varieties of seeds, growing and monitoring their viability in different soil types, altitudes and prevailing climates. In his case it was the tomatoes on which we'd feasted so heavily for the past month. The enormous 'pineapple' tomatoes were our favourite. Bright yellow and the size of a horse's hoof, they were a meal in themselves.

Still, as winter approached they all went into the sauce, which was then divided into well-boiled jars and simmered for another hour inside the glass to make sure it was sterilised. We did the same with other fruits and vegetables, making all manner of preserves and pickles in the same simple, timeless way that so many people have moved away from nowadays. We adored it, making the most of what nature provided and seeking to reduce waste before winter struck. We also joined a large and festive group who came together to harvest grapes by hand, picking all day and tossing the plump fruit into a huge vat to mush into pulp and kickstart next year's vintage.

Bizarrely the land owner didn't want to let us help at first. In a group full of dreadlocks, scruffy stubble and baggy clothes, with our clean shaven appearance we were considered the outsiders in a very telling moment of societal role reversal. It was only when Cyrille personally vouched for us that the owner of the vines smiled and gave us a big hug.

The harvesting of the grapes marked a watershed moment in the year. All around us the land was changing fast. The sun was taking longer to reach the farm every morning and burn off the overnight frost that had started to form. At close to 1000 metres above sea level and with clear skies, the night-time temperatures were becoming fiercely low in Guillestre and we could feel it inside Homer. As we took to the wooded hillsides with our new friends to forage for mushrooms, walnuts and apples in abandoned orchards, the world of the farm was slowly winding down.

Cyrille was still busy indulging his other passion, building things by hand. During even our brief time with him he'd already constructed another apartment above the stables using only materials taken from his own land. But in terms of farming, things were definitely coming to an end.

We used some of our increased spare time to roam further afield, visiting Magelie to learn about the flowers and herbs she picked and dried from the mountainside. We also spent a fascinating afternoon with Regis and his bees, donning full protective gear to delve into the hives and learn about queens, workers and the plants that fed them. It had never crossed our minds before that the taste of honey changed with the flowers the bees took their nectar from. Regis was only a one-man operation, but he still had several sets of hives dotted around the hills to produce a variety of honey flavours.

"It is possible to do this without protection, if you're really in tune with the bees and unafraid" he explained to us as he handled layers of honeycomb bare-handed, each one swarming with bees.

"So you don't get stung then?" we asked.

"No, I get stung all the time" he laughed. "That's why I still wear the rest of the gear."

We learned a lot about honey that day, but mostly about the possible symbiosis of industry and nature. For instance, while mass producers take all of the honey from their hives, finding it cheaper to feed their bees on cheaper sugar or to make totally synthetic honey without any bees at all, Regis would only take 20% of the honey from each hives so that the bees could still thrive. It was enough for him to make a living he told us.

It was the end of October when we said our final goodbyes. There was no pomp or ceremony, just a final shared lunch and a farewell hug. We'd prepared a few handmade gifts and received a box of the preserves we'd helped to make in return, plus an armful of the little remaining fresh food.

"You can come back any time you like" said Cyrille, smiling in his usual peaceful manner as we climbed into Homer. And with that we drove off into the sunset. We'd arrived for a single evening and ended up being farmers for the best part of two months. Who knew what adventures we might stumble into next?

Gorgeous

We drifted south and west slowly after leaving the farm, hopping between various small villages that were separated by the rolling foothills on the western fringe of the Alps. We weren't going anywhere in particular; just bumbling around wherever the fancy took us. We had it in the backs of our minds to head back towards Spain for winter, but we still had weeks in hand for that, so haste was relatively unimportant. Life on the farm had slowed our pace right down to a sedate gentleness, a significant change from the impatient mindset we'd carried with us out of the UK so many months earlier.

Perhaps it was our perspective from the edge of the mountains that calmed us. From the outside looking in the Alps looked timeless. An unchanging monument, at least compared to our momentary human existence. Yet, as most of us know, that just isn't true at all. It might be difficult to comprehend how much the Earth has changed across the aeons but that doesn't mean it hasn't. Or that the ancient changes carved into the bedrock don't still affect us now.

The area we were touring through, for example, was once covered by a sea, during the Triassic period over 200 million years ago. That's how the thick limestone deposits that cover much of the region (and Provence) came to exist. During the subsequent Jurassic period (which inspired Richard Attenborough to build his infamous park), the sea became shallow, warm and filled with corals. Then, in the Cretaceous period, the whole area rose out of the water, a movement that fractured many of those earlier limestone deposits. Another sixty millions years and a few hundred trillion raindrops later and 'voila', the region is home to some of the most surprising geography on Earth.

The Gorges du Verdon is probably the most famous example, and it was to that deep gouge in the firmament that we found ourselves unknowingly drifting. It wasn't until we pulled up in the village of Castellane at the very opening of the gorge that we realised where we were. We'd heard of the gorge but had never made a special effort to go and see it, mostly on account of the fact it's a massive tourist trap in summer.

Then again, it's not hard to see why. At twenty-five kilometres long and up to seven hundred metres deep in places, it's often described as Earth's second biggest canyon after the Grand Canyon in the United States. This earth-bound testament to nature's patient craftsmanship was carved out by the vivid turquoise-green waters of the Verdon River, a colour from which the river takes its name. With winding roads cut into the layered limestone cliffs that enclose the gorge, visitors can drive, cycle, climb or even kayak their way along its length. That's why it's such a mecca for sightseers and outdoor enthusiasts alike.

We'd taken Homer to some special places in the previous eighteen months but few that matched Gorges du Verdon for close-up impact. Distant glaciers and snow-bound summits are one thing, but swooping and carving along roads where the history of the planet is written in foot-high layers just inches from our wing mirrors was an altogether different experience. It was much more frightening for a start. Praying that nothing big was coming the other way at each blind corner, the starkness of the bare, beige limestone surfaces was offset by the bright gold and red leaves on the trees that had taken hold in every nook and cranny they could cling to.

After about ten kilometres of slow driving, 'oohs' and 'aahs', we stopped in the tiny hamlet of La Palud-sur-Verdon. The road had swung away from the river here, emerging onto a flatter plain of endless trees and shrubs that smothered the now undulating terrain. We honestly thought we'd seen most of what there was to see and, while it had been undeniably beautiful, we were mostly ready to continue on in search of a place to sleep for the night.

It was, as so often happens with us, pure chance that we spotted a small brown sign indicating a viewpoint that claimed to be just a few kilometres away. We decided to cycle, partly because it wasn't far but mostly because we didn't trust the road to be Homer-proof. If we'd known it was going to be such a leg-busting climb we might have thought differently. Then again, if we'd known what a treat we had in store for us, we probably would have been willing to cycle ten times as far.

That's the great thing about travelling without mobile internet or even a brochure to hand. Treasures, when they're found, are made even richer by virtue of the fact they're so unexpected. So it was when we leaned our bikes against a small brown viewpoint marker and stepped out onto a little man-made terrace with little more than mild inquisitiveness and low expectations.

It was called 'Sublime Point', which tells you all you need to know about the image that confronted us on the small brick terrace. Hundreds of metres below us, cutting unheard through the tree-lined floor of the gorge, was the apparently tiny thread of water responsible for so much of what we could now see. It was as though a giant had taken an axe to the Earth, chopping out a rough, curving wedge that split the land open into a white-walled furrow of mega proportions. Extending away from us in both directions, the hills and plateaus that hemmed in the gorge merged together into a soft and green landscape that lent the perfect contrast to the sheer-sided suddenness of the gorge itself. Above us, wheeling gracefully in the blue autumn sky, a host of enormous Griffon vultures circled, their lazy arcs further emphasising the peacefulness of the overall scene.

I can't say how long we stood hypnotised at Sublime Point. I do know we eventually tore ourselves away, zig-zagging further uphill along a string of viewpoints we later learned made up the so-called 'Crest Route'. Eventually the climbing ceased and we swooped downhill on the uneven and narrow road, racing with the late afternoon breeze in our faces as the November sun began to cast a subtle pink hue onto the limestone. With each pause we looked down into the beautiful abyss, sharing each viewpoint with just a handful of other late-season visitors who stood equally enraptured.

There was just so much detail and colour to take in that it was impossible to do so. The best we could manage was to let our focus soften and try and absorb the essence of the moment as best we could.

Three hours had vanished in the blink of an eye by the time we rolled back to Homer, our minds in a trance-like state of calm. We didn't even resist the necessary departure, driving into the falling darkness towards a motorhome aire a little further north. Our visit to the gorge seemed to have infused us with a serenity that stayed with us over the next few days, and then we stumbled into another.

The Gorges de Méouge came next, a smaller but no less intricate limestone canyon on the eastern fringe of the Hautes-Alpes department. Again, the presence of this geological marvel surprised us. We'd only come this way after seeing a poster for a late autumn festival taking place nearby.

Starting at Châteauneuf de Chabre, a winding road gradually took us into the heart of the Baronnies Provençales Regional Natural Park, following the line of the turquoise Méouge river. On one side the road dropped sharply into the bubbling water, just a few tens of metres below us, while on the other side of us the tarmac was bounded by enormous layers of limestone that shot out of the ground at an acute angle before curving vertically upwards for over a hundred metres.

For ten kilometres the road continued like this, the naturally ornate stone never more than an arm's length away from our seats as we journeyed through this lost world in miniature. If a Brontosaurus had plodded through the water it wouldn't have looked out of place (well, maybe a little bit).

Once we arrived in the village of Barret-sur-Méouge we found a smattering of tents and a few optimistic musicians tuning up beneath a greying sky. By midday the heavens had opened into a torrent of powerful rain, through which a determined mayor struggled to bid everyone welcome. An hour later and most of the stallholders had already packed and gone home, leaving just a few dozen remaining visitors to enjoy the handful of indoor activities. It was all a little sad.

After each weaving a rather fine-looking small basket out of wicker (which would go on to become Christmas gifts for lucky grandparents), we joined a small gaggle of elderly ladies who'd signed up for a 'nature foods cooking class'. To be honest, I couldn't really follow what was going on. It seemed like we were all supposed to make some sort of nettle and chive omelette, plus a dessert that sounded like it translated as 'vinegar pins?', but without enough pots and pans to go around we were slowly edged out by the more determined locals.

Afterwards, however, we approached the instructor Isabelle and asked a few questions about what we'd missed.

"I live nearby" she told us in perfect English. "Give me a call if you stay in the area and I'll give you a tour". So we did, meeting up again a few days later in the town of Laragne-Monteglin. For the next three hours Isabelle gave us her time freely and abundantly, walking us along the banks of the Méouge and pointing out the few plants that were instant death and the many that were safe and pleasant to eat.

"It's so sad" she told us. "A hundred years ago almost everyone knew what they could and couldn't eat. Most things are safe, but now, because there are a small number of very dangerous plants, everyone's afraid of nature. This knowledge is dying."

Certainly, for us, it was almost all new and exciting. It was our first encounter with the ear-curling tanginess of sloes, the juicy sweetness of ripe rosehips and the sharp pleasure of épine-vinettes (the vinegar pins that had so baffled me at the festival. They're called barberries in English).

Having gotten used to picking food at the farm and gathering apples, pears and walnuts whenever we passed them, this felt like the next step, the ultimate in self-reliance. It reminded us of a documentary we'd seen years earlier about 'preppers'. These are folks who're convinced that civil unrest will one day sweep the globe, for whatever reason, destroying society and any semblance of order. As a result they spend their days dedicated to becoming totally independent from the world, stockpiling food, water, power systems and plenty of guns to defend it all with.

"So, could you live off the land if you had to?" we asked Isabelle.

"It would be very hard" she told us. "That's why we need community. People working together are so much stronger. One person alone in the wild is unlikely to last very long no matter how skilled they are. One injury. One bad winter. One poor summer and it's game over. People need to work together. The same with climate change and poverty and all the other big questions. Looking out for one person, or even one country can't fix these things."

We agreed. Meeting Isabelle was another breath of fresh air in a year already chock full of eye-opening meetings. We'd started the year focused on what we could 'get' out of our travels by blogging about them and showing off, but increasingly we were finding ourselves looking outwards at what we might 'give' to the people we met. As far as we could tell, people's actions could be identical but the intention behind them determined their nature and potential impact. We kept meeting people who gave so freely and generously, but were taken care of in other ways. Isabelle wouldn't even let us give her a single euro cent for her time.

"But this is your job" we pleaded.

"I'm more than happy to use my time passing on this knowledge to a younger generation" she said graciously. "Meeting people like you that are interested makes me hopeful that things can still change. I do believe the world is going to crash like a train one day. I just don't want to be staring at my phone when it happens. If more people start looking up then perhaps it won't be so bad, and maybe we can help more when it does."

Our final gorge of autumn was the Gorges de la Nesque, another wild canyon studded with caves a little further west, close to the foot of Mont Ventoux. At only 1909 metres high, the fearsome 'Giant of Provence' that has lit up so many Tour de France stages across the decades isn't on a par with many Alpine climbs in terms of absolute altitude. However, its isolation in the relatively flat heart of Provence ensures that it stands out like the proverbial sore thumb. There are three routes to the top, two of them crushingly hard and one of them merely difficult.

Over the course of the next few days we tried them all, each time setting off beside dusty fields and pine-trees in order to climb towards the exposed, bare summit that hovered at the tops of our eyes. Every time it felt like the weather was conspiring against us, the lateness of the season ensuring a crushing cold that left us shivering and exposed by the time we reached the bleak upper slopes.

On one ascent the wind was so powerful that it blew me clear off the road, dragging me into the scree and rubble that lines the route close to the top. On our right we'd just passed the memorial to Tom Simpson, a Tour de France cyclist from the UK who collapsed and died at that same spot during the 1967 race. It was an ominous moment, reflecting on that tragedy and the unforgiving nature of the mountains, a reality that is so easy to forget in our modern, sanitised world. Nature doesn't care who you are or how much your bike costs, if you push too far it will exact a price.

We didn't stop though, three times reaching the mountaintop lighthouse that marks the pinnacle of this dramatic road towards the sky. The views in the Alps had been one thing, looking up at sharp creases of slanted earth, but staring out from Mont Ventoux at never-ending miles of rolling vineyards, faded lavender fields and the hazy outline of the Alps in the east was a totally different reward. It was a change that felt symbolic of the changes in our own lives over the preceding months, from jagged sharpness and short horizons to smoother plains and distant perspectives.

Everything that had happened since we'd arrived in the Alps seemed to have guided us towards a calmer, humbler and less self-obsessed approach to our lives and we'd become undeniably happier as a result. I only hoped that we could keep hold of the same calm serenity.

Clearing Out

"Bullnuts" I exclaimed as a giant splinter pierced through one of my fingers, almost making me drop the filthy box that I was trying to lift onto my foot.

"What is it?" shouted Esther through the hole in the ceiling.

"Aaahh!" I explained helpfully. "Let's just burn everything and be done with it."

"We'd still have to take it out of Barry's attic first. He'd notice."

It was April 2016, the day after we'd moved back into our Durham flat and just a week after we'd landed back in Britain. After another winter of beach-hopping, aimless paddling and a spot of occasional skinny-dipping, our return to Durham was part of a major resolution. It was finally time to cut loose the life we'd left in storage so abruptly two years earlier.

In the years before we travelled, owning properties and accumulating stuff had felt like one of the more visible symbols of our successes, a testament to the hard work we were putting in to pay off debt in addition to giving us a layer of security for the future. It had felt both important and sensible, the creation of an apparently solid foundation to protect us against economic wobbles and unforeseen life challenges. It's also why it had felt so important to store and protect most of those possessions when we'd first left Durham, sealing away our previous lifestyle into a sort of time capsule that we could reopen whenever we chose. It had been reassuring to know it was all still there waiting for us, either as things we could use or at least wealth we could unlock.

Two years later and we no longer felt the same way. There was no one thing or special event that had changed our minds, just a gradual process of sharing half a dozen small cupboards and learning to make do with less that had taught us the twin joys of simplicity and self-reliance. As our wanderings had shown us time and time again, the people and things we needed just seemed to keep cropping up right when we needed them and in ways we could never have planned or prepared for.

At the same time we also felt selfish, hoarding so many useful things that other people could be using while they rotted away or became obsolete in an attic. That's why, when the tenant in our flat handed in his notice during winter, we decided not to see it as lost income and uncertainty, but as an opportunity to take an action that was in line with our evolving worldview.

It might not have made solid financial sense since we'd technically be worse off, reducing our monthly income, but we decided to sell the flat instead of finding a new tenant to pay our mortgage for us. It might sound mad (or at least stupidly sentimental) to some people, but we genuinely preferred the idea of a young couple building their own new life there, just as we'd done.

We didn't consider ourselves crazy though. We'd still release some cash in the short term but, more importantly, it would give us more of the mental freedom and clarity we enjoyed. That's why we also wanted to move back in temporarily and give away all of the possessions we'd happily lived without for two years, passing them on before they crumbled away.

Our hope was that by the time we were finished we'd own just one home, which we still needed for various boring administrative reasons related to insurance and healthcare, but we'd have less debt and paperwork to worry about and no longer have surplus 'things' to care for. Esther's childhood VHS tapes were probably going in the bin, but our hope was that we could find a new, useful life for everything else.

Selling Homer, so that we might buy another motorhome while living in the flat, was a bit of a last-minute addition to our plans. We still loved her plump cushions, homely beech-effect veneer and cluttered interior, but our second winter of touring had further underlined the fact that she wasn't quite right for full-time living. Two years of cold showers and sitting in the dark had deepened our desire for solar panels and a refillable gas system, both of which we could retrofit, but there were other issues too. The lack of outdoor storage, for example, and her under-powered engine.

We weren't sure how long it would take to completely change the material content of our lives, but we were optimistic it would be a matter of weeks. In fact, Homer had gone before we even got back to Durham, sold for the asking price within forty-eight hours of landing at Dover. The retired couple who bought her were so excited, showing up just minutes after I'd finished emptying our things into Esther's parents' garage. With a carrier bag containing seventeen-and-a-half thousand pounds worth of twenty pound notes, they'd come over on the train absolutely convinced that Homer was the one for them.

We'd gone to the nearest bank together, assured the cashier that I wasn't an international money-launderer by inviting him for a cup of tea in Homer (who was parked outside), paid in the carrier bag and handed over the keys on the street. It was that simple. The next day we'd hired a car, filled it to the brim with Homer's contents and driven north.

"Just this" we agreed as we emptied the hire car outside of our flat building. "We only use these things. Everything we fetch from Barry's attic stays in a pile. We just don't need it!"

Unlocking our own front door after so much time away was exactly like opening the time capsule we'd imagined. We'd bought the flat a decade earlier, our very first home together, and neither of us could deny the wave of nostalgia that slammed against us as we stepped across the threshold again.

Initially, when we'd first committed to moving to Durham in 2005, we'd been looking at houses. We even got as far as having a survey done on an old terraced house to the north of the city. Unfortunately, when the survey suggested the place was busy sliding from its own foundations, we'd found ourselves at a loss. In a few days' time I was supposed to start my PhD, our rented accommodation was horrible and expensive, and we had an agreement-in-principle from a bank who wanted to lend us a surprising sum of money (nine times my PhD bursary, our only income at the time! It's like they were giving away sweets. And people wonder how the mortgage market crashed!)

Personally I was ready to give up and carry on renting, but thankfully Esther has always been made of sterner stuff than me. Inviting her mum to come and stay, they visited every single new-build estate within a twenty mile radius, explaining exactly what we could afford and that we wanted it immediately without any nonsense. After whittling down the options, all I had to do was show up and decide if I liked any of them.

It didn't take long. The first time I saw our home-to-be we'd walked up from the city centre together, a relatively stiff climb up the hill towards Gilesgate. It was misty that day, a thick fog that blocked out the sun and turned buildings into little more than gloomy silhouettes. After fifteen minutes or so of unfamiliar pavements and uncertain directions, a three-storey building appeared out of the mirk. With pointed towers just visible on either of the smart, red-brick building, I turned to Esther and said "can you imagine living in something with a turret like that?" Esther just smiled.

A few weeks later we moved into our top floor flat, a hundred square metres of two-bedroom loveliness with a living room turret that startled me every time I came home. It was big, light, airy, and it was ours. When the builders had agreed to accept what little we could afford, we thought we were just lucky. Three months later they went into administration, by which time we were fully settled in and getting on with our lives. Most of the rest of the flats and nearby houses were snapped up by an investment consortium, but we remained safe, secure and delighted in our smart new home together.

More than ten years later and we experienced that same thrill of excitement when we returned. We'd rented the flat out fully furnished, not having the time or inclination to remove any of the furniture before we left, and we were selling it exactly same way. As a result, our home appeared to have been in stasis for two years. Apart from a couple of pictures the tenant had hung and left behind, we might as well have been stepping back in time.

Wandering from room to room, every surface, cupboard and chipped mug reminded us of a story. The birthday parties we'd held here, the movie nights, the places where our house rabbits had nibbled the furniture, even the arguments, all were writ into the fabric of the rooms. This has been the scene of our shared lives for almost a decade and it was impossible not to be moved by the moment.

Still, resolved to our task, we unloaded our minimalist supplies, dropped off the hire car and made a plan of action. The flat had already gone on the market shortly after the tenant gave his notice, and we'd already agreed a price with a first-time cash buyer by the time we showed up. It was indeed a young couple moving up from the south, both about to start their PhDs just as we'd been when we moved in. All we had to now was get over to Barry's attic and start shedding stuff. We'd need his help to shift things back at the weekend, but we could at least start cutting out the most obvious junk up in the attic itself.

Hence the reason I was scrabbling about on my knees, getting covered in dust and sweating like a marathon runner in the desert. It was only spring but the sun outside was already turning our mate's attic into a dirty sauna. Frankly, the sheer volume of stuff we'd left behind had shocked us the first time we'd climbed the ladder. What we recalled as a few car loads was, in fact, a veritable mountain of clothes, knick-knacks and forgotten memories. Vacuum bags had expanded into oversized multicoloured balloons of fabric and teddy bears, while battered holdalls spewed forth all manner of personal treasures and tat. Who knew we had once displayed bicycle ornaments made from old Pepsi tins, two dozen sheep figurines, and photo frames full of cinema tickets from our earliest years together?

But that was just the surface layer. Beneath was a minefield of obsolete, broken or overlooked devices, tools and gadgets. We still had a TV circa 1994, a fully-functioning Sega Mega Drive, and a Hi-Fi so out-of-date it could play minidiscs. There was a Tupperware full of keys in various states of decay, few of which we could identify, and, of those we could, one was definitely for a bike lock I'd lost in 2002. Don't even get me started on the carrier bags of cables and defunct chargers.

After an hour in the roasting half-light, it had become clear that little progress was being made. It felt like we were playing a giant version of a sliding-tile puzzle game, the kind where you try and recreate a picture by clicking tiles around one-at-a-time. For every three boxes we piled up in a patch of empty floor, three more were waiting to fill the space left behind.

Perhaps, if we hadn't been so determined to send as little as possible to landfill, we could have made progress. Instead, we gave up, enjoying a nostalgic stroll back home in the afternoon breeze. It was the weekend before we got a couple of car loads up into the more comfortable setting of our second bedroom, thanks to Barry's ever patient nature.

113

It was perhaps only a quarter (or less) of our things but it was enough to make a start.

Except we didn't. We looked at the stuff fairly often, especially when I fetched another car load with Barry, and occasionally we spent an hour unloading some of the boxes and bags into increasingly specific piles. But nothing ever seemed to actually leave.

Just a fortnight after our return and we had settled into a rather pleasant and peaceful routine. With a city full of old friends to spend time with, a county of hikes and cycles to revisit, and a comfortable flat to do it all from, the sudden lust to 'just get it all done' had faded away. We'd even re-joined a gym we'd once belonged to, a place where our faces had been recognised the moment we walked back in.

"Esther. Dan. How're you? Good to see you back."

Part of the reason we'd fallen so in love with the North-East was the easy friendliness so many people were willing to share. We'd made friends in the supermarket, the gym, even just walking down the street. During the year we'd spent working in Cambridge the casual openness of the north had been the feature we'd missed the most. And, after two years of often isolated travels, it was a powerful drug to suddenly rediscover.

Despite convincing ourselves that we were ready to let everything go, the moment we'd stepped through our old front door we'd effortlessly slipped back into the life we'd walked away from, or at least the many positive parts. We might have convinced ourselves otherwise at times, but the truth was that we'd lived a good life in Durham. In reality, the only people making it hard for us had been ourselves due to our constant pushing for more and ever-expanding expectations. With the absence of work and deadlines combined with the deeper sense of mindfulness we'd been cultivating over the past year, life in Durham wasn't so much a delay as a delight.

Still, that didn't shake our underlying commitment to return to life on the road fairly quickly. The fact we didn't actually own a motorhome for the time being, or have a specific date until the flat sale went through yet, simply removed any pressure.

Another reason for going slowly was our differing attitudes and emotions around objects. As kids, my brothers and I had once cut the Cluedo board in half using the set's tiny metal dagger, just to see how sharp it was. Most of our other toys met similar fates. My parents never kept any of my exercise books from school, or even trophies from childhood sports victories. Some of them lived on windowsills for a while, but when it was time to redecorate they tended to get put away and left in boxes. Where they eventually went, I just don't know, nor have I missed them. I'd once seen a documentary about Marie Kondo and her 'method' for decluttering that had left me baffled. I'd never felt that attached to a 'thing'. The objects of my childhood seemed important for a while, then they weren't. To be honest, I felt the same about most of the things Esther and I had left behind.

The suggestion that I might hold a pair of tatty old jeans and see if I felt 'joy' before deciding to keep them or not was a nonsense to me. Either I wanted an extra pair of jean or I didn't. The main deciding factor was "which of these jeans have the least holes in? Will I fall out of any of them in an embarrassing way if I crouch down?" Since I now chose to live mostly in a tiny space, my default answer for ninety-nine percent of everything I saw around me was "no chance, that's going".

Esther was different, however, and while I occasionally felt frustrated at how long things took, it was through this shared experience that I finally began to understand why some people find it so difficult to let things go. The emotions and memories bought up by old objects, especially gifts, remained powerful to her. It wasn't the thing she was scared of losing, but the memories and feelings of love they invoked.

I'd been one of three sons sharing a chaotic household while Esther had been an only child with severe eczema. She'd spent huge chunks of her childhood alone, even in hospital for weeks at a time. 'Things' were sometimes her only link to the outside world. They symbolised love and safety and that wasn't a bond that could easily be severed. Some mornings we'd wake up enthused to tackle 'the stuff' while on others we'd pretend it wasn't there, preferring to walk in the woods or ride our bikes to the coast. Sometimes we both felt frustrated at our inability to 'just get it done', but most of the time we just felt peaceful and secure.

By the time a completion date was agreed, everything I considered 'mine' had been dealt, as had most of Esther's old clothes, all delivered primarily to charity shops or donated away on Freecycle. Teddy bears, photo albums, trinkets and unused wedding decorations still dominated a lot our flat, however, and they weren't proving so easy to shift.

It took the extra impetus of the deadline to blitz into the final emotional hurdles. Inevitably, most of it went to charity shops in enormous and disordered bin liners, having been systematically photographed, appreciated and let go. We would have liked more things to go to friends, but everyone had already received as many 'gifts' as we could reasonably give them.

And then, one fine day it was suddenly time to leave. We'd been back in Durham for almost three lovely months, time we'd filled mostly with making new memories, but now it was over. Our ambition had been to become single-home owners again and to fit all of our personal possessions into just ten plastic tubs, all of which would come with us when we next travelled. Choosing ten rather than twelve or fourteen tubs was a totally arbitrary goal of course, one that came from a touring cyclist we met in the Lake District years earlier. We recalled him telling us how everything he owned (that wasn't attached to his bike) was in ten tubs stored with his brother. We liked that idea, except in our case we'd take the tubs with us.

We'd managed the first goal and, although we hadn't quite made the 'ten tubs' cut-off, we were definitely down to less than twenty. Of that number, just four boxes would now need to be stored with family because they contained sentimental items.

All of our clothes, kitchen equipment, memorabilia and electronics could now fit into just a single car. It felt amazing, just as we imagined it would. In Homer our happiness had often been inversely proportional to the number of things around us, and so it felt now. It was as though a weight had been lifted from our shoulders. No longer were we the legal owners of far more than we actually needed. The principle of keeping only things that were practically useful plus a very small number that filled us with inspiration and joy had been adhered to. The rest had been sent forth into (we hoped) a new life.

Unfortunately, the fact that we hadn't actually gotten around to buying another motorhome yet was suddenly a big problem. We'd really meant to do so and had assumed it would be just as easy as buying Homer had been, yet every time we'd looked online nothing had seemed quite right. Prices had also shot up, or so it appeared to us. We'd kept kicking the can down the road, always intending to look again 'next week', but now there was no more 'next week'.

In the end we left Durham in a hired transit van, our boxes and bicycles lying in the back as we trundled across Britain to spend a celebratory week touring in the Lake District. Hopping from Travelodge to Travelodge, we basked in the sensation of freedom that flowed back into us the moment we got out of the city. We never regretted the time we'd spent back in our flat, but at the same time the

117

physical separation from Durham wiped away the attachment instantly.

For two people living out of a transit van, it also surprised us how relaxed we felt about our circumstances. It was a mark of how much we'd already changed as people that we revelled in the blankness of the canvas our lives had become. Then Esther received a request. After hearing about our joy at culling so much clutter from our lives, Esther's parents asked if we could help them do the same thing. So we did. We spent three days living with them while they earmarked things we had authority to rehome, then three more weeks actually doing the rehoming, happily interspersed with playing with their dog Sam in the garden while they went on holiday.

If any further explanation of Esther's attachment to objects was needed, it came in the form of every single scrap of paper, toy and teddy from Esther's childhood we discovered boxed and labelled in her parents' attic. From home-made monopoly sets to plasticine food she'd crafted thirty years earlier, it was all there. We even discovered a dozen chocolate Easter bunnies, all decades old, that she hadn't eaten. It all went now though, photographed and sorted into the bin, charity or eBay piles. Car load after car load left the house, emptying the attic and freeing up huge amounts of space.

By which time it was mid-July and we still didn't have another motorhome. We drove around several southern dealerships and private sellers to take a look, but still nothing grabbed us. Everything we saw seemed overpriced or under-equipped for what we really wanted it for. We wanted our next motorhome to be the kind of thing we imagined full-timing in for the foreseeable future, not a rushed, last-minute decision imposed by our own lack of planning.

Perhaps that's why we ended up doing something else that was totally unplanned instead.

Turn Left At Mont Blanc

As the soft light of dawn began to filter through the green and orange material of our cheap, single-poled tent, we rubbed our eyes and shuffled around to face each other. Like stiff-limbed caterpillars encased in lime-green cocoons, we gently held hands through the padding and said the words that would become our daily mantra for years to come. "What adventures shall we have today?"

After sliding reluctantly out of our nests, we slipped into our damp and dusty clothes, unzipped the narrow exit from our shelter and crawled out to be greeted by an awe-inspiring sight. Right in front of us, across only a few dozen miles of crystal clear Alpine air, was Europe's highest mountain silently bathing in the pink rays of morning.

During the previous seven days of trekking from the shores of Lake Geneva, we'd encountered challenges and highlights in abundance. We'd faced rain, blistering sunshine, more uphill metres than we could remember, mosquito-bitten bottoms, stomach troubles and overly friendly cows. We'd even slept in a real teepee. But it was when we'd first crossed the 2257 metre Col d'Anterne the previous evening that all of the doubts, blisters and bruises had finally faded away, crowded out by the bewitching paradise we'd walked up to.

The imposing bulk of the Mont Blanc massif is a majestic sight from any angle, but seen from over 2000-metres on a remote and isolated hillside, it's a perfect yet private scene. It draws the eye like a magnet, along with any idle thoughts and worries that happen to be fluttering around uninvited at the time. That's why we'd decided to camp just below the col. That and the fact we'd just hiked for nine hours and it was getting dark. Never before had an impulse decision seemed so perfect as in the moment that

119

we crested that rise. Everything made total sense in this phenomenal landscape.

In stark contrast to the months of tedious preparation we'd invested into our abandoned honeymoon-hiking plan, our knee-jerk dash to Geneva was about as under-cooked as you could imagine. We knew there was a long-distance hiking route through the Alps because it would have been part of our honeymoon route and we'd found the still-unopened guidebook while clearing out our stuff. We also knew we owned the gear required to camp in the hills, most of which had joined us on our ill-fated attempt at the Tour du Queyras. It was just a short mental leap to put the two together.

We started packing late one night and by the following evening had arrived in Switzerland. We spent our very first night in a thirty euro hotel room just across the border in France. Arriving to find a silent crowd of truck drivers staring at us as they chain-smoked in the entranceway, we checked in and made our way along narrow corridors to our small and basic room.

Never before had we stayed in a place where both the beds and chairs were bolted to the floor. Nor could we open the window any wider than two-inches, a problem as it had been over thirty-degrees Celsius all day and the room was south-facing. Lying nude on our hard single beds, stewing in our own juices, it wouldn't have been hard to question if we'd made such a wise decision.

Other teething troubles followed. Within a few hours of leaving Lake Geneva it became obvious that we weren't in quite as good shape as we'd thought. Our unconditioned bodies, softened by four months of urban comfort and access to abundant dairy-free ice cream, had been forced to harden up quickly. We also hadn't made the wisest packing choices, ending our third day by spreading out all of our gear and easily discarding four kilograms of bumph (that's the technical term by the way) which we posted back to

Britain. Then, to top it all off, we'd been trying to walk much too far every day.

The one slightly extravagant thing we'd decided to do with the cash released from our flat sale was booking an all expenses tour of Egypt at the end of August. The rest of the money was going into our general living fund and clearing some debts, but for reasons I'll come back to in the next chapter, Egypt was something we really wanted to do. That's why we'd booked a flight from Geneva to Cairo (via Athens) on the 20th August.

Now, as you already know, we weren't exactly used to having deadlines in our lives any more, especially not deadlines that only gave us 29 days to complete a 31-day guidebook itinerary. As a result, we'd spent the first week always trying to get ahead, constantly trying to put some time in hand. We might have considered ourselves more mindful after two years of nomadic life, but it's amazing how scenarios manage to repeat themselves in disguise, almost as if life is checking up to see if we've really learnt our lessons yet.

"Ah, so you think you've learned to slow down do you?" said life. "What if I give you a physical / sporting challenge? Will you still make sensible choices then?"

"We'll go faster than the guidebook" had been our initial response.

Eventually, just as in our rat-race lifestyles, it was the pain and tension that our haste created which forced us to reassess. This wasn't supposed to be an egoic dash through the hills to add a notch to our mental trophy wall. It was about staying slow, smelling the flowers and appreciating the scenery together.

Hence why the sight of Mont Blanc on that seventh beautiful evening felt like such a watershed moment. It soothed our limbs and calmed our minds equally. Whatever had come before and whatever came next, wherever our feet took us, we'd have shared this view for just one night. That in itself was enough to make the entire adventure memorable and good. Perhaps we'd make it the Mediterranean Sea and the end of the trail? Or perhaps we'd need to catch a bus? Who cared? Either way, this moment could never be taken away.

We lingered the following morning, watching the rainbow colours of the sunrise play out across the snow-bound tip of Mont Blanc and the surrounding spires. As the morning dew began to burn off from the grass, we packed away our portable home, stuffed our sleeping bags and shouldered our burdens. Rush or no rush, today was to be another big day. It had to be, because our food had run out and it was at least twenty-one kilometres to the nearest village, a trek that included a thousand uphill and two-thousand downhill metres. All being well that would carry us across the summit of Le Brévent and down into the Chamonix valley, right up against slopes of the Mont Blanc massif itself.

It would prove to be a day of beauty but also of hardship. A day that involved an alarmingly crowded summit thanks to a busy cable-car, an unexpected brass band concert, and a roasting three-hour descent on a parched mountainside devoid of streams. By the time we directed our unsteady feet into the village of Les Houches, gazing up at the steep and rugged face of the 3842 metre Aiguille du Midi, our minds were consumed by thoughts of penguins dancing on icebergs and juggling ice creams. So vivid were our daydreams that I was beginning to reach out and stroke them, which you really shouldn't do, because penguin hallucinations do not like to be touched.

In the end we had to settle for several bags of frozen mango, inhaled on the kerbside right outside of the shop. As our bodies cooled and our dehydrated cells swelled again with the welcome arrival of fluids, our thoughts turned to the days ahead. For the next forty-eight hours (at least) our route would share paths with the most popular multi-day hike in the world, the Tour du Mont Blanc. At over 162 kilometres long, with almost ten kilometres of ascent included for good measure, this loop around the entire Mont Blanc massif is no mean feat.

That said, every year tens of thousands of visitors from all over the world set out to tackle all or part of the loop. Some carry a tent and all of their supplies on their backs, but many rely on a network of well-serviced mountain refuges, restaurants and occasional towns and villages to meet most of their needs. In the grand scale of the mountains these human elements are (mostly) blended sensitively into the scenery, with the ski-resorts of Chamonix and Courmayeur as the main exceptions. However, it's still true that in high summer the well-trodden tracks of the 'TMB' are some of the busiest in the world.

That's what was worrying us. After seven days of near total isolation, rarely coming close enough to another human being to say hello, the prospect of being surrounded by hordes of fellow trekkers on paths cluttered with rest stops and refuges was not a welcome one. We didn't like to think of ourselves as anti-social. There are many beautiful sights in the mountains and we'd long believed that a warm smile and a friendly 'hello' should be one of them. We'd never ignore or deny someone else's right to share our joy of the outdoors.

However, we also always believed that solitude and silence was one of the most essential ingredients of our personal experience when it came to enjoying nature. That's why we liked to choose the paths less trodden. Our uninformed mental image of the Tour du Mont Blanc was of a 'Disney-style' parody of what the mountains really are. A place where unfit, unsafe and disrespectful droves can blunder into the wild and go home bragging about how 'rugged' they were. In our arrogance, we couldn't have been more wrong.

Our eigth day of hiking began with a stiff and stony climb towards the saddle of the Col de Voza. It wasn't an especially long climb at a 'mere' 650 metres of ascent, a tiddler in Alpine terms, but as the rain began to lash down and dark grey clouds crowded out any trace of blue above us, we found our mood sinking quickly. This was something we'd already come to half expect after our first week, that our tired limbs and hungry tummies could play havoc with our mental outlook. Moods, we were increasingly realising, were passing events. That's why we did our best not to react outwardly, not to put any momentary frustrations into harsh words that could degenerate into an argument. It was something we'd read about in many mindfulness books as well. Practice is a lot harder than theory though. Then we met Rotem.

We'd been slowly gaining on a small green dot for most of the climb, a dot that had gradually grown arms and legs, then a head and finally a shock of red hair. We were just beneath the top of the Col de Voza when we finally said hello, falling into what could have been a brief exchange but effortlessly continued into something more.

Rotem, it transpired, was from Israel, and this was her first day of hiking from Chamonix. She'd stopped off at Mont Blanc specifically to hike for four days around the tour, hopefully reaching Courmayeur before continuing on to a summer work placement in Germany.

I suppose, since Esther and I had only had each other to speak to for more than a week, anybody new would have been a novelty, but Rotem also happened to be especially intelligent, funny and interesting. She told us about her job as a teacher, about the politics of her homeland, about the work she'd be doing in Europe over summer, and about her hopes and dreams for the future. We, in return, told her of our lives before setting off to travel, of the various things we'd done since and how so many of our old certainties were dissolving the more time we spent as nomads.

Although we'd only just met, it seemed our shared objective of simply walking and taking in the scenery made the conversation far more open and flowing than it might otherwise have been. Bonded by this mutual activity and appreciation, we talked like old friends meeting after a long absence. It was actually a very sad moment to part company, which we were forced to do at an otherwise nondescript trail junction because our destinations for the night weren't the same. We'd chatted for two happy hours and suddenly it was over, leaving behind a hole in our day that we hadn't even noticed before Rotem had filled it.

It was a pattern that soon began to repeat. After a first blessed rest day, sheltering from a day-long storm in the comfortable, clean and cat-filled home of a lady who offered rooms in a tiny hamlet, we re-joined the TMB feeling refreshed and hopeful. After meeting Rotem and smiling at countless other tour-goers, we'd used our rest day to re-evaluate our preconceptions and intentions. We knew there was no way we could make it to Nice within our time limit, at least not without making ourselves ill. Nor were we overly keen to part company with Europe's tallest mountain now that we'd arrived and fallen in love with its glaciated flanks and monumental spires.

In short, by the time we said farewell to 'Fan-fan', our cat-loving rest-day host, we were no longer heading due south but were swinging left around Mont Blanc.

It was one of the best decisions we ever made. As the sun returned to the sky we didn't find ourselves surrounded by noisy throngs but quiet and respectful souls, all of whom wanted the same thing as we did, a dose of nature's energy. There were families walking with small children, groups of friends, solo trekkers, and other couples like us. There was no one 'type' to be found here and certainly no parody or diminished sense of wilderness.

While we'd naively anticipated crowding, what we found instead was camaraderie and friendship.

By the time we pitched our tent outside of the Refuge de la Croix du Bonhomme at 2443 metres that same evening, the highest we had ever camped in our lives before, we knew in our bones that we'd made the right choice. The hulking giant of Mont Blanc looming above our left shoulder for the past two days had continued its magnet-like presence in our lives, drawing us away from our previous plans.

A challenging night of sub-zero temperatures ended with a stunning dawn. Gritting our teeth against the bitterly cold air that was freezing our lips and nostrils, we struggled out of our sleeping bags, contorted ourselves into our moist and crumpled hiking clothes, and emerged into the new day. Shivering in the shade alongside our frosty tent, we watched the light silently chase the shadows away from mountain peaks and push them further and further into the valleys below.

A family of ibex appeared to wave us off when we finally got going, the very last pairs of feet to leave the terrace of the refuge and head into the great green-and-white unknown. Positioned as they were, magnificently framed against the brilliant blue sky, it was like a wildlife photographers fantasy moment. All we'd done to deserve it was to eat our breakfast slowly.

We crossed the 2665 metre Col des Fours that day, a variant of the 'main' TMB route that we'd chosen primarily because it was so engagingly high. As you might expect, it was a place of monumental proportions but also of startling contrasts, both of scale and of time.

Gazing into the far distance we could make out saw-like, jagged summits decorated with snow patches as far as the haze would allow. Looking a little closer, but still far below us, we could make out the various pathways that snaked along the Vallée des Glaciers between Les Chapieux and the Col de la Seigne, where France turned into Italy. Closer still, on the slopes immediately all around us, were boulders and scree of all shapes and sizes that served as a reminder of how even these enormous mountains wouldn't last forever, broken down over the millennia by the gradual but incessant cycle of hot and cold. Then, much, much closer, between the soles of our feet we found several incredible fossil impressions of sea creatures embedded in the fabric of the Alps, a relic of former aeons when even the ground beneath our feet was beneath the waves somewhere or other. It was a very special moment, reflecting on the complex and awesome timescales of nature compared to our own time in the universe.

Two days later, having crossed into Italy and finding our way through the unexpectedly charming town of Courmayeur, we climbed up almost as high again onto another invigorating variant, the Mont de la Saxe crest. For three blissful hours we walked through a world of near unrivalled splendour at close to 2500 metres. We could have easily done it in half an hour, but to have done so would have been to race through one of the highlights of our hiking lives.

As we pottered and paused for a leisurely lunch, we gazed out on a scene that encompassed four full days of the TMB experience. On our left was the broad saddle shape of the Col de la Seigne, the French-Italian border that we'd crossed two days previously, while to our right was the Grand Col Ferret which we planned to cross the next day in order to enter Switzerland. In between lay a feast of alpine delicacies topped with the iconic skyline of the Mont Blanc massif, all underlined with a valley floor carved by glaciers. It was awe-inspiring in the extreme and was even made that much more special by the symphony of alpine flora and fauna that fluttered and whizzed around us.

If we could have paused that moment forever I believe we might have spent a very happy eternity. As it was, we eventually roused ourselves and raced the weather to the Rifugio Bonatti where we braced ourselves for our very first encounter with communal sleeping. A night inside of a solid refuge had seemed a great idea from afar while contemplating the forecast thunderstorm, but up close the reality of narrow, adjacent mattresses arrayed in long rows felt even more frightening than a few lightning bolts.

There's no time here to go into the roots of our respective 'privacy issues'. Suffice to say that feelings ran deep on the subject, almost to the extent that we dashed straight back out into the rain to huddle on the wet hillside.

Thankfully, we didn't. Not only because of the rip-roaring storm that smashed through the mountains that night but also because we might otherwise never have experienced the humbling environment of a mountain dortoir. In a global society that so often seems rife with division and mistrust, here was a multi-national, multi-cultural planet in miniature. A place where old and young, male and female, rich and poor could be safe and sleep soundly side-by-side, their life-giving possessions and supplies piled alongside each other. It was a world of trust and companionship, even if it did force us to confront some of our childhood demons.

For the remainder of our hike we continued to exist in a happy, friendly cocoon of smiles and companionship. The weather continued to challenge us, as did the gradients and uneven surfaces. It was an extreme landscape and the heat, cold, rain and wind mirrored those extremes. Yet because of the way everyone was moving at a similar pace, we were also part of a transient, ever-moving tribe. Right around the Mont Blanc loop we were surrounded by the same faces and smiles.

Whether it was the American military girls on leave from the navy, the older gentleman with a cigar hanging out of his mouth ("I don't smoke it, I just like the disapproving looks people give me"), the Israeli couple we'd slept alongside, or the Texan couple we spent laughing evenings with, there was an unspoken but undeniable bond that grew as we all shifted ourselves along the same winding route. It was a beautiful connection.

By the time we marched into the concrete jungle of Chamonix, startled by the sudden return of cars and exhaust fumes after almost three weeks of continuous walking, we'd notched up close to 300 kilometres with 17 kilometres of ascent. Our bodies had become leaner, our minds sharper and our boundaries had been broken down by a series of unexpectedly powerful encounters and experiences. Technically we were the same people who'd left the shores of Lake Geneva with love handles and too much kit on our backs, but as with every phase of our travels so far, we'd also been left altered in countless subtle, hard to fathom ways.

Egypt

Careering through the streets of Cairo in the back of a taxi, it was hard to believe that just hours earlier we'd said farewell to the tranquil magnificence of the Swiss mountains. One step at a time the sense of peace we'd felt among those wondrous glacier-bound peaks had been chipped away, first on a busy bus, then a noisy train, then a chaotic airport and now, two plane rides later, we were being driven through the night by an aspiring Formula 1 driver who loved Phil Collins music. This was not at all what we expected.

Not that I mind Phil Collins music I hasten to add, but if there was anything 'in the air tonight' it was the imminent sound of sirens. The fact that the driver was grinning so broadly as he hit his horn, grazed past bumpers and kept turning round to make conversation was not helping us feel at ease.

Gripping each other's hand tightly on the back seat, we tried to distract ourselves from our imminent meeting with the Grim Reaper by looking out of the window. We'd honestly expected that landing in Cairo at 1 a.m. would see us arriving into a city half-asleep. Not totally lifeless, because it is a national capital after all, but it'd never occurred to us that we'd be arriving into a metropolis still going at full speed. It might have been the early hours of the morning and the sky was pitch dark, but the roads were rammed, shops were open, street vendors plied their trade and five-a-side football centres were alive with hordes of young men chasing around AstroTurf pitches.

The reason why was obvious, now that we were here. It'd been obvious ever since we'd stepped out of the air-conditioned airport terminal in search of the taxi rank and been greeted by a waft of semi-roasted air. Even during the day's darkest hours, the temperature of a Cairo night in

August simmered somewhere between pleasant and a bit-too-hot. We trembled to think what it would be like when the sun came up. Then again, I guess we'd soon find out.

Thirty-minutes of hair-raising speed beneath road signs we couldn't even begin to understand carried us to our destination, the towering elegance of the Nile Fairmont Hotel. Rising high out of the ground next to the banks of its namesake river, the Nile Fairmont dwarfs most of the other buildings and hotels that can be seen nearby. It's an imposing monument of glass and modern architecture, with more than 500 rooms spread across 25 storeys, 8 restaurants and a sprawling health club that occupies the uppermost floors. Yet none of that was really catching our attention when we first arrived. It was the two enormous machine gun emplacements enclosed by sandbags that we'd just driven through that were dominating our thoughts.

We definitely weren't in a world of mountain lakes and butterflies any more. We'd arrived in a land of heat, history, guns and tension.

It says something about our tunnel vision at the time that the 'Arab Spring', as it's commonly known, and Egypt's 2011 revolution had largely passed us by. The popular uprising, in which hundreds died and the autocratic leader Hosni Mubarak was forced to step down from the presidency, morphed into a military takeover. Years of unrest followed, with continued protests and elections called into doubt, not to mention more tragic loss of life.

It's impossible to condense such an intensely complex topic into a simple paragraph. Suffice to say, although matters had apparently settled down by 2014 when Abdel Fattah el-Sisi was elected president, attacks on government forces by armed groups continued. By the time we arrived in the summer of 2016, tourist numbers at the various Red Sea resorts stood at just 50% of the pre-revolution figures. At inland historical sites and temples the numbers had fallen by up to 90%!

131

It sounds like big news doesn't it, because it is. It's the kind of news that people travelling to an unfamiliar destination might expect to stumble across during even the most basic background Google search. Yet we didn't have the slightest clue about any of it before landing in Egypt because we hadn't done a basic background Google search. We hadn't done any research at all, unless you count learning about pyramids at school twenty years earlier. That's why the sight of two enormous guns guarding the entrance to the luxury hotel we'd been booked into was a total surprise.

Pulling up in front of the hotel entrance, a smartly liveried porter collected our still dusty and grass-stained hiking packs from the taxi and posted them directly into a metal detector by the revolving door. Stepping back out into the heat, we cut striking figures in our hiking boots and well-worn trekking clothes. Esther had bought an extra shirt at Geneva airport, but apart from that and a single set of swimming gear, the only clothes we had with us were those we'd been wearing every day for the past month.

We may have been joining a five-star tour for the next fifteen days, but any opulence would not be extending to our wardrobe choices. After our Egyptian odyssey we were due to fly back to Italy and resume our backpacking lives, unless something else came up first. Picking up extra gear simply couldn't be part of the program for us. Besides, with almost two dozen temples and historical sites to visit, looking like Indiana Jones' poor relations didn't seem like such a bad thing in a nation of sand and sunshine.

Pausing briefly in the marble entranceway, we were further surprised to find the young and beautiful of Egyptian high society swirling around us. Mercedes and BMW cars jostled for position on the forecourt while short skirts and cleavages bounced around us in every direction, with long legs tottering on high heels and keen-eyed young men vying for their attention.

In preparation for our trip Esther had been specifically advised to dress conservatively in this predominately Muslim country. The only exceptions, we'd been told, would be inside of certain hotels and at the seaside resorts we were due to visit towards the end. Evidently the Nile Fairmont counted as one such exception.

Stepping through another metal detector ourselves, the chaos of smiles and lithe bodies continued inside the reception area. A base beat throbbed through the walls and it didn't take us long to realise that the Nile Fairmont also boasted a nightclub in its basement. This, in addition to the fact Egypt had no indoor smoking ban, was suddenly an enormous problem for us. You see, although we had a room booked for the 'night' ahead as part of our package, we didn't actually have a room arranged for the night of our arrival.

Our plan, which had seemed inordinately sensible back in Esther's parents' kitchen, had been to save money by spending the early hours dozing in a quiet armchair while we waited for the rest of the tour group to show up at lunchtime. "How hard can it be" we'd thought, "we'll have just spent a month camping and it'll be the middle of the night in a swanky hotel. We'll just find a quiet corner somewhere and wait." In the end it took less than five minutes of excessive smoke inhalation and body-shaking bass beats to drive us up to the main reception desk.

"Hello. I hope you can help us. We're part of a group that's arriving later today, but we've arrived ahead of the others. How much for a room for tonight?"

The receptionist smiled at us warmly. "Welcome to the Nile Fairmont sir, madam. A room tonight will be $300 American."

"Oh. Ok. We were told it was $150 extra by our tour organiser, but we originally said no. We've changed our minds. It is almost 3 a.m. now. Is there anything you can do on the price?"

133

"I'm sorry, we are very busy tonight and a booking now would have to be outside of any group discounts. We only have $300 rooms left."

Retreating to a vacant sofa we took stock of our situation. We had a credit card in our pockets and we did have the money in the bank, but we'd never paid $300 for a room in our lives. We hadn't even paid half of that. It just felt like so much money. Yet what choice did we have? It was either that or we spend up to twelve hours in a smoke-filled, vibrating marble hall echoing with the sound of high heels and laughter. Exhausted from our journey and still stressed from the pulse-pounding taxi ride, we trudged back over to the reception desk and did the only thing that seemed sensible at the time.

"Erm, hello again. We have hiking equipment with us. Would it be okay if we spread out our sleeping bags in a corner?"

"But of course" they smiled. "Might I suggest over there by the plants?"

Imagine walking into the Ritz in London and asking to blow up an air mattress. I'm still amazed they said yes. Not only that, but they even went out of their way to make us comfortable by sending over a porter to move a few of the huge ceramic pots around, just to make space for some untidy trekkers and their shy credit card.

Perhaps if the same thing had happened two weeks later we wouldn't have been so surprised. We experienced unrelenting friendliness everywhere we went in Egypt, and not only from people being paid to look after us. It would turn out to be one of the most welcoming places we'd ever been. We still should have paid for a room though. It was foolish not to, but our tired minds just couldn't cope with the extra outlay. We were still somewhat uncomfortable about having already spent so much to be here at all.

In total it had cost us £3500 for the tour package, plus £500 for the flights that we'd arranged ourselves (hence all of this middle of the night silliness). Considering that included transport throughout Egypt with several internal flights, a three-day Nile cruise, all entrance fees, five-star accommodation wherever we went and enough meals to triple our body weight, we didn't doubt this was good value for two people. That said, we'd never had a five-star holiday before so we didn't have else anything to compare it to.

The last time we'd planned to use hotels for a holiday was during my PhD when we'd eagerly awaited a Travelodge £9-per-night room sale. We'd waited up until midnight for the rooms to get released and then spent several hours trying to book fourteen consecutive nights in places that were sufficiently close together. Two nights in Barrow-in-Furness were followed by a night in Kendal, a night in Carlisle and then back down to Kendal etc. Actually paying somebody else to do the organisation for us was a totally new experience.

Yet none of that, not the itinerary, the luxury, or the novelty of being taken care of, were the real reasons we'd come to Egypt at this precise moment in our lives. It wasn't even the fact that we'd both longed to see the pyramids. The main reason that we were in Egypt, in this specific hotel on this specific evening, was because of the origin of the tour group itself.

Ever since Esther had been hit in the head by Eckhart Tolle (or at least his book), we'd continued to broaden our reading on the subject of mindfulness and meditation. We'd even started meditating a little ourselves in addition to keeping a journal and trying some yoga, which Esther was predictably fantastic at while I had the flexibility of an iron bar. Not that I didn't feel the benefit of waggling my fingers optimistically at my distant toes.

Almost a year later and there was one particular author who'd really appealed to both of us. His over-arching message was to "don't listen to your worries, go with the flow and, whatever you do, just be nice to each other", a message that closely matched the evolution of our own outlook on life. He still said some things that my brain filtered into the 'woo woo' category occasionally, but the core of what he had to say was practical, sensible and uplifting. As a result, we'd often tuned into the weekly guided meditations he streamed online via the 'spiritual community' he'd founded three decades earlier.

That's how we'd found out about this tour, because they were organising it. Plus, even more excitingly, the head honcho himself was definitely coming along. More than anything else, we really hoped that during our time in Egypt we'd learn something new about meditation, life, meaning, or whatever other intangibles came our way. Our own preliminary dabbling in meditation and mindfulness practices had convinced us that they were powerful, so we were excited to have the chance to spend a fortnight surrounded by like-minded people, many of whom we assumed would be much more 'advanced' than us, whatever that meant.

The main group eventually arrived in the early afternoon, eighty jet-lagged Americans, half from New York and the other half from California, and all of them with copious quantities of luggage. They were poured out of two coaches into an empty conference room, where they lingered in a state of what appeared to be tired annoyance (not the author we liked though, he was peacefully asleep in a chair). Aside from an abundance of colourful trousers, my own first impression of a meditation community was that they looked hungry and irritable.

In reality the eighty-odd people in the room that day were some of the nicest (and most interesting) we'd ever meet, and they were indeed united in a commitment to greet the events of the world with equanimity, hope and love. That said, when faced with empty stomachs and sleep deprivation, everyone's human.

The chaos of that conference room never really settled down, not for the next fortnight. Introductions and hasty amendments to the itinerary were announced, suitcases and bags were frantically dispatched into the hands of an army of porters, and everyone was loaded back onto the buses for a whirlwind tour of the nearby Egyptian museum.

With tens of thousands of artefacts crammed into the sweltering building and only a couple of hours left before closing time, our visit was necessarily focused on the obvious showstoppers. Simultaneously making introductions to our fellow travellers, we perused the dazzling golden death mask of Tutankhamun, wondered how they'd really managed to fit so much 'stuff' into such a tiny tomb, and marvelled at the immaculately preserved remains of those who had once been considered Gods upon Earth.

Some of the mummies on display had not endured the millennia as well as others, but those that had were enchanting. A bit on the skinny side, undeniably, but with their rich heads of hair and pointed cheekbones you might almost expect one to sit up and ask if anybody had fed the royal cat. It was all intriguing and fascinating, though in a curiously sad way.

By the time we all got kicked out, a ridiculously spacious expanse of Nile-facing luxury was waiting for everyone back at the hotel. We bathed twice in our room, just because we could, and then made use of the rooftop gym. Sleep would have been a better idea, but like kids high on candy-floss this opulent fairground felt too engaging to waste in slumberland. Not after what we'd paid to be here anyway and not even with an impending 4 a.m. wake-up call the next day.

Balloons & Hot Air

Two hours of private access inside of the Great Pyramid of Giza is a good reason to get up early. Otherwise known as the Pyramid of Khufu or the Pyramid of Cheops, the Great Pyramid was built four and a half thousand years ago and, for most of that time, remained the tallest man-made structure on the planet. It would be another 3700 years before Old St Paul's Cathedral in London would exceed it, and then only by a few metres, by which time the pyramid had actually lost almost ten metres in height through erosion. That's how long it's been standing in the desert, a man-made mountain being eaten by the wind and sand.

We arrived at the pyramid complex just as the red sun rose out of the surrounding desert, bathing that iconic, near-timeless triangle in soft pink light. Like most British schoolchildren, I'd seen plenty of pictures of pyramids over the years, including this one, but seeing it 'in the flesh' was frankly disarming. The sheer scale and ambition of quarrying, shaping, hauling and stacking so many tonnes of stone into such a gigantic heap out here in the parched desert is staggering enough as a concept. Seeing the result looming towards the sky as you stand at the base of it is quite another matter.

Put simply, there's a sorcery about the pyramid that I find hard to describe, as though it bends the space around it to create a beacon-like magnetism that captures one's gaze and doesn't want to let it go. From half-forgotten books and insomnia-soothing documentaries over the years, I was vaguely aware that the geometry of the pyramid and riddles about precisely how it was built had occupied minds for generations, yet none of that seemed the least bit relevant when confronted with the solid reality. It was there. It was amazing. What else really mattered?

As soon as the tour buses had stopped moving, our fellow travellers, some of whom were already becoming fast friends, started to fan out around the otherwise empty plateau with their cameras, as did we. Slowly but surely the ebb of bodies started to drift towards the gaping hole in the side of the pyramid. It would be easy to assume that the large and most obvious void in the Pyramid's face is the way in, but it's actually a relic of a ninth-century treasure hunt. Unfortunately for the Moors who hacked their way in, even back then only empty chambers remained. The public entrance nowadays is a much more discrete hole created by other enthusiastic sledgehammers in 1925.

As I ascended the human-sized steps chipped into the mammoth blocks that crowd skywards towards the pyramid's pinnacle, I found myself running my hand over their surface. Feeling the gritty sensation of the sandstone against my palm I wondered how many millions of others had done precisely the same thing. The stone around me was covered in hand-carved graffiti, with names and dates that stretched back over the centuries. How many of those that left their mark on this giant statement of existence stood in this exact spot asking the same questions that I was?

I closed my eyes and tried to imagine those who had hewn the rock from the quarry, transported it, shaped it and, ultimately, laid the first stone. What had their lives been like? How did they feel about the work they were tasked (or forced) to do? Pride or resentment? And did it matter now?

The sun was already well above the horizon by the time Esther and I slipped inside the pyramid, entering a narrow corridor of hacked-out rock that meandered into the darkness. Dim lamps were strung out along the tunnel, providing just enough light to see by but not enough to chase away the many shadows that remained in the cracks and crevices around us. Like a metaphor for the tomb that encased us, a lot more remained hidden than could be seen.

The group's first destination was the rarely visited Subterranean Chamber, an apparently unfinished void roughly hewn into the bedrock some 30 metres beneath the pyramid. Like most things pyramid-related, its exact purpose remains uncertain and hotly debated. Some say it was a decoy to fool grave robbers. Other suggest the architects simply changed their minds.

Either way, the narrow but arrow-straight passage that plunges into the ground is alarmingly petite. With the dim lighting, the length of the tunnel and the fact that our fellow travellers were closely packed both ahead and behind us, once the descent began it was impossible to be certain how far we'd gone. After even just a few metres of shuffling our world had shrunk to the space of a kitchen cabinet. There was smooth, solid rock on four sides and sweaty bodies completing the movable box we'd climbed into. The going was slow, with long periods crouched in the semi-darkness not moving at all. If I stopped to think about it, I could almost feel several billions tons of pyramid weighing down from above. Then again, I didn't think about it too much. Partway down, someone started singing 'This little light of mine…" and everyone joined in. It was corny, but lovely nonetheless.

Reaching the bottom was like stepping into a primitive sauna. The accumulated desert heat of several millennia was being intensified further by the close pressed human radiators packed in against the walls. Somebody had set fire to some incense, filling the limited air with a cloying pungency. A few people were praying, others were hugging, but most simply sat and stared. There was an overwhelming happiness in the air, a positive energy that totally erased the obvious fact that we were all stood in a deep and tiny cave with a single narrow entrance.

A talk and history lesson preceded the equally slow and halting upward progress that began after twenty minutes or so, with the group clambering back up the steep entrance tunnel towards the more famous Grand Gallery and the King's Chamber. This is the space at the heart of the pyramid where an empty stone sarcophagus sits silently in a room lined with 30-ton blocks of hard red granite. These are blocks so finely shaped and aligned that it's impossible to put even a sheet of paper between them. According to some folks, that's a level of precision that would be difficult to reproduce today, which is pretty mind-blowing if you really stop and think about it.

By the time we blinked back into the desert sunlight after two peaceful hours in the unchanging heart of one of the most sacred sites of the ancient world, the previously quiet plateau outside had morphed into a chaotic marketplace. Other visitors were arriving steadily, all of them being followed determinedly by clusters of vendors waving all manner of goods at them, from statues and figurines to clothes and headdresses.

We'd been warned that we'd be approached by lots of people with things to sell in Egypt and it wasn't hard to understand why. The stark poverty and desperation on display, even in Cairo during our first full day, was extreme. Manicured footpaths and sprinkler-dusted hotel lawns butted up directly against stinking rubbish heaps and homeless encampments, further enhancing the sense of unease that the ever present machine guns, car horns and shouting created. When we got to know our Egyptian tour guides better, they opened up a little about their changing world. The comfortable middle-class, they explained, had all but vanished now, with wealth flowing ever-upwards to a tiny number of families while the majority of people slipped closer to poverty.

That said, we were totally unprepared for our first encounter with the hawkers. Things were shoved into our hands, people refused to take them back and sums of money were shouted loudly in our faces, the figures changing constantly as we tried to make our way back into the relative quiet of the bus. The sums were so small it wasn't even about the money. We knew that some of our fellow travellers had bought totally empty suitcases with them with the sole intention of taking home gifts and souvenirs in abundance. We felt the exact opposite. We just didn't need or want anything, especially trinkets and ornaments.

Many times in Egypt we chose to pay several times the value for a bottle of water to disguise a donation, or bought something anyway only to slip it back on another trestle table later on. We may not have wanted the stuff, but walking through crowds of desperate people broke our hearts every day and underlined how incredibly fortunate we were, and how insignificant our imagined problems really were.

Back on the bus and that magnificent and private visit to the Great Pyramid was only the first event on a bulging itinerary. After the pyramid came a camel ride across the Giza plateau, then the Solar Boat Museum, which houses a complete and original royal barge over 4500 years old, then a pause at the world famous Sphinx standing, or should I say crouching, in the shadow of the Great Pyramid itself. And that was just the morning! After lunch we visited tombs, lots and lots (and lots) of tombs in the area surrounding the Sakkara Step Pyramid, which was our final destination of the day.

It was all fascinating and intriguing, but with each stop the pace seemed to accelerate. On the bus, drive across Cairo, off the bus, herded towards a specific collection of hieroglyphs or doorway, quick explanation, back to the bus...all in the growing heat of the day. We were some of the youngest on the tour but by the time we returned to the hotel the sun had set, we'd missed dinner and we felt absolutely drained.

There was no reduction in pace the following morning, which started at 12.30 a.m. That's not so much an early wake-up call as it is simply not being allowed to go to bed. Two internal flights came next, carrying us almost 1000-kilometres south to visit the stunning temples at Abu Simbel, right on the border with Sudan.

With morning air temperatures in excess of 40°C, we had just an hour to appreciate the two giant, 3000-year-old temples carved directly into a mountain by Rameses II (ancient Egypt's greatest self-promoter) before we had to go back to another airport and fly to Aswan. Incidentally, it was because of the construction of the Aswan Dam in 1958 that the Abu Simbel temples were cut into enormous blocks and moved 2 kilometres away from the river's edge to save the monument. Like an epic 3D jigsaw puzzle, even the placement of the smashed and broken fragments was perfectly recreated.

Our hotel in Aswan was another luxury development, the only peculiarity being that we were obviously the only guests. The location was undoubtedly beautiful, with another large room overlooking the waters of the Nile, plus every other possible amenity. There wasn't a single thing we disliked, apart from a strange feeling that we were somehow out of place in an otherwise deserted hotel capable of catering for hundreds more.

It was a feeling that was sadly underlined that evening during a much anticipated visit to an authentic 'Nubian village'. It was touted as an opportunity to see how the indigenous tribes along the Nile had lived thousands of years earlier thanks to an invitation from one of the few traditional communities that remained. To say thank you for the gracious invitation, everyone had also been encouraged to bring gifts for the villagers who would be hosting us, with toys for the children and clothes being suggested as the most appropriate.

From the moment we stepped out of the water taxis and entered the 'traditional' village, something didn't feel quite right. Souvenir stalls and shouting hawkers crowded all around and, as night was falling, the atmosphere was worryingly tense. We were ushered through the throngs quickly as a group, with traders reaching out to grab hands, arms and shoulders, demanding promises of purchases later in the evening. After almost an hour waiting in a courtyard with brightly coloured walls, being offered sweet tea by an army of young ladies, an elderly man appeared. This, we were told via a translator, was the headman and he was here to speak to us. His words were as powerful as they were unexpected.

Bidding us welcome he began speaking of traditional Nubian values, telling us about the history of his people and the simple life and respect for nature that had been handed down for generations. However, he then changed his tone, talking about how a growing desire for the trappings of western materialism was edging out those traditions. Change, he told us, was inevitable, but the pace of change and the wastefulness that was creeping into the world scared him.

The young people of his village wanted Coca Cola and McDonalds now, not because they were 'better' than what they already had but because they were considered symbols of prestige. Respect for the land and each other was waning while a lust for city life was rising. That made him scared for the future, not just of his village, but of the world.

As if to underline the point, the subsequent giving of the gifts instantly descended into chaos. Excited adults began barging into the room to grab handfuls of 'stuff' and run off with it. We left quickly and unceremoniously after that, bundled back to the boats and sailing into the night in shell-shocked silence, straight back to the waiting arms of luxury hotel rooms. A handful of people complained about the villagers' greed and lack of respect, but to our minds we were there ones that had carried materialism into that village. The end result was on us.

From Aswan we spent three days cruising down the Nile, pausing at various riverside temples and historical sites with a welcome drop in the pace of movement after such a frenetic few days. Food and song were available in epicurean abundance on board, but mostly we sat in the shade on the deck to stare out at the slowly passing riverbanks. Mile upon mile of green shoreline slipped by, often with lean, weather-beaten farmers wading with oxen as they worked a stretch of land. Every now and then we'd pass a rotting flotilla of half-sunken cruise ships next to villages and small towns.

As staff on our boat explained when we asked about them, a few years earlier there had been literally hundreds of similar ships ferrying passengers up and down the Nile. Now there were almost none in operation. Even the ship the 80 of us were on, which could have taken 300 people, hadn't been used for several months before our arrival. There were no bookings at all after we left.

We disembarked in Luxor, enjoying a nocturnal stroll around the majestic and illuminated expanse of this sprawling 3500-year old temple site. With the modern city spinning around its edges, we walked beneath pillars and alongside obelisks, culminating in a starlight stroll along a five hundred metre avenue lined with sphinxes. Today the avenue ends abruptly in a wall, but thousands of years ago this was a ritualistic highway between Luxor temple and the nearby complex at Karnak some three kilometres away.

"Walk alone and meditate on the experience" was the suggestion, but we chose to walk together, holding hands and reflecting on all of the beauty, busyness, history and decadence we'd experienced already in Egypt. We still had several days left to go, with many more temples to visit, but out there in the momentary peace we experienced a rather unexpected but shared epiphany.

Whether it was accumulated tiredness from the itinerary, the daily moments of sadness we'd felt at the inequality we saw, or the occasional disillusionment we'd experienced from the unconscious behaviours of people we'd initially looked up to as 'experienced and spiritual', I can't say. Probably it was all of those things. However, that night among the sphinxes we found ourselves melting into a deep and all-pervasive sense of calm about the life we'd be returning to the following week.

We'd realised by now that we'd come to Egypt looking for something 'more' again, looking for another purpose for our lives, albeit a more spiritual one than at other times in the past. Using the ruse of meditation and mindfulness as a cover, our egos had sneaked back in through the back door and started to make us feel uncomfortable about our life choices again. It was a subtle trick, but a trick nonetheless.

However, where we'd hoped and expected to be carried towards transcendental insight on the backs of a crowd we expected to be 'better' than us, instead we'd just met people: normal, kind, good, flawed, over-sleeping, disorganised, wonderful people. Ironically, it was exactly what we needed. Meditation and mindfulness were indeed useful and powerful tools, but that didn't mean there was anything wrong with us without them either. Why were we rushing again to be different rather than being grateful for all the changes we'd already made?

That night, on our 'pilgrimage of togetherness' as we called it, we realised how much we loved the life we already had. That we had no need to search for a deeper meaning beyond loving each other and appreciating the many gifts we already shared. In other words, we'd had to leave behind what we really loved to discover how much we loved it.

The tour continued to unfold the next day, just as fast and furious as before we'd boarded the boat. Millions of hieroglyphs blurred before our eyes, so much so that at the vast temple city of Karnak, where the main pillared hall is still the largest room of any religious building in the world, we wandered alone, away from the guides. Rather than focusing on a specifically unique shrine or scene on a wall, we felt happier to gaze in uninformed awe at the gargantuan pillars and intricate symbology that adorned every surface.

Later that same day we blitzed through the Valley of the Kings like a whirlwind, spending just forty-five minutes there. We spent even less time at the Valley of the Queens. It wasn't nearly long enough to appreciate a single ancient tomb, never mind the three we managed to charge in and out of.

Hidden away from the scorching sun, the incredible colours of the wall decorations here have survived like nowhere else in Egypt. Above ground the Valley of the Kings is bleak and deathly hot, but below ground most of its 63 tombs are vibrant, artistic masterpieces. It's hard to imagine that such vivid colour and detail once existed across all of the beige, eroded temples we'd already seen.

Early the following morning we rose high above the Nile in a deep wicker basket, feeling the searing heat of the hot air balloon's burner as we ascended into the dawn sky. It took just moments before the lush green snake of the Nile River began to stand out from the otherwise barren terrain beneath us. Like a trail of life and abundance in a sea of hot beige, the raw facts of life in the unforgiving desert world were laid bare.

We watched in silent awe for the next hour, enjoying the breeze on our faces as we skirted below 3000 feet with little more than some tangled sticks between us and rapid oblivion. It was all going wonderfully well, drifting like human seeds caught on the morning breeze. As we began to lose height and glide towards the desert landing site, we crouched down in the basket as instructed, bracing for the feeling of sand beneath us. It was at this point that the ever-smiling Captain Khaled gasped something that we couldn't understand, but which we later guessed was the Egyptian for "Oh Bollocks!"

Catching a pocket of low pressure, the balloon suddenly dropped earthwards at high speed. We looked up from our brace position just as the Captain flicked on the burner and the basket slammed heavily into what we later learned was a boulder of enormous proportions. The basket was flung sideways, with Esther headbutting the wicker hard with her forehead before the recoil sent the back of her head into the bridge of my nose. By the time we stood up again, Esther half-conscious and my nose gushing blood, we were several hundred feet back in the sky.

We did land, eventually, and spent the afternoon in hospital. I was fine, just a headache, but as Esther had wobbled unevenly back into the hotel the tour boss had insisted she get an MRI. Thankfully the balloon company was picking up the bill given that our travel insurance specifically didn't include hot air ballooning!

As we were ushered through a humid and crowded waiting area towards an ancient MRI machine, it struck us how much we took for granted the luxury of on-demand healthcare in our European lives. We'd been specifically told to expect the best care available, but as we entered what looked like a normal house, passed through a living room turned into a waiting area and saw the stained and battered instrument, it reminded us how fortunate we were.

As doctors reassured Esther that her brain was still present and in once piece, but that she had a severe concussion, the police showed up, as did the balloon company owners. Everyone wanted to know whose fault it was, or at least to hear Esther say that she didn't blame anyone, which was fine because she didn't. It was just one of those things. We actually felt grateful that Captain Khaled had avoided a much worse accident by reacting so quickly. But with half a dozen burly men shouting across her hospital bed, the only woman in the room, the doctor

148

was having a hard time reassuring Esther that all was well. We did get a 'holiday snap' of her brain as a souvenir though.

By the time Esther got discharged the rest of the tour group had gone ahead to the Red Sea. It was a long and deathly quiet drive through the Sahara Desert that afternoon, just the two of us in the back of a car, the owner of the balloon company driving and a man with a machine gun sat in the passenger seat. Every now and then we had to stop at a remote checkpoint, where bored-looking teenagers with even bigger guns waved us through with little interest.

After a week and a half of relentless heat, hieroglyphics and long bus journeys, the next forty-eight hours at Hurghada was like stepping into a parallel universe. The heat remained but long dresses transformed into bikinis and the sand no longer went on forever, plunging instead into the warm waters of the Red Sea. Also, we weren't the only people on 'holiday' any more. During the daylight hours deck chairs and loungers were filled with happy families, with waiters in white suits carrying cocktails through the masses, while in the evenings restaurants and bars overflowed with laughter and live music. It was like a materialistic world in miniature, a strip of western decadence edged up against the shores beneath the Gulf of Suez.

We had just a couple of nights left by the time we got back to Cairo, with a repeat visit to the Great Pyramid promised as a symbol of closure and reflection on the odyssey we'd shared. Unfortunately, like almost everyone else in the group, we were physically and mentally exhausted at this point. The whirlwind of temples, food, shopping and salesmen had reduced us, at times, to automatons, taking photos and moving on. We'd overeaten and under-slept our way around Egypt's most holy places and, sadly, that did diminish the end of our trip slightly.

Not that we didn't still feel the magic of the Great Pyramid when we stepped out alongside it in the light of dawn for a second time. Nor did we regret a moment of our Egyptian adventure. We understood why the itinerary had been so full, not only as the guides wanted to showcase as much of Egypt's beautiful history as possible but also to spread the tourist-dollars out to their compatriots as widely as possible. They'd told us as much. Most of our fellow travellers had wanted to shop, and in turn the various bazaars, stores and stalls had been desperate for footfall.

On reflection we chose to see it as a life lesson, specifically that less is more and that taking the time to savour beauty is a gift that shouldn't be taken for granted. All things considered, we'd had a wonderful time in the heat and the sand, but more than anything else, as our time in Egypt drew to a close, mostly we couldn't wait to return to the life we'd left behind.

Now What?

Of course, actually defining the life we'd left behind was like trying to throw stones at a cloud. Boarding the plane out of Cairo in the early hours of another balmy African night, we were once again backpackers with no fixed plans. What came next, we really hadn't a clue beyond getting to Venice airport and getting a lot of sleep, not necessarily in that order. It was a situation that looking uncannily similar to many others spread out across our shared history.

For example, how could we forget the night that we tried to cross the Finland-Sweden border in 2005? Our Lonely Planet guide made it look like the train went directly across the boundary, but it didn't, leaving us stranded in the middle of thunderstorm. We'd visited a few bed and breakfasts but refused to pay forty euros for short-term comfort, so instead sat on uncomfortable plastic stools for eight hours in an all-night 'Scanburger', slowly and reluctantly eating various forms of fried meat in burger buns until the staff realised what we were doing.

"You don't have to eat any more burgers" they'd said to our bloated younger selves. "You could just sit, if you like."

Then there was our ill-fated 2008 attempt to tour the Scottish Highlands in Esther's Nissan Micra. With no advanced planning we'd simply loaded the car with stuff and driven north, confident it would all work out. At first it did, we had a lovely walk when we arrived. However, cowed by the prices of both rooms and campsites, we'd resolved to sleep in the car. Two nights later we were home again, covered in hundreds of mosquito bites and so sleep-deprived that Esther had needed to drive home in half hour stages (I still couldn't drive at the time).

There are other examples as well, including our most recent decision to spend an uncomfortable twelve hours in a smoky Egyptian foyer rather than part with $300.

I've said it before, but it really is amazing how life has the ability to keep replaying certain situations in this way, waiting to see if you can finally start making better choices. The scenarios reoccur in disguise, adjusting to suit the changing circumstances of life, but that's all part of the trick. The underlying challenge is always the same. Truth is, Esther and I have never been very good at paying for a place to stay, at least not when a cheaper, less comfortable option is available. That's why it felt so momentous when we finally bucked the trend, landing in Athens at 6 a.m. with a seven hour wait until our connecting flight to Italy, determined to rest whatever it cost.

We spent ninety euros that morning for the sum total of four hours sleep in a hotel room we scarcely touched. So desperate were our bodies to become horizontal after our flit through half the temples in Egypt that we handed over our credit card with barely a grimace and passed out within three minutes. It was wonderful. We didn't even use the shower.

When we landed in Venice later the same afternoon, our plan was simply to stay still for a few more days before working out what to do next. We had no commitments but we did have a renewed sense of confidence and mental clarity regarding our simple, uncluttered, nomadic lifestyle. Whatever came next, our intention was to make sure we didn't introduce any unnecessary complications.

Unfortunately for our still tired bodies, peace and quiet wasn't in high demand or supply on Camping Village Jolly, the first campsite we'd stumbled into after stepping off the airport shuttle in Mestre. It was mostly beer, boobs, beach balls and bottoms that surrounded us rather than birdsong and slowly waving palm trees. Still, we didn't mind too much. Or at least if we did, the prospect of moving again so soon was much worse than a few late night party-goers and dive bombing students in the busy pool.

Safely ensconced within a flimsy plastic camping hut, where the paper-thin walls left little of our neighbours' activities to the imagination, it was heaven simply to be able to close our own door, shut the curtains and not have a single engagement waiting for us. No more wake-up calls in the middle of the night, lost suitcase dramas or hustling through sacred sites in an effort to stay on schedule. We were back on our own clocks again, something we'd taken far too much for granted until we spent a lot of money to confirm that we really quite liked the life we'd stumbled into. We even preferred the plain cheapness of our twenty-eight euro camping shed, with all of our still dirty, tattered hiking gear spread out around us. This was us. No frills but a lot of love. Having tried it ourselves for the first time, we now knew that we didn't really need or want the mostly unnecessary baubles of five-star life.

Of course, we still visited Venice, twice in fact. With its chequered and often bloody past, there are few places that can boast so much history as this floating city strung between tiny islands and poles driven into marshland. From the sublime beauty of St Mark's Basilica, founded almost a thousand years earlier and richly decorated with beautifully painted frescos and sculptures, to the Rialto Bridge, the most famous crossing of Venice's Grand Canal, Venice is simply flooded with scenic marvels (if you'll pardon the pun).

It was also hot, crowded and expensive, but we didn't have any desire to queue for the many museums and cathedrals, or even to eat pizza in one of the boutique restaurants on St Mark's square. We remained content, as usual, to meander through the narrow streets, looking up at the blue sky framed by the tall buildings around us and lose ourselves in the suggestive aura of mystery that cloaks these ancient byways. We were fulfilling our goal of holding hands and smiling at the world passing by.

It took us five days to tire of living in a shed alongside randy students, so we decamped to a quieter stretch of nearby coastline on the Adriatic Sea. It was there, among the half-empty sands and deck chair ranks of Caorle's beaches that we began to consider our medium-term future in earnest. We'd soon be approaching our third winter as nomads and we definitely felt more at ease than we had at the same time in either of the previous two years. With the combined knowledge that we no longer had an unwanted life gathering dust elsewhere, and that we could happily exist with little more than the clothes on our backs, the question now was in what direction should we point our lives?

Did we still want another motorhome, for instance? Did we want to settle down for a while? Should we travel even further afield? Almost everything was on the table. We obviously didn't have expensive tastes and so, with the resources we had available after our flat sale, most of what we could think of was a genuine possibility. It was a happy position we found ourselves in, 'making ourselves rich by making our wants few' to paraphrase Henry David Thoreau.

I won't dwell on the many discussions we shared over the course of our fortnight by the sea. Truth be told, talking about options was easy and fun. It was committing to a course of action that was daunting. Still, we got there in the end. As the late season sun began to set on the final remnants of Caorle's summer footfall, we also drifted away, back towards Britain with a plan of action crystallising in our minds.

The short version is this. We wanted another motorhome, but not just any motorhome, we wanted a small, 'adventurous' motorhome. After a summer of backpacking, revelling in the lightweight freedom of having so few things to think about, we were ready for just a touch more stability. A tiny little bit of extra comfort, such as access to a toilet and a shower when we felt the need. However, what we didn't want was another cumbersome living room on wheels. We wanted a little van, something we could use specifically to lose ourselves in the deepest, most remote patches of wilderness we could find. A van we could leave behind when we set out with our tent, but also a van we could use as a car when nomadic life felt too much and we did some house-sitting or similar. In a nutshell, we wanted a vehicle we could sleep in, not a home that moved.

It took us two busy weeks in Britain to find what we were looking for. It came in the form of a professionally converted transit van. Yes, it was cramped inside when the door was shut, but as we'd learned with Homer, campervans and motorhomes are essentially rolling compromises. With a toilet, shower, fridge, kitchen sink, hob, dining table and a double bed, there's really not a lot more space left inside of a 6-metre-long vehicle. It was also, much to Esther's chagrin, fitted out with dark wooden cupboards which, even I had to admit, did cast a gloomy mood across the interior. However, functionally at least, it was everything we needed and more. It was a good price and it was available there and then, so we took it.

I confess, we started having doubts on the very first day, just minutes after starting to pack our travelling possessions into the cupboards. With only a handful of our things on board the initially reassuring sense of newness and tidiness had already vanished, along with most of the residual comfort or space. But we'd made a commitment now. There wasn't time to change our minds.

We left the UK at the beginning of December, charging at full speed through France and right to the bottom of Spain where the weather remained fine. Driving wise, Ithaca (which is what we'd called our new home) was a dream. With a bigger engine than Homer on a much smaller vehicle it was like stepping out of a tractor and into a sports car. Singing at the tops our voices as we drove, we sailed through Europe with the proverbial wind at our backs.

We only stopped a couple of times all the way to Granada, right at the foot of the Sierra Nevada mountains. With the Alhambra as one of the most renowned buildings of Spain's Islamic history, plus a great wealth of Spanish-Islamic art, Granada's a popular tourist destination for many reasons, but it was the white-topped horizon that was catching our eye.

Sierra Nevada literally means "mountain range covered in snow", and this particular ridgeline pressed up against the Mediterranean Sea contains the highest point in all of continental Spain, the summit of Mulhacén, at 3,479 metres. That's what we wanted to get a little taste of, so we did, braving the chilly winds as we pedalled all the way to the snow-packed end of the road at Pico Veleta, Europe's highest paved road at 3400 metres and, consequently, the highest cycling climb too (without needing any extra bits of tarmac to qualify).

As we set off from the outskirts of the city and wound our way into the pine-tree slopes beneath a kind sun, it was hard to believe it was winter unfolding around us. With a maze of forests, crags and ancient terraces weaving together across the mountainsides, we ticked off the long but smooth kilometres to the top in grateful appreciation of this red and rugged landscape scattered with shrubs. Towards the top, as we approached the end of the portion of road accessible to cars, we emerged onto an exposed stretch of ridge where the winds and altitude conspired to make us feel very small and vulnerable, but we plugged on.

Ducking under the barrier that keeps out the cars from the final twelve kilometres, we wound up one switchback after another, snaking towards the cold summit above us with little idea how this could possibly keep going. We could rarely see a way ahead, yet every time it looked like we were approaching a dead-end we'd turn a corner and find still more chipped asphalt threading upwards, a bit like how we were living our lives really.

I can't say exactly what height we reached before the tall snow drifts cut off the route entirely. It was at least 3200 metres, maybe more, but it was enough. Standing in the now biting wind and looking out over hundreds of miles of rolling Spanish plains, it felt amazing to be back in the hills, not to mention nice to know that our cycling legs still worked after a summer of hiking, riding buses and eating Egyptian buffets.

We spent the next week exploring the fringes of the Sierra Nevada mountains, riding up a few more long hills and appreciating the picturesque network of valleys and rolling foothills that play home to remote villages, tumbledown farms and wandering herds of sheep and goats. We would have stayed longer but we had a rare appointment to keep. Just a short hop away Esther's parents had arrived in the Cabo de Gata Natural Park for their own winter break and we were heading over to join them. Family time had been a rare commodity over the past few years, for obvious reasons, one of the few real downsides of a wandering life.

They'd booked into an apartment in San Jose, the largest of the Cabo villages, and we'd arranged to move into a lovely house nearby, excited to experience a short dose of family closeness for a few weeks. With winter rents being so low in the area at the time, we'd be paying just 400 euros for a comfortable month of sea-views, sofas and a bathtub. It would be one last dalliance with urban living before our exciting van life really, or so we told ourselves, a way to make sure we hit the road fully-charged and hungry for adventure.

Or at least that was the plan.

Leela

Easing ourselves into the white plastic garden chairs of the shoreside café, we used our slowly improving Spanish vocabulary to order some drinks. "Café con leche, dos, uno Polio Menta y uno Agua con gas por favor". The waiter nodded, smiled to confirm that we hadn't bodged the pronunciation too badly, and then sauntered slowly inside to fetch the drinks. So far, so good. All we had to do now was sit back, bask in the morning warmth and watch the colourful boats bobbing around on the shimmering sea.

I expect there are few places more idyllic to while away a sunny December's morning than the miniscule fishing village of La Isleta del Moro. With a jumble of white houses clustered together on a dusty spit of land and a short jetty that juts out just beyond the stony beach, the scene is framed by a background of red cliffs and the sparkling clear waters of the Cabo de Gata Natural Park. In other words, visiting La Isleta is like stepping into an especially charming postcard.

A few moments of quiet reverie slipped by when Terry, Esther's dad, suddenly added "Hmm, I think I'll have a cheese and ham toastie as well. Would anyone else like anything?"

A quick round of head shaking confirmed that, since we'd all only just enjoyed breakfast, we were quite happy to wait for our drinks and enjoy the moment with a little companionable chatter. Terry, however, was undeterred. We were 'out', and going 'out' meant toasties, breakfast or not. "Just me then" he said with a smile, getting up and heading inside to add the food to his order.

A few minutes later the drinks arrived along with an alarmingly large length of steaming baguette, liberally smothered in melted cheese and bright pink strips of ham. "Wow" exclaimed a delighted Terry, rubbing his hands

158

together before swiftly setting to work on his elevenses. It wasn't long though before his pace was slowing.

"I'm not sure I'm going to be able to manage all this on my own you know, are you sure that no-one else wants any?" Another round of head shaking followed until a new voice suddenly joined the conversation, a soft, feminine voice with a strong hint of Mexican.

"Give it to dog" said the voice.

We looked down and there she was, the dog I mean, not the voice. A small, sleek, ginger cylinder of fur, with a white nose and a tufty Mohican running along the length of her upper back. I could say that she was wagging her tail expectantly in the general direction of the toastie, but that wouldn't be wholly accurate. Better to say that she was wagging her entire body in excited ripples that extended right from the end of her shaking nose to the white tip of her beating tail, her front paws padding quickly from side to side as though she was only just managing to restrain the explosion of excitement that the mere existence of "toastie" was creating in her mind.

This being southern Spain, the presence of several street dogs wandering around a café or perusing the nearby dustbins was not an unfamiliar sight. Nor was it uncommon for other dog owners to simply allow their own pets to roam at leisure while they supped and chatted somewhere in the vicinity. Sort of zoning out and accepting their usually benign presence was an easy habit to fall into. Occasionally you might reach down to provide an ear scratching service or complement a nearby owner on their "lovely dog", but certainly, being British, actually feeding somebody else's pet wasn't usually on the agenda, not without permission anyway.

The owner of the pleasant Mexican voice turned out to be a lady named Blanca, well-tanned with a shock of white frizzy hair, who was sitting just across the café from us with her friend Kathy. Quite naturally, since she was dishing out permission so freely, we assumed she must be the owner of the cute excited dog. It was wearing a collar after all. A short while later, after delivering a fair amount of cheesy-hammy bread into the increasingly excited ginger dog, we stood up to leave.

"She's really lovely" said Esther, reaching down to give the expectant happy face a final fuss. It was true, she really was. Gentle, soft, quiet and persistent but without being a pushy nuisance. In fact, as much as the melted cheese had clearly delighted her, fuss and cuddles seemed to invoke just as much response. The slightest touch had her rolling on her back for a tummy rub and, if we had the gall to try and stop, she'd jump up and push her muzzle back into our hand to remind us that there was still more rubbing to do. Clearly, if fuss wasn't coming to her, then she'd go to the fuss. Even Sam, Esther's parents' dog and an occasionally grumpy elder statesman, had willingly accepted her energetic presence from his own quiet station beneath the table.

"You want her?" came the unexpected response from Blanca. "She was only found in our village last week. I've taken her in for now and tried to find an owner but we can't keep her. We already have several cats and another dog of our own, Lily". She nodded towards a large Alsatian-type dog that had been running back and forth on the nearby beach for the past quarter of an hour, barking loudly and continuously at the disinterested seagulls.

"We call this one Chiquita."

I was immediately on my guard, spotting a certain contemplative look in Esther's eyes that I could recognise from the days when we'd first started adopting abandoned rabbits. We both loved animals, no doubt about it. At one time we'd had a dozen heartbeats sharing our Durham flat, with two humans, six rabbits and four hamsters (all adopted from various small-animal rescue centres). One particular ball of ginger-white fluffiness (also with a Mohican hairstyle) even melted my own initially sceptical heart. His name was Thumper (what else?) and he had no known limit for human attention. All we had to do was drape an arm out of the bed at night and a few seconds later he would appear, nuzzling at our fingers and demanding a head massage.

Parting company with our house rabbits had been the hardest part about leaving our old lives behind, so the sudden and casual offer of an unsought dog was hardly something I welcomed. Yet it planted a seed.

For the next fortnight we couldn't quite put the issue down. Outwardly I was the more reluctant, but the more we talked the clearer it became that we both felt exactly the same way. Yes, we liked the idea of a having dog. Yes, we could definitely offer a dog a good life in our new little van. But was the love and companionship we'd be giving and receiving worth the necessary curtailment of our freedom, even if it was only minor? We were young. We'd still only just sold our flat and given away most of our stuff. We had money in the bank and an urge to explore. And we'd just bought the very vehicle we wanted to do that exploration in.

No, we eventually decided, we couldn't do it. We weren't going to get a dog. Eventually, as the New Year approached, we finally felt able to put the matter to bed. The answer was no.

And then, just hours after agreeing 'once and for all', we met Gustav, a travelling Englishman tramping through Spain who turned out to be a former academic himself. He'd walked out on his 'old life' eight years earlier he told us, in search of something he couldn't define, and was now making his slow way north again to try and resume something of his previous lifestyle combined with the simpler existence he'd lived as a traveller.

We met him just as he was bedding down for the night in the cold comfort of an empty shop doorway. We swiftly fell into an easy conversation, talking about all sorts of things as well as offering him some help, which he turned down kindly. But it was the moving bundle of rags by his hip that had the most profound impact on our lives that night. It was a tiny, crying puppy that Gustav was keeping warm beneath his tattered clothes, gently offering it scraps of food. He'd found it, he said, cut and bleeding after being attacked by larger dogs. Gustav's hope was that he could nurse the puppy back to health and then either keep it himself or find a suitable home as he headed north.

It was that moment that would change our lives. Turning to Esther when we reached our rented house, I asked the question that I couldn't get out of my mind. "If he who has so little can offer help to that tiny puppy, then why are we, who have so much, struggling to offer help to an animal in need?" I wanted to try, and so did Esther. We always had; we'd just been too scared to admit it.

The very next morning we called Blanca. I'd only half-heartedly saved her number by calling it from my ancient (but indestructible) handset. If I'd made a single other call her number would have been lost to us forever, and there could have been no Chiquita. But, as luck would have it, Chiquita was still very much with them, terrorising their cat who had now started peeing on the furniture in protest. Blanca was delighted that we wanted to try giving Chiquita a home. Two days later our travelling duo became a trio.

Two days was all the time it took for us to tell our supportive landlady, who released us from our contract without a qualm, find a dog-friendly place for the remainder of our time in San Jose and move our entire lives across town in a jumble of half-packed tubs and carrier bags. We tossed everything into the van at one end, cleaned and scrubbed the place we were leaving, and then poured everything back out at the new place. Having hardly any possessions definitely had some major advantages.

Blanca was ready when we arrived, with our new partner's few worldly possessions waiting in a pile by the door. A small striped basket contained a mangled teddy bear and one of Blanca's bright orange scarves, plus a half bag of the kibble she was used to. That was it, an even lighter traveller than we aspired to be. Blanca told us that she was just happy that her temporary friend had the chance of a good forever home, but she couldn't hide her watery eyes completely behind her broad smile. It was a brief parting, functional but friendly, with Lily the crazy Alsatian sniffing noses with her sidekick for what would prove to be the last time in a long time. Maybe she knew?

Stroking and soothing the alert ginger bundle perched on my knees as we drove back to San Jose together, I found myself pondering if this was how new parents felt driving home from the hospital. It was the closest we'd come to such an experience, suddenly entrusted with the care of a living, breathing being that carried with it an uncertain future. Did they also feel zoned out and numb, as I did, as a means of coping with change and the fear that comes with it? We had a dog. Now what?

Every few moments I glanced over at Esther as she drove, caught her eye and smiled. Occasionally, I squeezed her knee for good measure. Neither of us said very much while our new addition sat still on my lap, whining quietly. She hadn't resisted leaving Blanca's little house, or fought to stay either. Now that we were on the move she seemed content to sit with a front paw on each of my knees, peering at the passing coastline. Perhaps she knew the places she was seeing?

According to Blanca, she'd been found with another dog, both dirty and emaciated, the morning after a heavy thunderstorm. They'd been sheltering together in a shop doorway. Blanca had taken in Chiquita while another kindly villager had given the male dog a temporary home, but efforts to find an owner (or owners) had drawn a blank.

"It happens a lot" Blanca had explained. "We're in a remote area so city people drive out, dump their dogs and

drive away. Once I saw a dog chase a car for over a mile."
Tragically, this was just the first of many such stories we'd
hear in the weeks and months ahead.

Within just a few hours of getting home, Chiquita
had become Leela. It wasn't a planned change, though
Chiquita had always felt like a cumbersome name for such a
small, well behaved little dog. Plus I felt like I was singing
an Abba song whenever I used it. The name Leela just
seemed to fit, falling out of Esther's mouth during our very
first stroll along the street together. Curiously, it worked.
The dog came back every time when we called her new
name.

More than a year later we'd have a chance meeting
with an Indian lady who was giving the keynote speech at a
European yoga conference. She stopped to fuss Leela in a
Swiss car park of all places, eventually coming to sit with
us and share a cup of tea. The fact people had come from all
over the world to hear her speak and we got to spend a
private hour and a half with her simply because she liked
dogs hadn't escaped our notice. The moment we told her
Leela's name, she started laughing. Turns out that in ancient
Sanskrit "Lila" translates as "the cosmic game". She was
certainly going to lead us on a merry dance in the weeks
ahead. But we had no idea of any of that yet.

Leela's generally high level of obedience and
gentleness (especially with children) suggested that she'd
started her life as a pet somewhere. She was also house-
trained, though she was heartbreakingly fearful. The first
time she saw us pick up a brush to sweep the floor she ran
and hid beneath a chair. She would submit to fuss at the
slightest touch of a finger, usually rolling onto her back, but
if we raised a hand above our heads to stretch or reach to a
high shelf, she would cower.

Whatever had happened to her, we hoped that she'd
be safe now. She slept in a basket by our bed. She sat
quietly with us when we read or typed. And she came

jogging with us when we went out on the beach. She was just so damned easy, fitting in with our existing routines and activities without a murmur. In fact, during our first few days as a trio, it was a mystery as to why we hadn't gotten a companion sooner.

Dog Nipples

Esther first commented on the size and fullness of Leela's 'nipples' on only our second day with her. My embarrassingly masculine, know-it-all response had been to make an entirely confident (and utterly uninformed) announcement that "that's just what female dog nipples are like". The fact that I knew nothing about dog nipples, beyond the fact that they existed, didn't overly concern me. Leela was a girl and she had nipples. It didn't even cross my mind to call them teats.

Still, as I'd learned during my few years in academia, it's amazing what you can get away with when you say it in a confident tone of voice. Just look at any prominent politician. It wasn't until other people started to comment that I became aware of a growing sense of dread. "Has she had a litter?" people would tactfully ask, nobody wanting to raise the possibility that we might, in fact, have just given a home to a pregnant dog.

And then someone did say it, "I think she might be pregnant you know". Oh? Crap!

During the many and varied dog discussions we'd had prior to offering Leela a home, the fact she was female and therefore might be pregnant hadn't come up. Not once. All of a sudden we became fixated on the shape of Leela's belly, which was showing a definite and non-trivial rounding now that we came to think about it.

Although Leela had been living for several weeks with Blanca after her unknown life beforehand, she was still very thin when she came to live with us, or at least that's what we'd perceived. She certainly looked nothing like we imagined a chubby, pregnant dog should do. Then again, what did we know? We were clearly clueless. 'Dog nipples' indeed.

"Was that a twitch?" one of us would say, followed by a minute of intensive staring as we tried to convince ourselves that what we'd just seen hadn't really occurred. Or that it was just an especially lively bit of poo working its way around her innards.

We'd collected Leela just before a weekend and national holiday combination, so it wasn't until the middle of the following week that we could get her to the local vet practice. On the face of it we'd come to have a health check, some routine vaccinations and a pet passport filled out, but by this stage there was really only one question on our minds. "How many dogs have we just adopted?"

Praying that the answer was 'one', but with little hope remaining, we made our way into the plush little boutique surgery, a satellite of a larger place in nearby Almeria.

Fortunately, Pati the vet was a charming young lady who spoke perfect English. We explained the circumstances through which we'd adopted Leela and she expressed her own gratitude that we were helping with what she knew, from first-hand experience, was a massive problem in the region. Yes, she sadly confirmed, the rescue centres in the area were full to bursting. Yes, they did their best to find good homes, but dogs often came in faster than they could go out. And yes, because of tragic necessity, dogs were sometimes destroyed on the flimsiest of reasons. There was simply no other way. Rehoming charities did the best they could, with many taking dogs to other European countries, but the scale of the problem was just too big.

Leela's health-check followed. Teeth, temperature, ears, eyes and joints all got a clean bill of health, and we got further confirmation that she was probably less than a year old. But it was when Pati began feeling her abdomen that we saw her face grow more thoughtful.

"Erm, some people said she might have already had a litter. Or even, ha ha, be pregnant?" I said nervously.

Pati didn't say anything at first as she continued to caress Leela's midriff with gentle fingers.

"Could be" came the quiet reply.

We were back at the vet's practice bright and early the next morning, with Pati bringing in an ultrasound machine from the Almeria surgery. By now we had little doubt what the result would be. We'd spent a foolish (but fascinating) hour the previous evening watching YouTube videos of puppies being born. With our hands resting lightly on Leela's middle, we could no longer ignore the gentle but bony ripples moving beneath our fingers. The vet may have reserved her official verdict until after the ultrasound, but even we could see the writing was already on the wall. We'd only gone and adopted a pregnant dog.

As Pati switched the machine on, the ever-biddable Leela lay on her back, incredibly relaxed about everything while the soft fur around her undeniably swollen teats was shaved off and replaced with blue lubricating gel. The probe and the official verdict followed seconds later.

"2, 3, 4,... 5,... 6,... I think, erm, maybe 7" declared Pati, slowly counting off the wriggling spectral images on the ultrasound screen.

"What do you mean 'maybe' 7?" we asked, clinging to the one remaining piece of uncertainty instead of the now unavoidable fact that our new dog, the one we'd collected a mere 5 days ago, was going to emit a lot more dogs.

"Well, the problem is they're packed in very tight, as you can probably see. Also, some are pressed up into the ribcage and they're moving all the time, so I don't want to pretend I'm giving you a definite answer. In my opinion though, and I've done this quite a lot, there are definitely 5 puppies, probably 6 and, although unlikely, there could be a seventh as well. There could even be eight, you can never be totally sure."

"Oh Shit!" we helpfully added.

"Yes" agreed Pati, "and I think you have about 2 weeks to go. After number 5 appears, expect a probable sixth, and if number 6 appears, expect a possible, but unlikely, seventh."

"Two weeks?!" we exclaimed, doing our best to make it sound like a question and not a cry for help.

"Well, dog gestation periods are usually pretty consistent at around 59 days. Some larger breeds take a few days longer, some small dogs a little shorter. But the average is a good indicator. Obviously, you don't know when Leela got pregnant, but based on the size of the puppies, fully-formed with strong heartbeats, I'd say they are between 45 - 50 days along already. So, around two weeks left to go. Maybe a little more, but probably a little less."

"You mean she could have the puppies today?"

"Well, theoretically I guess she could, but no, I really don't think so. There would be other signs as well."

There followed a crash course in dog birthing procedures, a process beautifully named as whelping, which involved Pati drawing diagrams on her whiteboard. We learned a lot in the next quarter of an hour.

It was the first time we'd heard that dogs show nesting behaviour in the days preceding a birth, for example, growing increasingly restless and uncomfortable as a birth got closer. We were fascinated to find out that each individual puppy was growing inside of, and would be born within, their own amniotic sack. And we were even further amazed to hear that as each puppy appeared Leela should break that sack open by licking it, as well as severing the associated umbilical cord by chewing through it. In fact, all being well, we wouldn't have to be involved at all during the birth itself. All we had to do was give her a quiet, safe space to do it all in while keeping an eye out for emergencies.

"What sort of emergencies?" we asked, anticipating blood and afterbirth dripping from walls of the rented apartment we were supposed to be moving out of shortly.

"After Leela goes into labour it could take up to 24 hours until the first puppy appears. After that there really shouldn't be more than an hour between successive puppies. So one problem, for example, might be that after a few puppies Leela gets too tired to push and the process stalls. If that happens, she might need drugs to get things going again. But don't worry. In the majority of dog births I've been involved in the mother dog manages everything. Really, don't worry about what you'll need to do."

But we were worried, and not just about the birth but also about what would be required of us in the weeks and months afterwards. Raising and rehoming puppies was not quite what we'd signed up for when considering bringing a single, house-trained, adult dog into our previously free-and-easy lives.

But, there was another option. An option that had been mentioned in passing the previous day and which we now needed to understand in detail. Basically, Pati had told us that if the ultrasound confirmed a pregnancy, then it still might be possible to abort the puppies as long as they weren't too well developed. At the time it had been a somewhat vague suggestion, since the number and developmental state of the puppies was unknown, but we'd pushed her for more details about what "too developed" meant. Her response the previous day had been to say that anything up to 40 days was 'possible'. Difficult and potentially dangerous for Leela, but possible nonetheless.

Well, now we knew, and we'd apparently passed Pati's 40-day threshold. It was the reason that part of my own initial reaction, when she'd declared 45-50 days, was to feel pissed off. If we hadn't dithered for so long about giving Leela a home in the first place then this whole thing could have been sorted out as part of a standard spaying,

170

whipping out a few balls of cells weeks earlier rather than bringing more dogs into an overcrowded world.

But then Pati seemed to change her mind.

"I think I could still terminate" she said, with an uncertain and worried look on her face. "Surgically, it's really on the edge of what's possible but the problem is so much bigger than I'd hoped it would be. With Leela being so young and this being her first litter, I'd hoped there would be only 2 or 3 puppies to think about, but I'm certain there are at least 6. They'll all need new homes and there are so many abandoned dogs in this region alone, not to mention the fact that if these puppies aren't sterilised by their future owners there could be even more dogs to follow. I know this isn't what you wanted. Maybe it would be better to try and terminate after all. What do you think?"

What did we think? What did 'we' think? Well, to be honest, my first thought was "why can't you tell us what to do? You're the professional. Why put this on us?"

What we actually asked, however, was "What precisely do you mean when you say 'risky'?"

"The puppies are pretty large now and that means more of Leela's blood flow is shared with them. Taking them out is riskier because of that, and also because the surgery requires a larger incision. It's basically a more major operation so there's more risk of complications like bleeding and infection and….."

The blank was left hanging in the air, because we all knew what it meant. Our new dog could die less than a week after coming to live with us, probably by bleeding to death during a drug-induced sleep. "And what happens to the puppies? Do they die quickly?" I asked.

"Most people don't like to know about that sort of thing." Pati responded.

"Well, I'd like to know."

"It's most of the reason I really don't like doing it. Because they are fully-formed they'll take about 3 to 5

171

minutes to suffocate. Then they will be gone. I'm only offering this because of the circumstances, with you but also here in Spain. But if I'm going to do this it has to be very soon. Waiting even a few days is not possible. I'd do it today but Leela has already eaten and everything has to be just right for such a major operation. Can you bring her to the Almeria surgery first thing tomorrow morning?"

"Hang on a moment" interjected Esther, "just to be clear, yesterday you said 40 days was the cut-off for termination, but now you're saying you'll do the surgery even though the puppies might be close to 50 days? Is that right?"

"I know it's frightening, but I have to think about the bigger picture as well. I spoke with my boss about this last night and he believes that part of our role as vets here in Spain has to be keeping the numbers of unwanted dogs as low as possible."

We understood of course. It was impossible not to see the dogs roaming loose along roadsides as we travelled in Spain, or the physical state of some of those we saw tethered up by skips and piles of junk with their skeletal frames and frothing mouths. We also knew that Pati was partly trying to look after us, stretching her own guidelines to help a young couple that had tried to do a good thing. Standing in the small, perfumed and colourful surgery room, we could feel the weight of lives weighing down us.

We left the surgery with a provisional appointment for a termination the following morning. Leela was as happy and carefree as ever, looking up at us with a trust and connection that belied our brief time together. Could she have even the vaguest concept of what we were talking about I wondered?

As soon as we got back to the apartment we phoned a UK vet practice we'd trusted in the past to ask for their purely medical advice. The opinion they expressed was unequivocal: "Never! We'd maybe consider a termination up to 20 days into a canine pregnancy, but only under extenuating circumstances such as a medical complication. At the stage you're at it is not only unethical but there is a considerable level of risk that the mother won't survive. Obviously, we understand the situation is very different in Spain regarding abandoned dogs, and that unwanted puppies in the UK almost always find a home one way or another, but we'd never, ever consider an abortion at this stage. It's just too late. Sorry."

We spent the afternoon apart, taking time on our own to consider what we each thought best. The idea was to avoid wasting time going in circles, or influencing each other too much. Whatever we decided, we hoped it would be a decision we shared, but also one we could both arrive at independently. If we disagreed, well, we'd just have to cross that bridge when we came to it.

Fortunately we both found a similar route to the same decision. We knew the facts and we'd checked the numbers, but we just couldn't find it in ourselves to risk Leela's life and starve it away from the unborn faces we'd seen on the ultrasound monitor that morning. Balls of cells was one thing, but for all we knew those dogs were just days away from entering the world. Nor did the fact Leela had only been part of our lives for a few days make a difference either.

All my life I'd prided myself on my ability to be rational, to detach myself from soft-hearted foolishness if a situation demanded it. But in this case I knew that I was choosing foolishness. Less than a week into our dog adventure and already things were about to get a lot messier.

New Life

Throughout all of our travels, there are two things that have never ceased to amaze us. The first is how kind people can be to those in need, even if they're complete strangers. The second is how often the right people seem to cross paths at just the right instant, sharing the knowledge, skills or compassion that only they can share at a fixed moment in time.

In the days that followed Leela's pregnancy confirmation, and our decision not to go ahead with a risky, late-stage termination, word began to spread among the English-speaking community of San Jose. It was a community we'd become aware of, even if only slightly, during our very first visit to the Cabo de Gata Natural Park two years earlier. With its calming landscape, picturesque, small villages, perfect beaches and total lack of high-rise developments, Cabo was indeed a haven for many Europeans seeking a dose of soothing winter peace.

Since we'd returned to San Jose we'd naturally and easily fallen into the periphery of this community, welcomed with open arms despite our relative youth and nomadic life choices. There were no boundaries we'd encountered, not of gender, age, nationality, or former careers. Retired German doctors mingled easily with British cleaners and Dutch lawyers, and everything in between. It was a community founded on friendliness and mutual support, coming together for hiking clubs, quiz nights and padel tennis mornings, a wonderful Spanish game that merges elements of squash and tennis (look it up on YouTube – it's great).

Pretty soon we found ourselves overwhelmed with kindness and offers of help. The estate agent looking after us, a British lady who lived permanently in San Jose, couldn't have been more accommodating. Upon hearing of

174

our sudden need for longer-term dog-friendly accommodation, she somehow convinced the owner of a magnificent three-storey villa to rent it to us until his next booking arrived in two months' time, despite knowing that we were about to have at least half a dozen soggy puppies on our hands. The price she negotiated for us was almost the same as we'd been paying for the small apartment we'd just left behind.

On the day we moved in, wrestling our jumble of bags and boxes through the smart doorway, we found ourselves gawping in wonder at our good fortune. This was to be our third place in as many weeks and it was by far the most opulent. With a prime position high on the sun-baked terraced streets of San Jose, it was a three-bedrooms marvel with a roof terrace and several balconies, all boasting an unhindered view of a sparkling blue expanse of Mediterranean Sea. From our bed in the morning we could sit and watch the sun rise out of those crystal waters, illuminating the rest of the village and the intricately beautiful coastline beyond. Even the ensuite toilet had a sea view.

After quickly unpacking our handful of things into the cavernous void of this tiled mansion, we set about passing our time as conventionally as we could. We continued to spend time with Esther's parents, visited friends in the village and at the nearby campsite, went jogging and took our increasingly waddling dog for slow walks on the beach in the cool winter sunshine. Now that we knew what was happening we could no longer deny the bulging curve of her body. The more we watched, the larger she appeared, expanding seemingly by the hour. She only had short legs and if she didn't give birth soon we joked that she was going to get stuck on a high kerb.

Yet she didn't really change, at least not in her nature. She still looked at us with a disarming trust that transcended the brevity of our shared experiences. She was

175

there in the mornings, wagging her tail and standing by the bedside waiting for fuss. She moved as eagerly as her rotund figure would allow if we so much as looked at her lead. And she slept on our laps every evening as we sat listening to music, quietly reading or watching Lady and the Tramp! We might have been counting down an unknown number of days until a life-changing event, but in those quiet moments it was easy to forget everything except the companionable love we already felt. Like the calm before the storm, any scepticism about taking Leela in, which could have easily turned to regret, was washed away with a single look at her trusting eyes.

In terms of practical preparations, we mostly felt out of our depth. We'd sat through a few more videos on YouTube and read a handful of supposedly helpful blog posts, but like all advice that can be found online, there was no such thing as a consensus. Pet care, like childcare, food choices, politics and religion, was just another minefield of conflicting and often angry opinion. In terms of puppy births alone, we saw everything from "put the mother in a quiet cupboard and walk away" to detailed instructions for the construction of palatial whelping boxes and military-grade first-aid kits. I'm not even going to get started on feeding, exercise and training methods.

I raided the cardboard recycling bins of San Jose in search of big enough boxes to make our own DIY whelping assembly, a safe space where Leela could give birth and nurture the pups through their first and most helpless weeks. I also taped a smaller backup version inside of our little campervan, just in case we ended up rushing to the vets with a bloodied dog and mewing newborn puppies in tow. Whether we'd need to use it or not, we hadn't a clue. We hoped not, but the truth was that we weren't entirely sure what we were expecting. And still, the days rolled forward with no puppies, blood or squelchy bits in sight.

On one exciting morning I was woken from an especially deep sleep by the sound of Esther's panicked voice shouting "Dan, Dan, quick, I think it's happening…." Dragging my blurry-eyed self, still semi-conscious, into the unlit living room, I stood next to Esther who was pointing down the dark staircase which led to the front door. "It's Leela. I think she's giving birth" she repeated.

Sure enough, down in the gloom at the foot of the stairs, I could just about make out a small four-legged creature whining loudly and turning in circles like she was in great pain.

"Are you sure she doesn't just need the toilet?" I asked hopefully.

"No, she went just before bed a couple of hours ago. I really think it's happening. What do we do? Should we carry her to the box?"

"Erm, maybe, but the blogs said we have to be careful not to stress her out or get too involved. If she's picked that spot she must feel safe there. What if she's already had some?"

"Quick. Quick. Find the light switch."

"No! Don't turn it on. You'll scare her."

"Well, we have to see somehow."

"Find the head torch then and cover it with paper to dim it."

Crashing around in the dark looking for a torch and a notebook, we eventually managed to shine a weak beam of light down the stairs just as the whining stopped and Leela trotted through our legs on her way back to her basket by the bed. Flicking on the light, there was a big steamy present waiting on the bottom step. So much for going just before bed. On the other hand, she had tried to let us know!

But then, it finally happened, just under two weeks after she came to live with us. We were just climbing into bed when it began, looking out of the open shutters at the gentle curve of orange lights created by San Jose on a deserted winter's evening. That's when Leela abruptly began crying with an intensity we'd not seen before and started dashing from room to room. Crouching in the whelping box, hiding under beds, turning in tight circles and then standing by the door asking to go out only to strain on the doorstep and produce nothing at all, she just couldn't sit still and was clearly in pain. The crying was harrowing, but there was also relief that whatever was going to happen had begun. One way or another, the next stage of our story was starting.

There was no point both of us sitting up all night, so Esther volunteered to take the first shift, sitting with Leela to make soothing noises as she cried, shook and strained in the room where we'd put the whelping box. We switched places at half past three in the morning, and four hours later I called Esther back in as events seemed to be nearing some sort of crescendo. Sitting side-by-side on a single bed, we held hands and watched as Leela started digging and tearing at the newspaper around her, her muscles taught with the exertion and her swollen belly cumbersome between her short legs.

There was absolutely nothing we could do of course, at least not yet and hopefully not at all. Near at hand we'd placed a stack of old towels (donated by the estate agent), our DIY emergency kit and a warmed hot water bottle wrapped in a tea towel inside a shoebox, just in case we needed to move any newborn puppies without them getting too cold. These were all things we'd read about online. If anything else cropped up, we'd just have to wing it.

In the final moments before the first puppy entered the world, as the full-body convulsions racking Leela's small frame somehow managed to intensify even more, I became aware of a new sensation I was feeling in addition to the concern and helplessness bought on at the sight of our 'cute little doggy in pain'. I think the best way to describe it was amazement and respect. Yes, Leela was a cute little doggy. Yes, she was in pain. No, she hadn't asked for any of this. But in those final moments it also struck me that she was so much more than a cute little doggy. This wasn't an injury she was dealing. It wasn't even really a 'problem', as much as we may have been conditioned to consider an unwanted pregnancy as one. This was what new life really looked like. Not the Disney version, with a graceful stork delivering fluffy bundles in a clean white sling, but the real-world version, with pain and mess and blood and fear. This was real.

As a man now in my mid-thirties, it had been many years since I'd first learned the mechanics of the birds and the bees, but this was by far the closest I'd ever come to the coal-face of creation. In that moment, as nervous as I was that I'd be needed in some way and would be found wanting, or possibly even more nervous that I was totally redundant and wouldn't be needed at all, I realised that I was in awe of Leela. She was doing something that I'd never, ever be able to do. She was creating new heartbeats, bringing new life into the universe. I think that's amazing.

The first puppy emerged with an ear-splitting cry from Leela and a splashing thud as a translucent green sack smeared with blood was dumped unceremoniously onto Donald Trump's grinning face. Not the real Donald Trump, as interesting as that would have been, but since we were still within days of his 2017 inauguration ceremony the donated newspapers lining the whelping box were pretty much dominated by his Tango-man smile.

Quick as a flash, Leela set about doing all of the things we'd been told she'd do, acting by marvellous instinct with a calm certainty that further amazed me. She may have been little more than a puppy herself but as she turned to lick and break through the amniotic sack, stirring life into the apparently formless lump of wetness that was about to take it's very first breath, she was something else as well. She was a mother.

179

From what we could make out, beneath Leela's busy tongue, the brown and wet lump had all of the necessary parts but was yet to make a sound or move any of its tiny limbs. We were, quite literally, on the edge of our seats, silently willing it to move, make a noise, or just show any sign of life as it lay immobile on damp newspapers.

Abruptly a soft squeak filled the air. A sound that was at first hard to hear but whose meaning was certain. It was a message to the world declaring "I'm alive".

A wave of relief washed over me as I became aware that I hadn't been breathing either. Leela continued to lick for a while longer, until the loudening squeaks seemed to be saying "Aw mum, get off", which of course they weren't. What they were actually saying, probably, since I don't speak fluent puppy, was "I'm hungry, feed me now". That's what Leela seemed to understand anyway.

Lying down on her side, she shuffled her belly forward as the tiny pup used its flipper-like front paws to drag it's blind, deaf and tiny 10-centimetre body forward, playing its part in this instinctive dance with grim determination.

Glancing quickly at each other and squeezing each other's hands, we turned back to stare in silence as the still soaking puppy began taking its first sips of liquid food. Leela lay completely still as its soft and gentle front paws pushed outwards to press out a pulsing rhythm on her milk reservoirs. "But how does it know?" I kept asking myself in wonderment.

The reverie ended half an hour later when Leela stood up and began to pace again, leaving her firstborn to wriggle and flap around in the now drying aftermath of its own arrival. The result was a worrying series of near misses as Leela's uncomfortable and rapid foot placement stomped around on all sides of the squeaking firstborn. Partly we wanted to intervene, to sweep up the puppy and hold it safe, but we didn't. Fear that we'd do more harm than good stayed our hands.

A while later Leela lay down again, cycling through several more phases of feeding and pacing as we waited uncertainly to see another pup land. By now the first arrival was pretty much dry, revealing a short fine coat of brown and white fur that closely matched Leela's own colouring. It also had bright pink feet, an equally pink soft muzzle, short ears that resembled tiny flaps of felt, and a limp little tail sporting a wisp of white at the very tip, again just like Leela. Everything about it was wrinkled, too small yet to fit inside its own skin. I couldn't stop looking at it as the minutes passed with a speed that masked the worrying delay of puppy number two.

And then it happened again, just as it seemed everything had stalled. A sudden jerk to her feet, a convulsion, another sharp crack of pain and before we knew it another greenish sack had entered the whelping box. Minutes later and there were two little wrigglers suckling quietly against Leela's wet and red belly.

Things began to speed up after that. The third puppy arrived just half an hour later, number four another twenty minutes afterwards, and number five only waited fifteen minutes before putting in an appearance. Our involvement remained blessedly minimal. After one birth we gave the umbilical cord a helping snip after Leela's own chewing left a tiny strand of fibrous tissue that she just couldn't seem to break. We also used our warm little box to put the already delivered puppies out of harm's way for the later deliveries. The risk of her stepping on one just seemed too high.

The first time I touched a minutes' old puppy my hands were trembling. What would it feel like? Would I hurt it? Would I frighten it? I gently scooped my fingers beneath it and lifted it smoothly but quickly onto the warm towel. Its soft, wet fur seemed to melt around my own coarse fingers and it felt so frail, almost brittle, beneath its skin as I touched the sharp contours of its ribcage.

"Hello little one" I found myself saying as I grew in confidence, pausing for a few seconds with each transfer, simply to revel in the miracle of holding new life in my hands. At every stage we kept the pups close and visible to Leela, speaking softly to her, reassuring her that we weren't taking them anywhere as they were never more than a few inches from her body. We had no idea if we were doing the right thing by getting involved at all, but after watching Leela tread on a pup for the third time, it felt right in the moment.

The big question now was how many more pups were there going to be? Two and half hours after it all began and we had five little puppies suckling quietly against Leela's ragged teats. The first pup to enter the world was now completely dry and seemed to have grown already, almost as though it were expanding with each passing minute, while the later arrivals still had their wet, floppy look. Seriously though, how did they all fit inside of Leela? She was only small herself. Could there really be any more in there?

The sixth, and final, puppy arrived almost exactly three hours after the first. One last push, a chew and lick, and the sixth of her litter came to life before our eyes. Six hungry tubes of noise now jostled gently for position against their mother.

And so our previously quiet, multi-storey, sea-view base became a canine nursery, our days punctuated by intermittent yelps of hunger and the sight of Leela slinking back to do her duty. The birth had left her beaten and emaciated, with loose fur hanging in curtained lines from her pointed hips and ribs. Where, just hours earlier, we'd had a rounded and soft puppy seeking play herself, we now had a blood-stained mother bearing a heavy burden.

Motherhood didn't sit lightly on Leela. Within days she was following us around the house, leaving her offspring to sleep alone while she gazed at us with a hungry and uncertain look in her eyes. We sought to fuel her struggling body with as much protein-rich, calorie-dense food as she would eat. For several days I plunged myself into research and calculations to make sure we weren't screwing things up too much, looking up the European guideliness on canine nutrition and the average nutrient density in all manner of different foods. Perhaps it was my forgotten inner-chemist trying to prove itself useful? To be honest, I did quite enjoy it, even colour-coding the spreadsheet I created. Evidently I was still a nerd.

After a while, however, we realised it was better to trust Leela's innate wisdom. We offered a variety of foods and she ate what she wanted. It seemed to work, her frame filling out and recovering quickly over the following weeks, even while her teats grew black and bruised with the demands of feeding time.

As puppies are prone to do, they doubled in size in the first week alone, and then continued to grow at an amazing rate. Friends told us not to name them, "it will only make it harder to say goodbye" they said. They were right. Within a fortnight George, Bella, Pati, Rose, Teddy and Jess were starting to open their eyes for the first time and it was impossible not to be taken in by those black and bleary pools of wonderment.

For us, our initial resolve was to step back, let Leela do her stuff and to get on with our lives as normal. Within a week that plan was scuppered by Leela's growing reluctance to be in the room with her children. By the end of week two she'd only enter the puppy room at feeding time, and then only after sustained and soul-wrenching crying for more than an hour.

That was when little George in particular, who'd been the smallest pup by some margin at birth, started to fade quickly. While his brother and sisters charged towards the 'kilo-club' (something Bella achieved after just 17 days), George's growth stalled and started to go backwards . Watching him struggle in vain to hold on to a teat as his larger siblings bulldozed their way to extra milk was simply too much for us to bear. At the same time Rose, who'd been growing quickly, became ill and screamed with harrowing intensity for almost forty-eight hours straight.

That seemed to be the final straw for Leela who trotted off upstairs and basically left us to it after that. In her haunted eyes we could see the puppy she wanted to be battling with the demands of her inner mother. Most, but not all dogs, have strong mothering instincts the vet explained to us when we called her for advice. As long as they're growing, she told us, try not to worry.

We searched our souls briefly, asking ourselves if we should step away and let nature take its course. Would all six pups have survived in the wild? Almost certainly not. Leela only weighed seven kilos herself and fairly soon she'd be responsible for her own body weight in puppies, a total that was only going to keep growing. All of their needs had to pass through her own tired body first and it was breaking her down. She'd already had a kidney infection since giving birth. But then we already knew the answer. We'd made our minds up weeks ago.

As bottle feeding and a constant attentiveness to Leela's presence (or not) became part of our days, including getting up for night-time feeds, it was hard to resist the pull of the bond that was growing between us and the warm, ginger-and-white, wriggling playmates we'd found ourselves shepherding towards infanthood. Eyes opening gave way to wagging tails, then standing and uncertain walking as we eagerly waited for the day when Leela, for her sake and ours, wouldn't be required to produce milk any more.

For the most part we loved every moment, happy to close the door of our unlikely luxury home and bask in this (temporary) immersion in puppy love. It was intense at times. There always seemed to be something that needed doing to stay on top of the food, the mess, our own needs, or some random task that jumped out and surprised us. Yet no matter how tired we felt, it took just a single glance into twelve excited eyes to lift our spirits back up. Others might not have made the decisions we had, or done things in the same way, but whatever we were doing on this crazy, unplanned, messy adventure, it just felt right.

Letting Go

Pirates aren't usually renowned for their punctuality. Or for making appointments come to that. However, unfortunately, thanks to a mild offshore breeze and some very minor waves, it looked like San Jose's very own pirates were going to be rudely late to the party. They'd been stuck about thirty metres offshore for nearly an hour by the time we joined the crowds, waving their tin-foil swords at the now exhausted 'villagers' still running about on the beach in mock panic.

Eventually the pirates had to be helped ashore by the villagers themselves, joining forces to haul on a tow-line like an enormous tug-of-war. It was only when the marauders had disembarked safely and in line with all proper health and safety procedures that they could set about mercilessly killing each other. It was all good clean family fun.

We'd actually been watching the preparations for the Pirate festival for the past week, sitting on our balcony to enjoy the sight of enthusiastic locals practicing their pirate moves, choreographing sword fights and feigning violent death on San Jose's pristine half-moon sands. It was the showpiece event that rounded off a happy day of music, colour, smiles and fun.

We'd never learned whether this was some sort of historic homage to the area's smuggling past, or simply a chance for the permanent residents to dress up and have a bit of fun. Not that it mattered. As tourists flocked into San Jose's springtime streets, we'd taken the chance to expose the now two-month old pups to a little more life and excitement, something they'd met primarily with calm disinterest unless food was involved.

Ever since their first round of vaccinations had been completed the local vet had encouraged us to go out and about with the gang. Like everything else dog-related, we'd seen massively conflicting opinions online about the risks of exposure to the outdoors versus the benefits of more youthful socialisation. We were, after all, taking our job as temporary puppy wranglers very seriously. We'd read the Happy Puppy Handbook more than once (donated by another kind winter resident of San Jose) in order to immerse ourselves in the minutiae of best puppy practice. We'd also studied confusing Spanish websites tracking the incidence of various pet viruses. As you might expect, we'd mostly discovered that consensus was still hard to come by.

In the end, confused and exhausted by a myriad of angry commentators, we'd plumped for the local vet's advice, trusting them to know the regional risk factors better than anyone else. Starting with the purchase of a large dog crate, we'd driven all six pups to different parts of the village and let them look out on their suddenly expanded universe with wide-eyed amazement. Then they'd fallen asleep.

We'd also started training them, indoors mostly. Esther was the first to master 'sit' and 'lie down', followed soon afterwards by 'give'. 'Go mental' they'd already discovered without any input or command from us. There was such a wild delight in watching them wrestle, chew, ambush and snuggle with their siblings that it was hard to remember how our life had looked before they arrived. Hadn't we once planned to take off around Europe in a nippy little campervan?

Two months in and it was hard to remember. As the pups eat-sleep-make-a-mess-repeat cycle had interwoven itself with our own feeding-cleaning-get-life-done routine, we'd found ourselves increasingly retreating into our opulent cocoon of laughter and smiles. It's hard to match the happiness that can be felt by lying on a floor and being mauled by half a dozen eight-week old puppies, all of them determined to lick, love and jump on as much of you as they can.

The difference in their individual personalities had been obvious ever since they'd opened their eyes, but had continued to grow with each passing day. Bella was the boss, the biggest and most energetic of the pack. George was the smallest, but he didn't seem to realise it, constantly wrestling with Bella or falling asleep up against her body. Teddy, the other male, was short and stocky, with a boxer's physique that made him look tough, despite his fearful and timid nature. Rose was happy on her own, often sleeping away from her siblings or playing solo with toys in a corner. Jess liked to be close to Teddy and loved human touch, even more than the others who already liked it a lot. Then there was Pati, our space-cadet, who seemed to see a world that nobody else could see. She'd stare at the wall or use her tiny bark at a patch of empty space as though a person was stood over her. Frankly, it could be bloody spooky.

Fortunately, by the time they'd transitioned to solid foods, Leela had warmed to their enthusiastic approach for life. Sitting atop a high box that we'd placed in their pen, which they couldn't reach her on no matter how hard they tried, she seemed increasingly happy to spend time in their presence. Watching with a quizzical look on her face as the pups played tug-of-war over a toilet roll tube, every now and then she'd hop down and join in, or at least nick the toy and take it up onto her box. It was as though she was learning to play for the very first time herself. Plus, she always won.

In addition to indoor tricks, we also dabbled with some basic recall on the quiet pavement outside the villa. Taking one pup at a time for a very short stroll, we'd distract them with a tiny treat and then, when they were looking the other way, we'd sprint off. The moment they gave chase we'd stop, spin round, shout "come" and reward them. They bloody loved it, and with six pups to cycle through three times a day, it was a workout Usain Bolt could have benefitted from.

We met a surprising amount of people this way, with passers-by and holidaymakers drawn by the sight of adults running off repeatedly from a heart-stopping ball of cuteness yapping happily along the pavement. One Danish couple were so in love they stayed in San Jose specifically to visit the pups (and us) for the next week. Like us, Annie and Kim had also packed up their day jobs back in Denmark and taken to the road in a motorhome. They were only a few weeks into their journey so we had a lot to talk about. In return, they took us free-diving.

Donning borrowed wetsuits and slipping into the pristine waters beneath the towering volcanic cliffs, Kim (who was a qualified diving instructor) led Esther and I out into an underwater world of startling colour and abundance. As a protected marine reserve, we'd always been told that the land beneath the waves around Cabo de Gata was special, but the sheer volume and diversity of what we saw down there was dazzling. We went out three times with Kim, holding hands as we floated face down, listening to the whoosh of air in and out of our snorkels so that we could stare for long minutes at the passing life.

The sea was only ten metres deep, at most, for our excursions, though even that was too deep for our novice selves to reach easily. Kim could spend five minutes or more floating effortlessly across the sea bed, and spoke with passion about reaching fifty metres once before, his personal depth record. Floating in the blue void looking up at distant sunlight, he explained, was like visiting another world.

I only got a tiny sense of the magic he spoke of when, after a few initially shallow dips beneath the surface, I eventually managed to overcome the buoyancy of my own body and wetsuit more effectively and got close to the bottom for the first time. Passing through five metres I recall the abrupt sensation of total weightlessness as the air in the suit and my tissues compressed allowing the sucking drag upwards to balance perfectly with the pull of gravity. Suddenly I no longer needed to work to descend but instead found myself suspended, totally free with just the sound of my heartbeat for company. It was utterly calm, peaceful and comfortable down there and, in that moment, I didn't want to be anywhere else. Using just the tiniest wave of my hands I sank down further, hovering just above the sand and looking up at the ripples of light that formed the ceiling to this blue world. I stayed for as long as my breath would allow, not more than a minute, before reluctantly rising back to the surface.

Kindness had also continued to flow towards us from the San Jose community. When the pups were six weeks old, we'd been faced with the possibility of moving seven dogs and two sleep-deprived humans back into the van. Our tenancy was expiring soon and, with the spring season picking up, even the most dog-friendly landlords in San Jose weren't able to offer us any accommodation. With the pups too young to move on, and no homes lined up yet anyway, we were just days away from living in a cramped space with six largely untrained puppies. We weren't really sure how we were going to manage that, though we reassured ourselves that we'd find a way. We usually did.

It was only in our final days of stability that a chance encounter with some nearby neighbours turned into a lifeline. As usual, it was Esther's innate friendliness combined with the allure of six beautiful puppies that secured our fortunes. What started out as a little chat over some tumbling furballs turned into an invitation to stay as long as we liked in their almost-identical villa when they went back to the UK. It was yet another surprise in the long line of delightful accidents and remarkable kindnesses that seemed to characterise our nomadic life, not to mention our fourth house in less than three months.

At the same time, we'd also received a handful of unexpected cash donations from both friends and total strangers, all wanting to contribute something towards the pups impending vaccination and passport costs. A raffle had been organised by some especially kind friends, with people painting pictures, making jams and donating other prizes for the next pub quiz night in the village. The winning quiz team also donated their prize pot, which they didn't have to do. With food, crates, pens and vet visits, we'd already poured a fair chunk of our savings into dog care, so these donations were not only deeply moving but also practically very helpful for us.

Then again, we felt grateful that we were in a position to help at all, even if it meant our reserves dwindled faster than they otherwise would have done. We were still far too young to think we were set up for life. Nor did we really want to be, as the pups' arrival had reminded us.

When we'd first set off three years earlier we'd been happy to excite and distract ourselves in search of an undefined feeling of peace. At times we thought we'd found it, but whenever we had to stop moving we'd experienced nagging doubts and restlessness. Our subsequent discovery of mindfulness and meditation had helped a lot, and we'd let go of many of our old and limiting beliefs along with our stored possessions, but Leela's arrival and her vulnerability had forced us to focus on something beyond ourselves and we were finding that far more fulfilling than many of our personal adventures. Perhaps this was the next step we'd really needed, right when we'd been on the cusp of vanishing into the wilderness in our little van.

Besides, if it had been about the money, we might have contemplated some of the offers we had from people who approached us asking to buy a puppy. All of the offers came from strangers, mostly when we were out and about, though twice people knocked on our door having heard about the litter and our address on the San Jose grapevine.

In reality, we had no intention of accepting money for any of the puppies. Whenever people told us how their dog had cost hundreds of pounds (or even thousands!), came from a litter of a dozen, and that the mother was pregnant again three months later because the owner wanted a new kitchen, we winced inside. We'd seen how hard it was for Leela. We'd watched her belly turn into one enormous bruise. We'd taken her to the vets when she was peeing blood and kept throwing up her food because her body couldn't take the strain. The idea of doing that to a dog to make a few quid was not something we could contemplate.

Sadly, such approaches weren't totally unexpected. More than once we'd seen people with a cardboard box containing puppies outside of the local supermarket, with prices ranging from 50 euros up to 200. It tore us apart every time, seeing those helpless tiny dogs, some of them just a month old (we asked) and at the mercy of a shopper's whim. It was a worrying reminder that although we'd been able to press pause on our lives to throw ourselves into dog care, that we couldn't count on the same attitudes when it came to finding them homes.

We've never been fans of the 'fur baby' mentality, but that didn't mean we saw the puppies as disposable now that they were technically old enough to leave the litter. It's unfair to generalise a nation, especially as we'd seen plenty of pampered pooches going about town with their Spanish owners. But we'd also seen the other side of the coin. Whether it was the initial warnings we'd heard from the rescue centres, the harrowing anecdotes told to us by friends, the vet telling us about how she'd once been asked to euthanise a dog to avoid a fifty euro bill for antibiotics, or simply the sight of frustrated pets chained and panting in the hot sun, we couldn't pretend that the average Spanish attitude to dogs was the same as in the UK.

Perhaps we were being overly cautious, but the weight of responsibility frightened us. These dogs had known us from their very first breath. As far as we were concerned, we owed it to them to see them safe and settled for the rest of their lives.

As the pups passed the traditional eight week marker, more and more people kept asking us the same question, "how are you going to get rid of them?" Yet the truth was that the last thing we wanted to do was "get rid of them". We wanted to find them loving and safe forever homes, however long that took, which we saw as a totally different thing.

In part we dodged the problem by declaring that we'd keep them until at least ten to twelve weeks old. We'd read a few articles about the stronger human-canine bond that can form with a younger puppy (which is why some people push for six week adoption), versus possibly improved health and behavioural benefits that come from staying longer with the mother. We knew it was a disputed issue, but it at least confirmed that the eight-week standard wasn't set in stone. That was enough for us in a country where we knew so few people and spoke so little Spanish. At least it would give us more time to make the right choices.

Wonderfully, it worked. By ten weeks we had four homes lined up, the options coming forward in a flurry that we would have missed if we'd panicked sooner. Sometimes patience is the most important part of decision making.

Jess, our beloved golden girl with her playful nature was going to live with George and Ina, a fantastic German couple who lived in Ireland but were spending winter in San Jose. Ted, the timid little scrapper, was going to live in France with a young family with two children. That home had been arranged via the grandparents, a fantastic retired couple who'd been instrumental in drumming up support for us since the pups' arrival and who were also spending a few months in San Jose. They'd look after Ted in the short term until he went to his forever home.

The other two homes we'd lined were back in the UK with immediate family. However, since the pups couldn't have their rabies vaccination until at least 12 weeks old and it would be a further three weeks after that before they'd be legally allowed to cross borders in Europe, that still meant we had at least five weeks left with Leela plus four noisy, rambunctious, face-licking troublemakers. To be honest, we didn't really mind.

Many of the spiritual and meditation books we'd read or listened to went to great lengths to talk about attachment and the art of letting go. They described a subtle balance of non-attachment that allows people to love fully and care passionately about things, yet not collapse into pain and suffering when loss occurs. "If you can dream— and not make dreams your master" as Rudyard Kipling might have put it. However, just because we'd read about it didn't mean we were any good at it. I think it's fair to say we'd fallen short of that particular balance when it came to these beautiful animals that had exploded into our lives.

We'd never set out to be dog breeders. The situation had fallen upon us unexpectedly and while there had been moments of despair and exhaustion, looking back we felt blessed to have had the opportunity. On the morning of the day that Jess became the first to leave home, we took the whole gang out for a final full-family walk on a tiny stretch of beach just outside of the main San Jose village. There, among the driftwood, weathered rocks and the shells of washed up crabs, we watched the six puppies and Leela play together for the very last time.

They couldn't know what we knew. As Bella wrestled with George, who watched Pati digging in the sand, who was joined by Rose, while Teddy and Jess ran in the shallow surf, we couldn't stop the emotions rising up. That all of this love and beauty had unfolded against such a perfect, Mediterranean backdrop astounded us and made the cuts that much more painful.

We'd come to San Jose with the simple intention of spending a brief time with Esther's parents before setting off for new adventures. Now, with May approaching and Esther's parents back in Britain for two months already, all of our previous ideas were in disarray. We had another month, at least, to wait. But after that, who knew?

Years earlier such a prospect would have worried us, but after so many fateful meetings and moments of good fortune, we were starting to realise that something always came up. All we had to do was try and listen for the moment that it did.

French Heaven

"Hi Dan. Hi Esther. It's Gordon here. How are you both?"

"Gordon, so nice to hear from you. We're good. How're you and Sue?"

"Fine, fine. Listen, I heard all about you and the puppies and was wondering if you might be interested in some house-sitting. I've been looking after a house near to us in France for years now, but it's getting a bit much for me. I've had a chat with the owner. Would you like to live there in return for mowing the lawn, looking after the pool and doing a bit of DIY? There aren't any bookings until late July so you'd have at least three months."

It never stopped surprising us how far our news could travel without us having anything to do with it. We hadn't even seen Gordon for two years, not since we'd waved him and Sue goodbye as we'd driven away from Cabo de Gata for the very first time. They'd been some of the first friends we'd made on Camping Los Escullos and had stayed in touch intermittently ever since. That said, we hadn't spoken personally for ages. Evidently the San Jose jungle drums and smoke signals were working well to have reached Gordon in the south of France.

A month had passed since Jess and Teddy had left the pack, and we were now counting down the days until the rest of the team could legally cross borders as per the pet passport requirements. Sadly, while Jess and Teddy had settled in marvellously, just as we'd hoped, the other two homes we'd lined up back in the UK were now uncertain. A totally flooded home in one case and a serious health diagnosis in the other had created the doubt, though we remained hopeful that matters would get sorted and that the homes (which we considered ideal) would be back on the table soon.

Gordon's call had arrived just at a time when we were weighing up our options for van living with five dogs, none of which made us feel overly cheerful. Naturally, we said yes to Gordon immediately.

Prior to ploughing north to France in two long hops, our 'nippy little campervan' had been serving as a car for almost five months. Perhaps that's why we felt so much nervous excitement as we wrestled our possessions and the accumulated paraphernalia of puppyhood back into the compact living space. What had been a space-age and stylish interior when we'd bought it was now transformed into an apparently cluttered junk shop, with extra bags covering the bed and loose items stuffed into every available nook and cranny.

With four puppies sleeping nose-to-tail in a crate they'd once been dwarfed by (and that now occupied two-thirds of our living space), Leela harnessed safely on the passenger's knees, and an immaculately clean villa left behind us, we were on the road again, albeit briefly.

It was a nice thought, as we drove for a final time along the dust and cactus lined roads that would take us out of the natural park's boundaries, that wherever we went and whatever we did next, we'd get to see it partly through the eyes of our canine companions. Their lust for life and inquisitiveness was a pleasure to watch every day and it helped to infuse us with that same bounce and vigour. We felt very lucky.

Sweeping by Granada, our knee-jerk ride up Europe's highest cycle climb now seemed like a lifetime ago. Turning north, we motored directly towards and then past Madrid, eventually coming to rest in a tiny village that was little more than string of houses beside the motorway. All along the route we'd paused every two hours to continue the house-training successes we'd been enjoying back in San Jose. They all seemed to get it, all except Pati 'Ironbladder' who was quite happy to trot around a truckstop for an hour, sniffing discarded food wrappers and ignoring any need she felt to pee.

Then again, Pati had always been special, with her undershot lower jaw and watery eyes that stared with such powerful intensity. At fifteen weeks old, all of the pups were going through a 'perm' phase, with an explosion of soft, brown, tightly curved fluff that would soon fall out, but which temporarily gave them the look of walking pompoms. It was a look that guaranteed smiles wherever we went.

It wasn't exactly a comfortable first night back in the van, with loose bits and bobs piled on every flat surface and bags still jammed around our bodies. It definitely wasn't something we could have done for any long period of time. With two humans and five dogs, the volume of stuff in our lives hadn't swelled by much, but in such a tiny living space every millimetre counted. Whether this would be a problem longer term remained to be seen. In the meantime, it helped knowing that we were going to a house, even though we hadn't a clue what that house was like.

We reached France at lunchtime the next day, driving a couple of hours north of the Pyrenees to the heart of the Gers Department. The Gers is a peaceful, agricultural region in the south-west that boasts various gastronomic specialities and is named for the river that flows through it. We were due to meet Gordon in the petite mediaeval village of Fourcès (pronounced For-sez), a place that was simply a name we couldn't pronounce on our first visit, but which would soon become the hub of one of the best times of our lives.

This particular circular village in the heart of Gascony was originally built around a now-vanished castle, replaced today by an arcade of trees to leave a theatrical setting of half-timbered houses facing inwards with their overhanging arcades and exposed beams. Stepping into the snug and rounded heart of Fourcès, it's easy to feel as though you've just stepped back in time several hundred years.

In our case, we parked on the outskirts, pulling into the park with a dedicated motorhome area. Releasing the mini-hounds to tumble and romp on the lush green grass in the rising afternoon heat, it was a dramatic reminder of just how far we'd come, both physically and mentally. The previous morning we'd driven away from sun-baked white houses, golden beaches and exposed rocky trails. Now we were in the fertile heart of France, surrounded by green fields, vineyards and enchantingly haphazard ancient villages. From scorched to sumptuous in an (almost) single bound.

While we were bowled over and delighted with the change, having arrived in the area at such a beautiful time, Leela and her pups seemed initially befuddled. "Where has the normal floor gone?", their faces and tentative steps seemed to say. It hadn't occurred to us until now that this was the first grass they'd ever seen. Dust, sand and stone had defined their world before, a fact that had made the distinction between tiled floors and pavements all the more difficult at toilet training time.

Still, it wasn't a lengthy transition. Within minutes their initial suspicion of the soft, green tickly stuff had been overtaken by their ever-present urge to chase and chew each other. Leela, for her part, lay down in the sun alongside the van without a care in the world. "They're your problem now" her pose seemed to suggest. "I did try and tell you to get shot of them."

Gordon rolled up ten minutes later, his smiling bearded face a welcome beacon of familiarity for us and a target for the puppies. They hadn't seen many bearded faces before and, from the way they tried to get at it, it was easy to imagine that they'd decided Gordon's extra 'human fur' made him an honorary dog. Thankfully, for him and us, Gordon loved it just as we did, slipping straight into 'official' puppy wrangler pose of half-lying on the floor and letting them climb all over him. In terms of discipline it was totally useless, as we knew all too well, but it was great fun.

Half an hour of fuss and catching-up later, we arrived at our next home base in convoy with Gordon. We'd bought our van almost six months earlier and we could still count the number of nights we'd slept in it on our fingers. Not that we were complaining. So far, every move we'd made had been an upgrade and, as we were about to discover, this was no exception.

During the five-minute drive from Fourcès we'd mostly passed rows and rows of vines studded with occasional tumbledown (but working) farmhouses. As we'd soon learn, all of these grapes would be used to make Armagnac, a distinctive brandy specific to the region and the oldest brandy distilled in France. A cardinal in the 14th century, for example, once declared that it had 40 virtues!

Turning down a tiny side-road from the already winding country lane, we crested a little rise and dropped down towards a sharp bend. It was here that Gordon's car vanished, continuing straight at the curve and ascending into a tight archway of dense bushes that disappeared into an apparent thicket of trees and hedgerows.

We followed him cautiously, hearing the tickle of leafy tendrils scraping along our sides as we progressed slowly up the rocky driveway, heading towards sunlight and an overgrown garden. Emerging onto a gravelled but weed-bound patch of flatness, we found ourselves unexpectedly confronted with a vision of pastoral perfection straight out of a movie set.

Stretching perhaps twenty metres side-to-side, and ten metres front-to-back, the mostly single storey, eighteenth century farmhouse before our eyes was like an island of homely charm set in a sea of vibrant green. Finished in light grey stone with an ageing terracotta roof and dark varnished shutters, a set of wooden steps on the right-hand side led to a second floor terrace that wrapped around a small upstairs extension. It was beautiful and the idea we were going to live here astounded us. From a millionaire-style villa to a rural idyll in less than two days.

Gordon was already inside, opening shutters to let in the afternoon sun. "Well, this is it" he declared as we stepped into the country-cottage kitchen, a spacious expanse beneath a mezzanine floor that connected to an open-plan living-room-cum-conservatory. "I'll give you the tour".

Following Gordon as he bustled off down a shaded internal corridor, we were shown five bedrooms, two in the small upstairs area and the rest downstairs. As we stepped into each one, Gordon opened the shutters and revealed a house that could best be characterised as 'rustic'. It wasn't just the accumulated dust and cobwebs of a long, cold winter spent unoccupied, though that had also been the case. It was the various rough edges, flaking paint patches and wobbling handles that gave the house a slightly unloved or lonely feeling. Nothing was dangerous. Nothing was even glaringly broken, simply in need of some tender loving care. And we were here to give it.

It was the same story outside, where a ten metre swimming pool was currently doing a good impression of a frog pond surrounded by mossy flagstones, while the tall grass had gone to seed some time ago. Personally, we loved the wild garden look, with white, yellow and purple flowers dancing in the breeze, but that wasn't why we were here. As Gordon explained, he'd cleared everything with the owner and in return for giving the place a good clean, staying on top of the lawnmowing and helping him get the pool cleaned up when the time came, we were welcome to stay. "What do you think?" he asked. We thought we'd landed in heaven.

Gordon left a short time later, handing over the keys and leaving us to get settled in. Three hours of vigorous cleaning, evicting spiders and mice (alive and dead) and warm embraces followed. It was hard to believe this was really happening. Sure, there was a bit of cleaning and tidying up to do, but we weren't being asked to do much more than basic DIY. In return we'd get to live in what could well have been our dream home. Through the dense bushes and trees that ringed the garden, we could just about make out a single other house five hundred metres away. Beyond that there was nothing until the tiny hamlet of Larroque-sur-l'Osse sitting at the top of a small rise more than a thousand metres distant. We could hear no traffic, just bees, bird song and tree-branches swishing in the wind.

Over the next few days we alternated between basking in the glow of our good luck and gradually making the house into a space we could most fully enjoy. We bought some mesh from a DIY store to create a barrier around a specific patch of grass close to the house, allowing the pups to play safely and still get back to their own space for their naps and feeding times. We also tackled the garden work and made a start on the handful of DIY jobs Gordon had specifically mentioned.

Driving a red sit-on lawnmower slowly back and forth in the meadow-like expanse of the garden, I found myself pondering on two things. First, that there was a deep serenity and sense of reward to be found in the repetitive act of moving at 1 mile-per-hour through this ocean of dandelions and buttercups. Second, and much more excitingly, I absolutely looked like Forrest Gump. I even had my own fan club in the form of four eager, ginger faces that sat fascinated behind their enclosure, seemingly hypnotised by the pulsing throb of the engine and the buzzing of the blades beneath me.

With so many weeks spread out before us, life soon began to find a happy rhythm. Each morning we'd wake just as the sun crested the eastern horizon, illuminating this fertile world with an intense orange glow as we lay in bed smelling the overnight moisture as it drifted through the open windows. We lay still, knowing that the moment we moved a single joint the stillness would erupt with a chorus of yaps and yips. Leela, for her part, remained unmoved in her basket by our bed, but the pups were like Jedi. Even though they were several walls, two doors and a long corridor away from us, they always knew the moment we stirred.

When they eventually settled down we'd go and let them out, smiling as they lunged into the 'little wilderness' we'd enclosed for them. They loved butterflies the most, especially Bella, who chased after every fluttering shadow that passed over the floor. She didn't care about the insects themselves, just the impressions cast by their wings and the sun.

Esther and I would usually go out in the mornings, either to explore the network of waymarked trails nearby or to take our bikes for a spin on the rolling roads that criss-crossed the countryside. The undulating landscape and extensive green horizons made us reminisce about Oxfordshire, the scene that had been the backdrop to our first falling in love.

On other days we took the campervan exploring, loading the whole gang on board and heading out to visit a nearby village. Fourcès had already set the bar high but with other stunning places right on our doorstep, such as Nérac (with its rich royal history), the Abbaye de Flaran (one of the best preserved Cistercian abbeys in France), and Montréal (ranked among the most beautiful villages in the country), there were just so many local adventures to be enjoyed.

It was hard to believe that while all of these castles, churches and village walls were first being raised, in the 12th to 14th centuries, Gascony was a hotbed of intrigue and rivalry, where blood was being spilt over competing French and English claims to the land. When we visited, it was as though an aura of peace kept the tumult of the world at bay, like a time capsule that carried forward only the quieter parts of its past.

At Larresingle, the smallest fortified village in France, we could let the dogs play together in the dried up moat, far beneath the thick and crenelated walls. As busloads of tourists arrived to pass into the keep and survey the 13th century castle and other mediaeval buildings, they also got to see our small herd of puppies pounding and panting through the flowers beneath the drawbridge. If we'd had a euro for every photo they must be in, we could have been millionaires long before autumn arrived.

Back at base, dog training sessions continued, almost entirely driven by Esther. In addition to reading many books on the subject, she even signed up for local dog training classes, never once wavering in her determination that whatever homes we found in the future, that Bella, George, Pati and Rose would be ready.

Individually, in pairs and as a whole group, she slowly mastered new commands and did her best to 'proof' those behaviours against as many distractions as our quiet rural setting could offer. The fact that we were really quite happy sharing our island of seclusion with five wagging friends was something we tried not to think about too much. It was still our absolute and fixed intention to rehome them as soon as the opportunity arose. The fact we hardly saw anybody wasn't really our fault, was it? Plus, we still hoped that our original plan to rehome at least two back in the UK might be resurrected. Or at least that's what we told ourselves.

And so the days passed, full, furry and happy. We ate dinner outside most days, either beneath the sun or hiding from the springtime showers beneath the broad kitchen porch. Each evening as the sky darkened and the sound of crickets filled the air we'd reflect on how grateful we felt. We may not have been trekking up mountains or standing in the shadows of pyramids, but in this rarefied and remote rural atmosphere we were experiencing an even greater gift, a simple gift but one that we couldn't remember even imagining before. Amazingly, for the first time in a long time, we didn't feel the need to go anywhere or change anything at all.

Pilgrims

May flew past in a flurry of excursions, short, sharp rain showers and exploding sunflowers. What had been tiny green buds just breaking the surface of freshly-ploughed fields when we arrived had raced skywards, blooming into stunning swathes of yellow beauty that filled the few gaps between the extensive rows of vines. At the same time, wild cherry and mulberry trees were now heavy with darkening fruit, allowing us to take Leela out for her 'grown up' walks and return home every day with bulging sacks of delicious goodness, while the evening air filled with intoxicating scent of jasmine.

When June arrived, bringing with it scorching sun and endless days of unbroken blue skies, the searing temperatures forced us to seek out shade for much of the day. Gordon came over to open up the pool, ostensibly in plenty of time for the first summer guests but mostly, we knew, for our benefit. As the previously murky and frog-filled waters turned slowly back from a green soup to clear with a hint of blue, we waited eagerly for our own chance to take the plunge.

"The most expensive hole you can own" is how Gordon described the pool while explaining the handful of maintenance requirements to me, and I have to say that our own personal opinion on maintaining a dilute chemical soup in a back garden isn't totally positive. The idea of dumping all of that bleach into the water was the reason I'd spent several days fishing mature frogs out in preparation for Gordon's arrival, relocating them to other ponds nearby. We also couldn't ignore the fact that so much of the agricultural abundance around us relied on petrochemical assistance. Every day we watched the tractors and their sprays going up and down the vines around the house.

That said, as temperatures hit the mid-30's, we couldn't deny the pleasure that the relative coolness of the pool offered. We soothed our consciences by reminding ourselves that it wasn't our house, that we were lucky to be here and that we had no right to call the shots, all of which was true. But if enjoying the facilities made us hypocrites then so be it. We couldn't pretend we didn't like it.

We all collude with the 'system' one way or another, be it where we buy our food or the modes of transport we employ. All we can do is our best, whatever that looks like for us and being as honest with ourselves as we can. The truth was, diving and bombing into the water, we felt like little children again. With no neighbours or visitors to worry about, mostly we just wandered straight out of the house with nothing but a towel over our shoulders.

From time to time we did meet people when we were out on our excursions. Stu' and Sue, for instance, were a British couple touring in their own motorhome. We met them in Fourcès when we took the pups there for a play in the park. Having a pack of young dogs is like a social magnet. Anyone with the slightest interest in animals was drawn towards them with their total and utter confidence that they'd be met with smiles and fuss (and possibly cheese). They'd never known anything different.

We invited Stu' and Sue back to the house for an afternoon, laughing so hard that our bellies hurt as Sue told stories with a skill that we'd rarely encountered. The tale of the stray pig their daughter bought home, that they then adopted, and that subsequently ran away had us crying so hard that we could hardly breathe. The image of a middle-aged couple chasing round the block after a squealing pig was straight out of a Scooby-Doo episode.

Then there was Catherine and Edith, a Swiss pair who ran the organic supermarket in Condom (which really was the name of the closest medium-sized town by the way). Amazingly, they'd actually grown up in the Val d'Anniviers!

Their passion for animals was so intense that despite having a shop to run, they cared for eight rescued dogs, forty rescued cats and two rescued donkeys back at the smallholding where they lived. How they made time to visit us and share lunch on several occasions we never knew, arriving with enormous smiles and then dashing off for vet appointments, stock-takes and staff management meetings despite being almost seventy years old.

What we respected the most about them, aside from their tireless energy, was their commitment to their principles. They wouldn't stock meat in their store, for example, because they didn't eat meat themselves, even though this was France and they knew it limited their customer base. Nor had they bowed to commercial pressure by moving away from their local suppliers of fresh produce, even though that could have increased their margins. As they explained to us, they'd founded their store in a time long before 'organic' or 'vegetarian' was mainstream. It had never been solely about the money, but about promoting a sustainable way of life and supporting a community. They wanted to keep prices as low as possible to encourage people to support a more sustainable food system. In many ways they reminded us of Cyrille and our time back on the farm in Guillestre. They had the same infectious but subtle sincerity, the sort that makes you want to be a kinder, more loving person somehow.

Paul, of Paul and Elaine, the couple we'd met years earlier on the shores of Lake Maggiore also came and spent a night with us on his way back to the UK. Elaine had passed away the previous summer and we could see the pain in Paul's eyes as we shared an evening full of travel stories and a lot of table tennis. His own dogs, Bombo and Sammy, loved our gang, especially Bombo who spent almost the whole time so excited that he was waving his 'lipstick' around like a wand. Thankfully, he didn't seem to know what else to do with it except make us all laugh with his poor aim and enthusiasm. It was just a few months later that we'd find out about Paul's own terminal diagnosis.

But of all the people we met who influenced us that summer, Lorin and Lena were perhaps the most surprising. If you've ever imagined what it would be like to meet a younger version of yourself, but a version that had taken a completely different life path, that was how we felt to meet this young Swiss couple as they trekked together through France, heading towards Spain along the Camino de Santiago.

Usually known in English as 'The Way of Saint James', or more simply just as 'The Way', the Camino is actually a vast network of pilgrimage routes. Converging like the tracks in a seashell (which us why a seashell is carried by many pilgrims), the various routes come together as they approach the shrine of Saint James the apostle in Galicia in north-western Spain. Tradition has it that the remains of Saint James are buried there in the cathedral of Santiago de Compostela and, apparently, pilgrims have been journeying there ever since the remains were discovered in 812 AD.

Nowadays the route remains very popular, both as a spiritual journey for many but also as a challenge for any hikers and cyclists who enjoy a long distance trail. Every year hundreds of thousands of pilgrims set out from their front doors, or other popular starting points, all planning to journey great distances. Most would be supported on their way by the kindness of strangers and by pilgrims' hostels offering cheap accommodation and food, usually run by churches. Many would also carry a 'passport' in which they collect stamps from each of the hostels they visit, recording their pilgrimage as they go.

As it happens, one of the main Camino routes starting in Geneva (the GR65) runs directly through the

Gers department, passing through both Larresingle and Montréal, among many other places. Ever since we'd started taking little trips out we'd been aware of slow-moving human snails winding their way through the peaceful landscape we were falling in love with. Then again, that's not where Esther first met Lorin and Lena. That happened on the outskirts of Condom while they were stoned and looking for pizza.

Esther often took little trips into our nearest medium sized town to socialise the dogs in the park, so much so that she was now a regular face among the cluster of regular dog walkers that gathered there. Sometimes she even took the whole team out for a run, usually linking up with the same acquaintances and walking around the pleasant green space at the centre of the town. Otherwise she would take a pair up into town to remind them what urban environments looked like on the steep cobbled streets close to the picturesque cathedral. It was at the end of one such trip that she bumped into Lorin and Lena.

Lorin, a tanned, bearded and muscular young man of 21, and Lena, a petite, blonde and energetic 18 year old, were very much the archetypal modern pilgrim. Decked in a collection of colourful clothes and carrying various items slung under their arms, they were infectiously happy and seemed to vibrate with the enthusiasm of their youth.

Lena was carrying a guitar that someone had only just given her, so offered up a stumbling version of 'Redemption Song' by Bob Marley as a gift to Esther in return for any help she could provide. Sadly, Esther had never actually heard 'Redemption Song' before, so had no clue if that's what it sounded like. She clapped anyway though.

It was with a heavy heart that Esther had to point out they were going in completely the wrong direction for pizza. However, since thunderstorms were forecast, if they preferred a hot shower, access to a washing machine, or even a soft bed for a night, then they were welcome to call on us while they were in the area. In the immediate moment however, they chose pizza, so Esther dropped them off outside of a pizza place and said farewell.

In addition to food, it was always cleanliness and temporary comfort that we'd craved the most during our longer hiking adventures. Also, especially when we were younger, we'd benefitted time and time again from the kindness of strangers ourselves. It wasn't just 'Scanburger' employees. It was older couples in motorhomes who provided boiling water when our gas ran out. It was the Munich campsite manager who gifted us a plate of food because we'd lost our wallet. And it was the Swedish café owner who let us sleep on her front lawn when we got lost in the woods and then left breakfast outside of our tent the next morning. In our times of greatest need somebody had always been willing to step in and offer us some help. Meeting Lorin and Lena felt like a chance to rebalance the karmic books a little. Besides, marijuana-smiles aside, Lorin and Lena reminded Esther of a life she might have chosen.

I can't deny that it was my own preconceptions and prejudices about what life was supposed to be about that saw us pursue postgraduate degrees, with all of the mortgages and other commitments that arose as a result. Esther had always dreamed of travelling. In Lena, she told me, she saw the person she could have been, if she'd been brave enough to just set off on her own at eighteen. For one reason and another, she'd been too afraid to take that step and so gone to university instead, meeting me and, well, you already know the rest. Lena, on the other hand, had just left school and gone walking, before obligations had expanded to fill her life. She'd only met Lorin after several weeks of walking solo.

It was late the following afternoon that Esther got the call. After filling themselves with pizza and sleeping in

211

a wet field, they'd made very slow progress to Larresingle where they'd decided to take Esther up on her offer.

We only had a few weeks left now before the first guests arrived at the farmhouse, a reality that had recently been casting a small shadow over our carefree, pleasant and plodding routine. While the pups had shed their perm-like coats and were now two months older, growing into their bodies and filling out, we'd essentially managed to totally sidestep the issue of where they might live long term. It had been beautiful and addictive to simply immerse ourselves in the moment, relishing the perfect days as a family, but with such a short amount of time remaining until we'd all be forced to move back into the campervan, we had to at least start thinking about it.

I knew that we could make it work in the van for a week or so, but only if we absolutely had to. We'd go mad in such a small space and, more importantly, it just wouldn't be fair on the dogs. They were like small, ginger nuclear reactors they had so much energy. Our current van simply wasn't a viable option, or at least not in any way we could see.

Esther remained of the opinion that we should still just wait and see, that something would come up and that I could leave it to her, just as our many experiences had proved. In contrast, I was struggling to 'keep the faith' so to speak. Letting something come up didn't have to mean putting our heads in the sand, I argued, and I wanted a plan of action right away. Esther, however, dug her heels in and said she felt sure something good would happen if we could just be patient. It wasn't that there was a lot of tension between us, but I was worried.

Lorin and Lena immediately lifted our spirits, spreading their infectious and carefree abandon like fairy dust. Not that we joined in with the 'actual' fairy dust I hasten to add. As non-smoking, tee-totallers ourselves, we couldn't provide any alcoholic or narcotic stimulation for our guests, just healthy food and shelter, though that didn't matter because they'd bought their own.

Although I've never tried it myself, and nor has Esther, we'd obviously seen and been around people smoking weed in the past, mostly at university. I didn't have anything in particular against it. I'm not a puritan, I just never felt the need to put it in my body when there are plenty of other ways of feeling good, most of which involve breaking a sweat. Lorin and Lena, on the hand, loved a good smoke and during their brief stay we enjoyed plenty of open and honest discussions about what they felt they got out of it and why they enjoyed it so much.

For Lorin in particular, drugs were not just a recreational, lazy route to a pleasant sensation, they were about being able to access another state of mind and have 'insights' that he wouldn't otherwise have about life. Yes, he could admit that in the evenings he smoked weed to relax, but for him other drugs he'd used were about accessing spiritual experiences and inspiring a new level of creativity.

For my part I was happy to believe that he absolutely felt that way, but I couldn't ignore the likelihood that somewhere along the invisible supply chain that he drew upon (whether he knew it or not), somebody was being taken advantage of in all manner of unpleasant ways. I don't want to dwell on it, but while I never doubted Lorin's sincerity, unless somebody has a totally self-contained means of production that's entirely for personal use, drug use will never be 'purely spiritual' to me.

Anyway, it didn't taint our time together as it was such a minor element. They were both excellent company, adoring the dogs and showing us a life we too might have sampled once upon a time. After the first couple of days it was like having a younger brother and sister around the place, with a communal peace and harmony extending over

213

the house. We ate together, fussed puppies together, talked, read poems and listened to music. It was all so effortless.

Saying farewell to Lorin and Lena after five nights of them living with us was emotional. At the speed they'd been moving we were quietly confident that they'd never make it to Spain before winter, though they proved us wrong. They didn't make it to Galicia though, choosing instead to hitchhike down to the south coast of Spain. Lena went back to Switzerland while Lorin continued travelling into Morocco. At the time of writing he's still on the road somewhere, smiling above an enormous beard and beneath a lot of dreadlocks. The last we heard he was trying to cycle around Africa. Lena also continues to be a free spirit, adventuring and studying to be physiotherapist back in Switzerland. The world could do with a few more beautiful, uplifting folk like them.

Yet while seeing a vision of a path we could have chosen might have been bitter-sweet, in reality it made us even more grateful for what we had done. Yes, we'd had pain and depression in our lives. Yes, we'd made decisions that trapped and divided us. But it was precisely through that necessary suffering that we became the people that we are, bound in a relationship built not only on brief shared experiences but mutual respect, underlying trust and a savage commitment that's weathered many storms.

Which is also what I believed we were potentially facing if we didn't do something about our van situation, the number of dogs in our lives, or both, very soon.

Holland

Something did turn up of course, just as Esther said it would. In fact, several things turned up all at once. Just after we bid Lorin and Lena farewell, literally within an hour, we got a text message out of the blue offering us another housesitting gig in another region of France. I immediately thought our prayers had been answered. We still weren't going to be travelling but at least we had more time to sort something out.

Unfortunately, just five days before we were due to leave the Gers, that new house-sitting arrangement fell through leaving us right back in the lurch. Mercifully, that was on the same day that the house's internet connection was activated for the incoming guests. Living without internet for three months had been great, forcing us to make trips to Fourcès post office if we wanted to send any messages. We'd enjoyed the lack of connection. That said, it couldn't have come back on at a better time.

Two hours after the internet went live, Esther was on the phone arranging a part-exchange deal on our campervan with a dealership in Sussex. She'd found an incredible motorhome on eBay, bigger than Homer and with all the adaptations on board that we'd ever desired. Most important of all, we reckoned it was big enough to accommodate two humans *and* five dogs (well, sort of).

I left the south of France on a Saturday afternoon, just as Esther began cleaning with a vengeance, driving for ten hours to reach Dieppe before sailing to Newhaven in the early hours of Sunday morning. By the time dealership opened its doors I was parked on the forecourt.

Having inspected the motorhome and shaking on the deal, I would have driven straight back to France that same day, except it transpired we couldn't insure our new wheels until Monday morning. At first we thought that was a huge

215

pain in the arse since it left only the narrowest of margins for me to get back to the Gers in time to collect Esther, the dogs and all our stuff before the first holidaymakers arrived.

Yet somehow even that turned into a kind of blessing. Using my unexpected half day stuck in the UK, and the last few hours with our campervan, I drove a little further north to Buckinghamshire to visit Esther's parents and drop off some flowers. I thought it would be a nice surprise for them. I arrived to find them in tears.

Unknown to us, they'd just taken the harrowing decision to have Sam, their canine companion of thirteen years, put to sleep the following morning. He'd already beaten cancer twice and was suffering for a third time, with large open tumours on his legs that were now bleeding regularly. He'd been battling it for months but the time had come to acknowledge that the pain was now too great.

I joined them on their last walk together, pushing Sam in a buggy, taking some photos and offering what little support I could. They told me it was a huge comfort that I was there. Sam had been part of our own lives as well over the past thirteen but I could still only imagine what they were going through. I'd just spent an unexpected six months falling in love with five dogs and the thought of something like this happening terrified me too much to seriously contemplate the possibility.

The following morning I returned to the dealership, swapped keys and charged south again via the Dover-Calais crossing. Driving all day and most of the night to reach Esther by 6 a.m. on Tuesday, I then took a quick nap while she piled our stuff haphazardly into our new motorhome and then we all got out of the way. A few hours later the first guests arrived from Toulouse airport. It had been a close run thing but we left behind a sparkling house, tidy garden and swimming pool, plus a gigantic pile of happy memories.

We spent the next week sleeping, getting to grips with our new home and reorganising our things on the ever-accommodating Gordon's driveway. Esther had a brainwave to strip out some of the cupboards and build an extra layer of floor beneath our bed to serve as a dog sleeping and travelling space. It was a good idea, but taking a hacksaw and a screwdriver to what was a very smart motorhome did irk me at the time. Still, the result came out looking very smart and practical.

But then, as if all of that wasn't enough, the pups had now reached an age where they really needed sterilising, especially if they were coming travelling with us for a while. We didn't want to be worrying about any more unplanned pregnancies.

Since we already trusted the vet back in Condom we decided to get it done en masse before moving on, leaving us with four surgically groggy dogs on our hands on the day of my thirty-fifth birthday. For some reason only little George had to wear a cone-of-shame. The girls got a heavy duty dressing strapped around their middle but my only regular male company was left banging around like a drunken Tudor with an over-sized ruff (ruff-ruff, get it? Never mind).

Yet somehow, within a week of buying our third home-on-wheels, after all of that frenetic driving and logistical juggling, we'd somehow pulled it off. We'd gone from an unsuitable campervan to a seven-metre-long motorhome with loads of storage space, self-customised to have a dedicated dog floor. It had solar power, a refillable gas system and all of the other features we'd longed for during the Homer years. And we had five healthy, sterile, fairly well-trained and loving dogs on board. It felt like we had the world at our feet again. It was turning into a very different year to the one we'd imagined seven months earlier, but it was undeniably a fun way to live.

We spent a final evening with Gordon and Sue, saying our goodbyes and preparing to set off the very next morning. We weren't sure exactly where we were going, as usual, but intended to head east and see where we ended up. Then we got a call to say Esther's grandma had fallen and broken her hip.

When Esther's grandad had died in 2011, we'd arrived in Holland thirty minutes too late to say goodbye. We'd taken the call in Durham, jumped onto the next available flight from Newcastle airport, run to the train platforms in Schiphol airport and rolled up at the hospital in Den Haag to be told that he'd only just slipped away. It was crushing and not an experience we ever wanted to repeat, which is why we started driving north as soon as the news arrived. Stopping only as often as the team needed comfort breaks, we were outside of Leiden hospital by the following lunchtime, twelve hours of driving and not a lot of sleep later. In the previous week and a half I'd driven as many miles as we'd done in Homer in the first six months.

Incredibly, at a hundred years old, the doctors had still judged Oma strong enough for surgery to repair the shattered joint. That said, anybody that knew her would have expected it. Esther managed to arrive just as she was coming round and was able to hold her hand and hear the good news that all had gone well.

A few days later Oma was moved to a specialised rehabilitation centre, essentially a residential hospital for intensive physiotherapy and round the clock care. It was an incredible place for her to be, by which time we'd also moved in with Esther's parents, dogs and all.

On the face of it, a two-bedroom, sixth floor flat to the south of the Hague (Den Haag) doesn't sound like the ideal place for four adults and five dogs to share. That's because it isn't. But this wasn't just any flat. It may not have been overly large and it may not have been fancy, but it was just a few hundred metres from a very special stretch of beach.

In case you don't already know, Holland is really quite small. It's the most densely populated country in the European Union and its geography is essentially dominated by water management. A quarter of the Netherlands is famously below sea level, with much of the land having been reclaimed over the centuries from salt marshes.

Nowadays an elaborate system of dykes, pumps (traditionally windmills) and storm barriers work to keep the water out, a big worry with the anticipated rise in sea levels. Much of the western coast of Holland is an almost continuous beach that runs from below the Hague up to Den Helder at the north-western tip. With natural, undulating sand dunes dividing the water from the land, it's largely a gentle, windswept and very beautiful place to visit.

That's what we were basically looking out over from our sixth-floor station alongside an especially calm piece of coastal beauty called Kijkduin. While large stretches of untouched beach do still remain between the various towns dotted along the Dutch coast, many of the towns themselves have become tourist hotspots. Places like Scheveningen and Zandvoort, for instance, have high rise tower blocks that cater for the summer exodus that arrives from nearby Germany every year, with inland folks eager to get out their buckets and spades.

Kijkduin, however, had largely resisted such expansion and change. With just a single hotel, a few low-rise apartment blocks and an old-fashioned shopping arcade populated by independent stores and colourful restaurants, stepping onto the beach at Kijkduin was a little like stepping several decades into a calmer past. (That's sadly changing now, in 2020, because developers have finally got their way, bulldozing the shopping arcade in favour of new apartment buildings.)

Waking each morning on the little sofa bed we were sharing, we gazed out over the foamy crests of the wind-whipped North Sea, our eyes drawn by the long yellow line that extended away to both the north and south. On the southern horizon we could just make out the boats coming and going from the industrial colossus that is the Port of Rotterdam, historically a powerhouse of the former Dutch Empire. To the north, if the haze allowed, we could see the pier at Scheveningen, but in between those two distant markers was a lot of sea, a lot of sand, and a lot of tall grass waving in the wind on the dunes.

In what is commonly called the Dutch Golden Age of painting, in the 17th century, freedom from Spanish Catholic rule led to a surge in Dutch economic and cultural prominence. Dutch artists also blossomed, with many focusing on scenes of everyday life. From Rembrandt to Vermeer, it was often the play of light in their scenes that these masters sought to highlight. Sitting in bed looking out over the sea, it was easy to understand why light is such a key characteristic of Dutch life. In a land of long, flat horizons and correspondingly vast swathes of cloud-filled skies, the Dutch landscape always seems to appear in high contrast.

Often, in the mornings, we'd all go to the beach together, four humans and five dogs, letting the pups discover a whole new world of fun. With dozens of other dog walkers pacing the broad beach at Kijkduin, our gang would both delight and be delighted with each new meeting. They'd dig in the sand, chase tails (their own and strangers), and run after the bundles of foam being blown from the tops of the waves.

Some days, for a change, we'd take them to a dedicated dog walking area, usually a stretch of inland green space fenced off specifically for 'off-lead' walking. Holland is quite a well organised and regimented country after all, mostly due to how densely populated it is. Some days Esther's Uncle Hans and his dog Zoe would join us, looking at her extended 'furmily' with some curiosity before trying to join in with whatever games the pups had developed between themselves. They were a tight unit, but Zoe soon began to be accepted too.

Sadly, we did encounter a little unexpected resistance during our visits to the dog walking areas. While Leela and her pups were all well behaved individually, after months in the French countryside they could be rather loud and boisterous as a pack. Unfortunately that upset some of the more reserved and regular visitors.

I suppose we were something of an explosion of noise and colour. In Holland, it seemed for some people at least that a dog was absolutely expected to be seen and not heard. This was quite a surprise to us after the laissez-fair attitude to dogs and their barking that we'd largely encountered in Spain and rural France (where guarding behaviour was actively encouraged). Still, there wasn't a lot we could do about it right now.

After a morning walk we'd do some exercise of our own, usually jogging on the beach with Leela (while the pups slept) or cycling along the dune paths as far as Rotterdam in the south or Zandvoort in the north. In addition to being a country of water and light, Holland is definitely also a country of wind and at no time is this more apparent than from the saddle of a bicycle.

From time to time, while visiting Oma and Opa, Esther had taken the opportunity to borrow their clunky (but well maintained) 3-gear bikes and take off for a few days into the Dutch countryside with a tent. Holland's efficiency definitely extends to its famous cycle network, with a nationwide system of dedicated cycle paths that cover every part of the country. It is, quite literally, possible to cycle the entire length or breadth of Holland and not leave a cycle path.

In fact, more than that, with an interconnecting series of numbered markers and local maps, it's not even really that necessary to plan the route. All you need to do is have a direction in mind, find one of the many maps beside the path (which will have its own number), pick another number on the map and then follow the relevant signs leading all the way to the next map. And so the process repeats.

In addition to pedalling around the mostly rural southern islands that sit between Den Haag and Belgium, we'd also completed a couple of multiday tours around the Ijsselmeer and northern Holland, all without making any plans in advance. We'd played 'spot the windmill' from our saddles while pedalling through such picturesque locations as Giethoorn (the Venice of Holland), Leeuwarden on the northern coast and Texel (the largest of the northern Dutch islands). Camping mostly on farms, our brief trips away from the intense concrete jungles of Den Haag and Amsterdam had always revealed a green land dedicated to farming, with cows and regimented crops extending towards the always distant horizons.

We'd also crossed over many of the immense storm barriers that keep out the sea, though none more impressive than the 32 kilometre long, 90 metre wide aflsluitdijk (pronounced 'aff-slowt-dyke' - literally meaning 'shut off dyke'). Up until 1927 the North Sea used to extend right into mainland Holland in the form of massive bay some 100 kilometres long, but then the Dutch government built a huge, straight barrier all the way across the opening.

The existence of the aflsluitdijk is largely taken for granted now, but a hundred years ago it utterly changed the lives of hundreds of fishing communities that had long made a living alongside the sea that was suddenly a lake. The Zuiderzee museum charts some of those changes and plays home to dozens of original buildings from the fringes of the lost sea, all reconstructed with perfect attention to detail to give a sense of the harsh life once eked out on those windswept shores.

In cycling terms, thirty near-arrow-straight kilometres with nothing but a narrow strip of tarmac and visually endless water for company is a tough ride, especially with the ever-present headwind. I swear we've crossed that dyke both ways on the same day and had a headwind both times, but that's just Holland. Whichever way you go on a bike, the wind always seems to be in your face.

On a more practical cycling note, like all good Dutch people, we also used our bikes for pretty much every other aspect of daily life, such as going into the centre of the Hague (Den Haag) for groceries. Every Wednesday morning during our unexpected summer visit we'd cycle right up to the front of the Dutch parliament building where an organic market was taking place (the processes of government seem much more approachable in Holland).

One stall in particular was run by a charismatic trader called Perry, a man we got to know very well during the six weeks we eventually spent in Holland. We'd show up with our empty panniers and load up with all manner of vivid, firm and eclectic examples of nature's bounty. Every time we visited there was a new delight to try, from cherimoya to starfruit, guava to durian. Perry took great pleasure in surprising us with new flavours, often gifting things to us alongside our standard stock-up.

But it was our afternoons that really defined our days in Holland when we visited Oma at the rehabilitation centre. As a residential facility, dogs were allowed inside two-at-a-time, so each day we took a different set with us. Wheeling Oma out into the café, sometimes with Esther's parents as well, we'd share a drink together while Esther dazzled other patients and their families with dog tricks.

From benches, wheelchairs and even hospital beds wheeled outside, people applauded as Esther ran through a little routine of wait, stay, fetch and other crowd-pleasing games. They may not have been model dogs in the sense of sanctioned walking spaces, but in terms of raising a smile they were more than qualified. Fairly soon the nurses and receptionists were calling them therapy dogs, which seemed rather fitting in their colourful high-vis harnesses.

As Esther grew more confident we started bringing all five dogs into the café area for their impromptu shows. With their similar looks and ginger fluff, they could almost have been a circus troop. We might not have had a clue what we'd been doing, but whatever had guided our choices since New Year, the fact we were able to bring a smile to the faces of both loved ones and strangers in times of difficulty made whatever came next more than worth it.

Our weeks in Holland disappeared in a cloud of sand, cuddles, ginger fur, tricks and chew toys. By the time Oma was discharged back into her regular assisted living apartment, we found that both spring and summer had somehow come to an end. Nothing about the previous months had gone according to plan, it had been much better than that.

A Grand Route

"It's not a particular place we're looking for, but a feeling". Those were the words we'd shared with family and friends as we drove away from everything we knew. Never before had those words felt so apt as when we'd headed south out of Holland with five dogs packed aboard a still unfamiliar motorhome. With our options somewhat restricted by the obligations we'd slipped into, admittedly through our own inaction and the 'soft-hearted foolishness' I'd once thought myself immune to, feelings seemed even more important than ever.

After three and a half years of moving around, if there was anything we'd learned at all it was that relying on plans was a mug's game. For years before setting off we'd obsessed about the details of our imagined future, always worrying about how our actions in the moment might influence the unknown years ahead. Foregoing happiness, even welcoming discomfort, was taken as a sign that we were 'doing something right'.

Likewise, taking decisions that were occasionally selfish, cynical or even manipulative had seemed like an unavoidable fact of adult life. We'd been to seminars on networking, negotiation and management, listening to teachings that had encouraged us to see those around us professionally simply as 'friend' or 'foe'. In our private lives we could volunteer, bake for friends and give to charity, but when it came to work, well, different rules applied. At least that's what the cut and thrust of business seemed to demand.

Looking back across the years, we hardly recognised ourselves now. Kindness had been showered upon us with no expectation of a return. We, for our part, had done our best to pass on that kindness. There was no direction or intention to any of it, just a willingness to greet each day with an open mind and an open heart. The truth was that the best outcomes of recent years had occurred precisely when we'd let go of planning. It was only when we'd tried to impose control over the weeks and months ahead that events seemed to have gone awry.

As the September sun cast its fading light across the French Alps, we sat beside our motorhome on top of the Cormet de Roselend mountain pass with steaming mugs of tea in our chilly fingers. Together, we watched the final patches of light get swallowed by the silent shadows that chased them. Light and dark no longer seemed like polar opposites, just two sides of the same coin. Had we really been those people? Those frightened, driven, ambitious individuals who mistook pain as a symbol of success? The answer, like so many others now, no longer seemed simple. It was 'yes', but also 'no'.

Still, sunset in the high mountains can do that to a soul. It grows philosophical, confronted with the reality of a cosmos so vast that vocabulary begins to fail. People can quote vast numbers or invent clever analogies involving a grain of sand placed six metres away from a snooker ball (representing the relative scale of the Earth and Sun, for example), but that's not even scratching the surface. It takes light eight minutes to cover that distance, but it takes four years for light from the sun to reach the next nearest star! And that's just the closest one, a single star among billions in a single galaxy. The galaxies are even further apart, and there are billions of those too, comprising just the part of the universe that we can see. Don't even get me started on multiverse theories.

Staring upwards as thousands of pinpoints of light emerged across the heavens, a window into the vastness of such a reality, I listened to the snuffling and scratching of our five young dogs around our feet and felt a warm glow steal over me. It felt comforting to be so very small yet connected to all of that enormity. Some people probably pass their whole lives without seeing a sky so dazzling in its clarity. The stars seemed so close that I could have picked them out of the air in front of me.

Given the time of year and the many unknowns thrown up by having so many canine companions on board, a return to the French Alps had been an easy choice to make. We were going south anyway, for winter, and the sense of familiarity and homecoming was reassuring when we looked at the five sets of trusting eyes who watched us from their respective travelling stations. Older, hairier and noisier (and that was just us), we hadn't a clue how the next few weeks were going to go. Perhaps we'd still find them good homes over winter but, then again, maybe not. We couldn't deny how much of a family we'd become. Soft-hearted foolishness indeed.

Picking up the mountains just beyond Geneva, we'd started working through a network of passes and villages we'd not come close to before. The Route des Grande Alpes is a collection of high roads and deep valleys that connects the gently lapping waters of Lake Geneva to the warm, sun-dappled waves of the Mediterranean. Taking in eighteen lofty cols, including some of the Tour de France's most fearsome 'hors categorie' giants, it has over 16,000 meters of elevation gain over its 700 kilometre length. We'd visited the French Alps several times before, in Homer as you know, both on our bikes and by foot, but as we were quickly learning, in all of those previous visits we'd barely tickled the surface.

The Cormet de Roselend, at just below 2000 metres, was our fifth pass in just three days, and the first we were sleeping on top of. Our routine was as simple as it was necessary, the only way we could juggle our desire to explore with the needs of our still youthful companions. One or other of us would set out early to ride the next climb along the route, preparing and departing while the other rotated through the various dog walking, feeding and training requirements. Later, after the first rider had returned, our roles would switch. Whoever was behind usually also drove to the top of whichever pass we were on, ready to prepare lunch before descending the other side. And so the days quickly began to find a new focus, aiming to meet the needs of all passengers and spend as much time outdoors as possible.

The dogs loved it. The pups had known four houses, three countries and two motorhomes in their six months on Earth. They, like Leela, seemed to adapt to new environments as standard. Nothing phased them, except for cats of course. And birds. And squirrels. In fact, anything fluffy that ran away created an immediate frenzy of ginger fur and barking. But apart from that, they were unflappable. Except perhaps for discarded food? And maybe strangers that showed the slightest interest in them....I think you get the idea. They were never scared, just perpetually excited. And, as a result, our own life was constantly more colourful and exciting than it had been a year ago.

Everywhere we took them, be it a crowded Alpine col or cobbled street in a storybook village, we were inundated with smiles and photographs again (we really should have started charging). Walking with five small dogs sniffing the air ahead of us made us into a bit of a spectacle, which at first I did find uncomfortable. For most of my life I'd been a private person. Slowly, however, I relaxed into the occasional clamour the pups could incite and, as I did, I found myself mirroring the smiles we left behind us.

There also always seemed to be a safe place for them to explore. Whether it was a riverside path, a quiet park, or even a deserted ice rink waiting for the temperature to fall again, we rarely struggled to meet their exercise needs. It was getting them to rest that was the bigger challenge.

Up on the cols themselves it was even easier. During the day it could be busy with hundreds of other cyclists, hikers and car tourists passing through, but when evening fell and we stepped out to enjoy the mountain silhouettes framed by stars, it was a world all to ourselves. No doubt in July and August these passes would have been crowded with other campervans and motorhomes, especially those places that the Tour de France had whizzed across. But for us, as late-September approached, we were largely alone, just the seven of us enjoying companionable isolation amid the bare rock and grassy banks that framed the far-reaching mountain views.

Up and down we went, from winding pass to verdant valley, pedalling, sleeping, playing and repeating. We also threw in a few detours to the main Route des Grande Alpes depending on whatever possibilities caught our eye. We initially veered west after the Cormet de Roselend, opting to tackle the sequential challenges of the 1993 metre Col de la Madeleine and the 2064 metre Col de la Croix de Fer instead of the loftier 2764 metre Col de l'Iseran (although we came back to try that one as well – it was very cold).

As we sweated and marvelled in the shadow of the exposed cliffs and towering summits that were constantly changing, even after so many other mountain landscapes in the preceding years, we couldn't help but become hypnotised by this majestic land we were whirring through. Moving so quickly down the range gave us a whole new sense of how the interlocking valleys and passes melted together into the beautiful, flowing scenery of the whole.

During previous visits we'd moved deliberately slowly, savouring individual villages and hillsides like gourmet diners rolling a perfect morsel around our tongues. Now we feasted on a seemingly endless supply of delicacies, each one different to the last. Neither speed of travel was better or worse, they were both wonderful.

As we continued to complete most of the climbs apart, we also began to develop a new appreciation for each other. Counterintuitively, with the new level of independence required by the dogs' youth, we felt a more powerful sense of connection in the shared moments that bookended our busy days. Plus a greater sense of fulfilment as we focused on their needs and not just our own.

For col after col we repeated the same routine, grateful for the kind autumn weather that was keeping the quiet roads warm and hospitable. Almost three weeks after arriving on the northern fringe of the Alps, having chalked up almost twenty thousand vertical metres of pedalling, we approached the Mediterranean Sea. In theory we could have stopped there. We'd completed most of the Route des Grande Alpes, passing through lots of new locations and a handful of pleasingly familiar ones.

Rolling back through the Queyras, for example, had induced a wave of heady nostalgia for the days we'd shared there, both together in the mountains and working down on the farm. Indeed, we'd taken Cyrille up on his offer and spent a comforting evening sitting back beneath the old gazebo with several of our old farm friends as the sun went down. Some faces had moved on and others had arrived, but Stephan and Cyrille remained, even cracking open a bottle of the 'vintage' we'd helped to harvest. It wasn't bad.

Likewise, passing through Puget-Théniers had invoked an even more powerful response. Had it really been more than three years since we'd danced in that same square and taken off on our first, fateful Alpine cycle? It had, but it was hard to believe. So much had changed yet here we were, doing the same things, in the same place, experiencing an ever deeper joy. In the intervening years we'd let go of so many things, old ideas and possessions. As a result, so much inspiring newness had been allowed to flow in. As the saying goes, if you don't let go of the 'old', there'll be no space for the 'new'.

We did go further south, eventually, passing through the Pyrenees via Andorra, the 16th smallest country in the world by land, and the 11th smallest by population. It only takes around 40km to drive right through Andorra, where an unappealing gaggle of 'tax-free' shopping opportunities crowd together at either end of the main road that starts in France and ends in Spain. Pas de la Casa, in particular, which sits at 2000 metres altitude beneath a magnificent cirque of mountainside, is ugly and garish against the natural splendour it taints.

Fortunately, although many French and Spanish bargain hunters might think so, cheap cigarettes and booze is far from the full Andorran experience. Andorra does produce a lot of tobacco, with farming there dominated by the crop, but with so much of the landscape taken up by vertical rock faces and craggy summits, there's only so much commerce can do. In a tiny country that's avoided conflict for a 1000 years, it's easy to get lost among the handful of deep valleys and winding access roads that snake across the rarely-flat terrain.

As you might expect, we climbed back into the saddle. From the 2305 metre Port de Cabus to the 2407 metre Port d'Envalira, we spent a wonderful week pedalling back and forth across this tiny mountain nation as the late autumn sun stayed the hand of winter for a while longer.

Spoiling ourselves with two hours in the three-storey Sport Wellness Mountain Spa, a place where wood panelled walls enclose an oasis of calm hidden between high peaks, deep lakes and the Valira river, we reflected on what a bizarre year it had been. Just twelve months earlier we'd been flying back to the UK determined to buy a little campervan and charge across Europe in a campaign of thrill-seeking and nomadic decadence. Now we were wallowing in a whirlpool with a chunky motorhome outside, home to ourselves, five dozing dogs, two well-used bikes and rather a lot of dog hair.

Summer of Passes

By the time spring returned to the beaches of Spain, rapidly transforming the wild winter winds into hot gusts that whispered of swimsuits and palm trees, we were marking the end of our fourth year on the road. As the pups had approached a year old, their lives and ours still showed no sign of diverging. Truth was, we'd stopped looking a long time ago.

If you'd asked us at the time whether we wanted five dogs in our lives, with all of the double and triple walks that still required, curtailed excursions and the prospect of fifteen more years of the same, we'd have said "no, of course we don't, it's too much". If you'd then also asked us which one we could say goodbye to, then we would have said "would you like a cup of tea?" We weren't so much keeping five dogs as we were avoiding discussions about rehoming any because there was always something else that needed doing first. And so life rumbled on. I'm not claiming this was the healthiest way to deal with the situation, but it was how it was at the time.

Our very first trips to the beaches of Spain seemed lost in a forgotten past, a time when we'd ambled aimlessly with our toes sinking into the gentle surf and nothing to do but go back to Homer and watch the sun set. Now our experiences had changed irrevocably, from tranquillity to controlled chaos (although the level of control varied). As we watched the pack chasing seagulls, digging to nowhere and running in crazy circles in an endless game of exuberant joy, we saw happiness in action.

For all of the strict training that Esther had adhered to in the motorhome and on quiet walks with just the seven of us, managing what other humans did when they came face to face with tongue-lolling cuteness was something we'd had to throw to the winds of fate. We'd decided early

232

on that we didn't want to be the kinds of owners shouting "STOP! Please ignore my dog...." as we raced along the beach. Trained enough to be safe, relaxed enough to be happy was the middle ground we were aiming for.

Then again, safety wasn't entirely ours to control. It was in February that we had to take our first fishing hook related trip to a vet. The deadly little needles seemed to be everywhere on the beaches of southern Spain, baited but forgotten where fisherman had cut them loose and thrown them into the sand. For five sensitive, hungry noses, they were like unexploded bombs. Some days we'd collect half a dozen in thirty minutes, usually with a tangle of fishing line still attached. Every time we saw the tell-tale plastic cord in the sand we unearthed it, cleaning up what we could, when we could. We'd always picked up litter on the beaches of Spain, ever since our first visit in Homer, but now we had a renewed and specific focus.

Pati was the first to need an X-ray, then George just a week later. Mercifully they both managed to pass the ingested fishing hooks naturally without any sign of the fatal internal damage that so terrified us. The vet we'd found had optimistically advised a fibrous tangle of asparagus and pumpkin mash as a meal before the (almost inevitable) surgery, hoping that such a concoction would cushion the sharpness within. She was even more amazed than us when it worked.

Without the more colourful distractions of summer to occupy us, we'd basked in a more sedate beach-hopping life. Working on writing and other projects that we cared about in the mornings alongside exercise, in the mid-afternoon heat we developed a charming siesta addiction. After lunch, we'd toss the whole team up onto our bed at the back of the motorhome and then climb into the mass of sandy fur and happy tongues.

Up there, together, in a tangle of arms, legs, paws and floppy ears, we became an indivisible unit. We looked after them and they, in turn, whether they knew it or not, continued to remind us how to appreciate the moment. They looked after us every day by showing us that we could take nothing for granted, definitely not some imagined future based on the events of a half-remembered past.

Floating slowly north as temperatures climbed, we continued shifting from beach to beach, crossing into France in late spring as the Pyrenean snows melted. Continuing north-east through Provence, we pulled out our map of Europe and pondered upon where to go. We looked again at Eastern Europe and Scandinavia, a journey we'd half-planned before meeting Leela, but we were surprised to find that it no longer called to us as strongly. In a way, we wanted to want to go there, but when we were honest with ourselves we just didn't feel the urge. In fact, we didn't really feel a powerful 'urge' to go anywhere. In every way that mattered, we were already where we wanted to be.

Still, we kept moving slowly, slipping into Switzerland with the vague intention to pass through, which we almost did. But then, like a impassable barrier, the allure of those majestically high mountains that dominate southern Switzerland once again stopped us in our tracks. Chugging along the familiar Rhone valley felt like a homecoming in many ways, a return to the very first wild places we'd ever visited and rekindling the same sort of exotic sensations.

Balancing newness with familiarity had always been a reassuring feature of our travels, allowing us to alternate intervals of relative restfulness with the excitement of totally unexplored terrains. It's also what happened when we first returned to Switzerland.

Familiarity came first in the form of a brief sojourn back up in the fantastic the Val d'Anniviers. Diverting from the motorway to head up the road that had once so terrified us (but now seemed rather tame), we decided to just keep going up this time, continuing driving right up to the end of the road at the Moiry Glacier.

Parking at 2300 metres above sea level, right in front of the small lake formed around the glacier's tongue, we stepped out to breathe in the intoxicating cleanliness of our surroundings. Even though it had been a while since we'd visited, we felt the same sense of instant renewal that we had on previous visits, the same sense of welcoming peace that always made it so hard to leave. We stayed for almost a week in that secluded car park. During the days we played with dogs on the grassy hillsides while at night, when the day visitors left, we could look up at the falling glacier topped by snow and feel as though it was all ours.

'Newness' came a week later in the form of a village called Anzere, high on the opposite flank of the Rhone valley. We had planned to leave the Val d'Anniviers and start touring again right away. However, when we found out that the same permissive 'tax' scheme that existed in the Val d'Anniviers applied to the cable cars and amenities of Anzere as well, we decided to take a quick look.

It was on our first night in Anzere that we met Tim. Having parked at the back of the village and visited the tourist office to excitedly pay the 'tax', we decided to use our newly acquired pass for a dip in the heated, open-air pool that looked out over the mountains, complete with jacuzzi and bubble chairs.

Having fallen into easy conversation with Tim, we soon realised we'd met a man infused with an overflowing love of adventure. Among his tales of paragliding near misses and helicopter landings on lofty summits, we basically gathered that Tim had come to Anzere with his family because he and his brother had recently inherited a brand new, totally unused chalet there from their father. Although Tim lived in Australia, he was basically in Switzerland to sort out the administrative side of things and put the debt-laden property on the market.

After the pool closed we invited Tim and his kids back to our own petite home to meet the dogs, who they

235

loved (naturally). Tim then invited us to pop over and see the place he was having to sell. Walking towards a three-storey vision of immaculately wood-panelled elegance, there was only one word that could possibly be applied to such a place: mansion.

After giving us a tour and lamenting on the various legal hoops he was now having to jump through to sell it, Tim put the kettle on and then promptly knocked us off our feet with an offer that blew our minds.

"You can stay here for a bit if you want" he said to us unexpectedly. "We're off tomorrow and it'll only be empty. I'm leaving a key with a local agent anyway and there might be some tenants now and then, but if you want to stay in the little granny flat downstairs feel free. What do you think?"

The 'granny flat', as Tim called it, was actually a self-sufficient two bedroom space on the ground floor with its own kitchen and sauna.

"Wow, that's so generous and kind of you. But, really, even with the dogs? This place is immaculate."

"No worries. What can they do? I trust you to clean up when you head off. Just don't let them up in the main house. Enjoy yourselves."

So that's what we did. Moving just a few bare necessities (plus dogs) into the pristine 'flat', we spent the next fortnight waking up to the sight of the golden sun shining through our windows as it rose directly out of the snow-capped mountains across the valley from us. During the day we'd take the dogs wandering across the hillsides while during the evenings we'd enjoy some human-only time back in the pool where this whole, unexpected but luxurious interlude had begun.

Perhaps if it hadn't already been high summer then we'd have lost ourselves in the arms of space and comfort for a little longer than we did. While it was a beautiful, rare treat to experience such luxury directly within a location we already loved so much, it wasn't really the luxury that fulfilled us, it was the mountains themselves. So we tore ourselves away, back into our usual compact base in search of pastures new.

With July temperatures climbing fast towards the mid-30's, the reality of life with seven heartbeats in a plastic box dictated that we seek altitude as a practical obligation. The moment the morning sun broke above the high mountain ridges that surrounded us, the surfaces inside of our motorhome began to heat up worryingly quickly. Parking under trees, closing all of the reflective window blinds, covering the front of our motorhome with sheets and even placing frozen water bottles on the floor for the dogs to snuggle up with just wasn't going to cut it. Even sitting out beneath our awning, gasping at what little breeze the rampant summer heat allowed us, was like sitting in a sauna on the valley floors.

So we headed high. As we'd already experienced, Switzerland is far more than a country of low taxes, investment banking headquarters and the world's number one producer of chocolate. It's also a nation where the powerful, gravity-defying scenery has been efficiently, and for the most part respectably, integrated into the comfortable lifestyle of Swiss residents.

Take the Grand Dixence Dam project as a prime example, where the meltwater from 35 enormous glaciers is funnelled via a series of pumping stations and man-made tunnels into a single enormous lake, the Lac des Dix. There, at almost 2500 metres altitude, held back by the world's highest gravity dam, 400 million cubic metres of water waits to be channelled through four pumping stations, producing almost double the electricity of a nuclear power station. And that's just one project. Whether it's improbable train lines, remote cable cars, or jaw-dropping roads, it seems the Swiss like their engineering large.

Our first new cycle climb that summer was the Furka Pass, a string of 2429 metre-high tarmac spaghetti that cuts across the now sadly diminished tongue of the Rhone glacier. The Furka Pass was actually used as a location in the James Bond film Goldfinger, though Sean Connery wasn't the first famous face to grace the area. In 1868 Queen Victoria made an incognito visit, staying at a hostel high on the pass itself and painting several watercolours of the glacier. Today, the smooth and cracked rockfall that spills over from the current tip of the ice flow is a saddening reminder of how much has melted since then.

Sometimes, looking upon the past century of warming as it's immortalised so vividly in the ice and rock boundaries of the high mountains, it's tremendously easy to imagine a world where there are no glaciers left at all.

The Earth's climate has always changed, of course, as most people know. Eight hundred thousand years ago, for example (as climate change deniers are all too happy to point out), carbon dioxide levels in the atmosphere were similar to what they are now in 2020. "How could that be?" they argue. "There we no cars back then! It's all clearly natural and your science must be wrong."

Alternatively, they pick holes in the scientific consensus by claiming that certain data points or feedback cycles haven't been considered. An obvious example is the fact that green plants will grow more easily with increased carbon dioxide and so help to rebalance the system. Some sceptical voices claim (rather loudly) that such considerations have been ignored.

It would be nice if that were true, however, it turns out that thousands of dedicated scientists working together actually tend to think of most things. Every single example of 'inconvenient data' or 'overlooked' factoids that I've heard of and looked up for myself was, in fact, already accounted for with a robust and thorough explanation.

I asked a good friend of mine who worked for the Met Office his entire career and has since made a hobby of understanding the mathematical complexities of climate science to summarise the situation for me. In his own words:

"Almost all of the Earth's glaciers are retreating. Photos from the 1960's are a clear reminder of how things used to be. The amount of carbon dioxide in the atmosphere has risen inexorably from 280 parts per million before the industrial revolution, and is now approaching 420 ppm. The Earth has warmed by about 1 Celsius since 1970, and sea levels are starting to rise. Perhaps the most worrying thing is the melting of the Arctic sea ice. Satellite pictures each year (at its early September minimum) show an erratic but relentless reduction in area. It seems that within 50 years the Arctic could be ice free in late Summer. And then, without ice to reflect the sunshine, this will mean it's almost impossible to turn back the clock. Like so many climate changes, these impacts tend to build upon themselves, becoming unstoppable.

But these changes are not uniform, they vary over land, sea and mountains. When the Earth's temperature patterns change, then the pressure patterns change. And those new temperature patterns alter the winds and therefore the rainfall distribution. It's a complicated World. When I was born in 1947 there were 2.5 billion people on the planet. We're now closing in on 8 billion. No wonder that when I go back to the field in Kent where I tobogganed as a child, it's very different now. All those houses! Who's to blame? Almost no-one is innocent! And life must go on. We need to be aware of our impact, but without letting it become an obsession or a "life-spoiler".

I accept that's just a single (very well-informed) voice. And I accept that the scientific process can be confusing at best, or abused at worst. I was an academic for a while myself. Yet for those people in the world who still claim it's all a hoax, I mostly just feel sad.

I understand that people don't want it to be true, partly because of the frightening consequences for future generations and partly because nobody likes being forced to make changes. However, I think it's important to bear in mind that most of the people doing this research aren't highly paid heads of public agencies with possible political agendas. In reality this data is being drawn together and amalgamated from hundreds of thousands of separate, otherwise 'normal' people, most of them working long hours on salaries that really don't reflect the decades of learning their jobs require. They do their research because they care about it and they believe in it. The fact that all of that separate, independent data points in one direction matters, and it's worth remembering where the numbers come from when people start calling it a 'conspiracy' by 'bad' people with vested interests.

Apologies, I appear to have climbed up onto a soap box. Don't worry, I'm down again now. After Furka we crossed the 2164 metre Grimsel Pass for a second time, cycling up both sides as we did so (something we hadn't felt capable of years earlier), and then turned west to cross the 2260 metre Susten Pass. Incidentally, taken together the Furka, Grimsel, Susten trio forms a high altitude driving loop that even has its own tourist bus. We didn't want to do that, but with summer stretching out before us like melting tarmac, the promise of dozens of lofty passes to explore began to jump out at us from the colourful lines of our Swiss road map.

The only question, however, was where we might stay? Pretty much every patch of Switzerland is owned by someone and, in the throes of high season, even the most basic campsites were excruciatingly expensive. Rare places like Grimentz aside, unlike France, it wasn't at all clear to us if parking up on the tops of passes was technically permitted, tolerated, or downright illegal? The best we could tell was that the rules and their enforcement varied wildly, leaving us in an uncertain limbo whenever the sun started to set.

Thankfully, most of the passes we crossed did have a hotel, café of gift shop right at the top, many of which allowed parking for a nominal fee. On the totally bare passes, clusters of motorhomes often gathered in the dusky twilight before shooting off early in the morning, though we never felt relaxed doing that. It felt disrespectful to us, in addition to the nagging fear that we'd get a nocturnal knock and a hefty fine. Handing over a few francs to bed down in a private car park was much less worrying. We even spent one night in the private car park of Chinese takeaway after paying them five francs.

Then there were private roads. We found our first just six kilometres away from the apex of the Susten Pass, spotting a narrow black line that wound towards a giant mass of ice labelled on our map as the Steingletscher. Pulling up at an automatic barrier, it turned out that for an access fee of just 6 francs per day, we could basically live at the end of this road for as long as we wanted to. It seemed like too good an opportunity to ignore.

Stepping out of the motorhome at the end of the road, it appeared that we'd found our way into an enormous cradle of ice, snow and rock. All around us were bare walls shooting upwards towards overhanging glacier tongues, their blue-white surfaces pointing down at us like the frozen petals of gargantuan flowers. Even though it was now July, snow was still thick on the ground beyond the parking area, the depth of the valley head having kept out the most punishing of the summer's rays and so allowing this little patch of winter to survive. Since we were totally alone, the only sounds we could hear was the whisper of the breeze and a collection of gently running streams making their way down the mountain before bubbling beneath the snowfields.

It was like a hidden, mountain idyll which, for a brief time at least, belonged only to us. There was a peaceful, soothing energy that infused the scenery, protecting us in its calming embrace as though the entire planet had ceased to exist the moment we ascended into this secret ice garden. Then we let the dogs out.

Throwing open our door they careered out onto the white, slushy surface with absolute and total confidence. I suppose we thought they might draw back, or at least show surprise, but they seemed to draw energy from the crisp coolness. They'd seen a few little snow patches before, but nothing like this football field of slippery whiteness. As the previously virgin snow became a puppy party, we smiled and held each other close as our furry family jinked, leapt, ducked and dodged in an unbroken frenzy of total, unmitigated joy.

After a time, when five bright pink tongues paused momentarily to pant en masse, we joined in, throwing 'magic disappearing toys' (snowballs) into the void and sledging down the gentle slope with dogs cluttered on our laps.

Immersed in our temporary haven, we punctuated our days of hiking and cycling with more intervals of play out on the snow. In cycling terms, the western side of the Susten Pass proved to be amazing. There's really no other word for it. With a vertical cliff face on one side and rolling crags on the other, it was like pedalling through a painting. With glacial outlooks, waterfalls and streams running into mountain lakes on display, it was a climb that I simply didn't want to end.

The eastern side is a little shorter at 'only' 18 km, but with a relentless gradient it was a solid wake up call for our still winter-soft bodies. With most cycling climbs, average gradients are useless, masking lumps and bumps that terrorise thigh muscles, but in this case it was just a straight and punishing ribbon of road. It was also raining that day, smothering the sky with forbidding clouds that worried but excited us as we cycled up into the drizzle. Well, we all get out kicks somehow. Plus, it was a beautiful reminder of the dramatic changes in scenery that can be separated by just a few hundred metres of ridgeline.

We also trekked up to the Tierberglihütte, a high mountain refuge nestled on the brink of the main expanse of the Steingletscher at 2795 metres. Following a series of faded paint markers up the exposed bedrock of the mountain, with protruding ice flows creaking close to the trail, we emerged onto an open plateau to be confronted with a sea of ice that vanished towards the horizon.

Behind us the ground plunged away sharply and dangerously, belying the fact that we'd just followed a genuine waymarked route, while ahead of us the power of so much compressed ice groaned across the air. In reality the Steingletscher is relatively small at 4 kilometres long, but the real beauty came from the shared surprise we experienced as we first saw it together. In a world of ubiquitous data and Google images, the fact we'd only chanced upon this isolated little road in the mountains made everything we'd done from our remote base an unexpected gift.

It's a sadly rare experience in the modern world to be utterly surprised by a new location. It's just so easy and tempting to look everything up first, way beyond the basic facts needed to arrive somewhere safely. But while photographs can heighten the anticipation of an adventure, for me there's nothing quite like the moment that a totally unexpected scene rises up out of the wild horizon. It's like receiving a present from a loved one, not because it's a special occasion but just because they wanted to make you smile.

One by one the passes of Switzerland revealed their untamed treasures to us, both on foot and from the saddle. There was the Klausen Pass (1948 metres), where we spent another magnificent and secluded week living in a kindly landowner's field, parked beside a riverside trail that delighted the dogs constantly. There was the Oberalp Pass (2044 metres), from where we hiked to the source of the Rhine river. The Flüela Pass (2383 metres), where we were terrified by hair-raising reams of cars and motorcyclists revving their way around the Grand Tour of Switzerland. The Bernina Pass (2328 metres), from where we ran right up to the 3207 metre summit of Munt Pers alongside the stunning Diavolezza glacier paradise.

Then there was the Stelvio Pass (2757 metres), the second highest paved road pass in the Alps after the Col de l'Iseran. Starting in the border town of Santa Maria in Switzerland, we cycled for 15 kilometres with a 9.4% average gradient to cross into Italy and reach the top of this epic cycling climb. There are two other ways up Stelvio, both of which start in Italy and that are longer but less steep on average. We didn't know that at the time, however. In fact, we hadn't a clue what we were getting ourselves into.

Battling the oppressive heat of now late July, we ground out one pedal stroke at a time through the lower tree-lined slopes, eventually emerging onto a meandering series of green hillsides that continued rising towards a world of open skies and even hotter temperatures. With no shade to be had, we pushed out the final kilometres in strained silence, sweat dripping from every pore of our bodies and running across our bike frames until, with a final struggle, we arrived into a land of carnival.

Before this day I'd honestly never heard of the Stelvio Pass. It had simply been another uphill road with a promising sign at the bottom of it. I'd never seen images of Giro d'Italia cyclists cutting through six-foot-tall snowdrifts up here. Or the iconic shoelace-like hairpins that decorate the eastern approach. It had all been totally new to us. That's why the sight of thousands of coach, motorbike and car tourists mingling with hundreds of Lycra-clad cyclists was a complete and utter surprise. Hot dog stands and burger vans were crowded with hungry customers (including some of the aforementioned Lycra wearers), while dozens of cluttered tourist stalls were doing a brisk trade in cycling/Swiss/Italian/mountain paraphernalia. You could buy everything from a fluffy St Bernard toy to a Pope-themed snow globe up there.

We stayed for only ten minutes, as long as it took to wait in line for our standard summit photo and eat the bananas that had roasted in our back pockets. Yet while the litter, exhaust fumes and cooking oil floating through the air at the top had tarnished the final moments ever-so-slightly, it couldn't diminish the gratitude that we felt that our bodies could complete such a feat. It was almost four years to the day since we'd tentatively and unexpectedly ridden up to the Col de Valberg. Or four-and-a-half years since we'd said goodbye to each in a hospital. Now we were hunting down pass after pass in the high Swiss Alps, revelling in the pulse-pounding simplicity that could be enjoyed by two wheels, two legs and two hearts working together.

Other passes continued to rise and fall beneath our various wheels, paws and feet. For a while we felt invincible, alive and invigorated every day by the ever-changing scenery and the apparently retreating limits of our bodies. It honestly felt like it could go on forever.

Breakdown

It finally happened, my nightmare scenario. Parked in the deserted car park of an empty supermarket, the dogs panting in the back as the dashboard temperature claimed 42°C outside, and the motorhome simply said 'no'. Actually, what it specifically said was "Gear Unavailable", but the end result was the same. We weren't going anywhere. Not a single millimetre. Damn automatic gearboxes!

Just a couple of days earlier we'd swept through the exclusive resort town of St Moritz, startled by the heaving crowds and boutique fashion stores after several weeks of losing ourselves atop mountain passes. We hadn't hung around, continuing directly south and over the relatively tiddly Maloja Pass at 1815 metres. Scooting alongside a handful of long, blue lakes, we'd crossed the almost unmarked border between Switzerland and Italy before weaving down a series of smooth hairpins that carried us towards the historic town of Chiavenna.

As a pivotal border point, the Romans built several important roads out of 'Clavenna', as they knew it. In fact, the name comes from the Latin word for key, precisely because it sits at the hub of several vital routes. And it was one of those routes we'd travelled here specifically to visit. The modern day Splügenpass (or Passo dello Spluga depending on which country you start in) would be our longest cycle climb of the summer, rising almost 1800 metres over 30 kilometres of challenging ascent. Then our motorhome decided to conk out.

As luck would have it, we'd broken down right at the start of an Italian National holiday, so there was pretty much nothing we could do to change the situation. Our breakdown insurance provider told us they could probably still get us towed to a garage, but since nothing was likely to be open for at least five days we'd be camping on a forecourt for the foreseeable future. With the baking temperatures showing no sign of easing off, that simply wasn't a risk we could take, not with the dogs on board. We'd been coping with the summer heat by staying high and had only come down for the night. We simply couldn't live comfortably at this altitude at this time of year, not without air conditioning anyway.

Thankfully, we'd broken down with our rear end poked beneath the shade of a large tree, just a short walk from a motorhome service point so we could at least empty out toilet cassette. As for the rest, we decided to stay put and hope. We arranged to call the breakdown people back when Italy reopened for business and until then, decided to act as though nothing had happened. It turned out to be one of the best decisions we ever made.

We cycled up the Splügenpass the next day, setting out very early to avoid the most intense heat and be back to let the dogs out long before the motorhome got too hot. Opting for the 'historic route', rather than a longer modern option, for ten terrifying kilometres in the middle of the climb we found ourselves sawing back and forth, ascending along short, vertically-stacked sections of road that seemed to defy gravity as they clung to the smooth cliff-face they'd been hacked into. Up, up, and up we went, following a thread of pot-holed asphalt that was just about wide enough for one-and-a-half cars on the straight sections but only three quarters of a car on the turns.

Every now and then an Italian Jedi Master in a Fiat Punto would graze past us at about two hundred miles an hour (or possibly more), as they participated in a world record attempt to see if they could complete the entire climb with less than four wheels on the floor. All of which would have been stressful enough if we weren't already battling a 9% gradient and a series of worryingly dark tunnel sections (because it's obviously not very masculine to use headlights in the dark).

Still, we made it, and with all of our limbs still attached. After three and half hours of knee-popping fun that left us gazing back into the mountainous heart of Switzerland, I even started to feel grateful that we'd broken down when we had. We hadn't a clue how much a repair would cost, but as we looked back at the land of Toblerone one things was certain. It would have cost a whole lot more if we'd broken down twenty-four hours sooner.

Back at our super-heated box-on-wheels, we discovered another treat in the form of a nearby stretch of sandy path beside a river, a path that lead straight to a small, secluded portion of riverside beach. With the intensity of the afternoon heat essentially shutting down outdoor activity between midday and 6 p.m., it made our lives so much easier that we could stroll just a few hundred metres with the dogs before letting them off the lead to exhaust themselves with play and padding for an hour or so twice a day. The rest of the time they dozed beneath the motorhome. Sometimes we worried that living out their days from such a small home was unfair, but the reality was that they played like mad and slept all day anyway. Having a large space to do that in wouldn't have changed their routine. Nor were they ever left alone for longer than a few hours.

Modern day Chiavenna turned out to be a delightful mix of churches, a ruined mediaeval castle, and tight cobbled streets hemmed in by tall, sun-baked buildings, all tucked up against the larger-scale vertical scenery of the mountains. Between here and Lake Como the valley floor was almost perfectly flat for thirty kilometres, dotted with tiny villages and farms, but at the edges of the flood plain the geography turned sharply upwards towards the bare stone summits that stood like sentinels standing guard over the national boundary.

We wandered through Chiavenna most days during our enforced pause, usually in the evening and always with a pair of dogs in tow. After a month of relative Swiss seclusion it was good for them (and us) to get a brief reminder of what urban life looked like. Like all of the other Italian towns we'd passed through over the years, Chiavenna was like a monument to the past tangled up with modernity. Age-battered buildings housed colourful shops selling all of the trappings of 21st century life, while ornate churches and museums looked on with an air of both pride and sadness. A happy atmosphere filled the streets and not just because of the smiling faces of the many visitors. It ran deeper than that, like an aura of optimism and independence left by the town's frontier heritage.

When the national holiday came to an end, we re-dialled the breakdown company and arranged for our entire lives to be collected on a truck the following morning. We didn't know where we were being taken, or what we'd do when we got there. We didn't know if they'd fix our home quickly or if it would take a while. And we definitely didn't have a clue where we'd stay if we couldn't live in it. Over the course of the extended weekend we'd largely put such concerns out of our minds, preferring to focus on the necessity of the moment, which was something we'd gotten much better at since the dogs arrived. However, as the sun began to set on what was probably our final evening living in a quiet Chiavenna car park, we couldn't completely suppress our intellectual doubts.

"It'll work out" I repeated, trying to convince myself. "It always has in the past. We'll deal with whatever comes up."

"Let's take the gang out for a longer walk" suggested Esther (who was still much better at trusting fate than I was), "we don't know how much time they'll get outside tomorrow".

Down on the now familiar sands by the river we threw sticks and paddled in the refreshing waters that bubbled by, appreciating the coolness that spread throughout our bodies in the still hot evening air. For days now we'd visited this beach and not seen a single other soul. Other dog walkers had used the path to get here, but never come out on the beach itself. That's why it was such a shock when our pack suddenly charged at an Alsatian that had appeared out of the surrounding bushes.

A minute later a small, middle-aged lady appeared, greeting us in Italian at the usual unintelligible speed.

"Parli inglese?" we replied.

"Yes, I'm from Manchester" was the unexpected response in a slight Mancunian accent tinged with Latin flamboyance.

As the team made friends with Blink the dog, who was big enough and confident enough not to mind their relentless attention, we got chatting to Max, who lived in Chiavenna with her Italian husband Giovanni. She'd been living in Italy for more than a decade now, she told us, having moved their lives away from the UK for all of the usual reasons: a chance to slow down; a desire to live more in tune with nature; and to be closer to Gio's family to name a few. And, from the sound of things, it had worked. Max effervesced with a radiant energy and happiness that we couldn't help but enjoy. We were actually sad we hadn't bumped into her sooner so that we might have spent some more time together.

"We'll be moving on tomorrow" we explained, outlining the reasons why. "We haven't a clue where we'll end up."

"Well, I do have a spare house" said Max. "We built a 'granny flat' at the end of the garden for my parents to visit years ago. It's just sat there right now. You can stay there if you need to. Here, take my number."

"Wow. Thank you. That's amazing, and such a huge relief to have that option. Let's hope we don't need to take you up on it though, and they can get us back on our way tomorrow."

We chatted a while longer, enjoying the sense of having a weight lifted from our shoulders as we watched the vivid red sunset, swatting at the sand-flies before we walked back towards our stationary home in the gathering darkness. We might not have known what the morning would bring, but it seemed that life had already stepped in with a solution. How did this keep happening?

A worryingly small flatbed truck pulled up bright and early the next morning, driven by a bouncy little man in immaculate overalls. He didn't speak a word of English, shooing us away with an optimistic smile and a wave of his arms that we interpreted as the global symbol for 'trust me, I'm an expert'. It was either that or 'stand back, this might not work'. I wasn't entirely sure.

As he set about manoeuvring his little yellow vehicle in front of our larger white one and lowering the ramp, I couldn't help but wonder how the hell he was going to achieve his goal. Our motorhome had a long overhang at the back, quite low to the ground. So low, in fact, that we'd occasionally heard it tap against particularly vicious speed bumps. We'd never cracked the moulding, but I was getting the worrying feeling that it was about to happen.

Sure enough, as the motor began reeling in the tow line and dragging our entire world up and onto the tow truck, we watched in horror as the bumper plunged quickly towards the hard asphalt. Thankfully, I also know a bit of universal sign language, so dashed forward using what I believe to be the signal for "Aahhh. Stop. Please. Stop".

The tow truck driver, who didn't seem the least bit phased by the sight of our motorhome's fibreglass rear-end flexing slightly as it pressed against the ground, smiled and waved his hands about to imply that everything was absolutely under control and going according to plan. He then produced several thick planks of wood and some chocks, wedging them under the back wheels before continuing to drag our home upwards. It was fairly obvious that he hadn't noticed the impending snap of fibreglass, but his solution still worked perfectly.

It was just half an hour's drive to the allocated repair centre, an enormous Fiat / Iveco truck garage close to Lake Como, though it felt longer. Hurtling along in standard Italian fashion, we sat in the cab watching with grim fascination as the driver steered with his knees so that he could hold his phone in one hand and wave the other around while he was talking. As far as I could tell, arm-waving was a pre-requisite for speech. We hadn't much clue what he was talking about but I had a feeling it was football. On the back of his truck the most precious elements of our lives were secured in their usual driving positions, totally and utterly helpless as HGVs came barrelling towards us, their wing mirrors at just the right height to take a chunk out of our house.

It was amazing to think that, once upon a time, just a few years earlier, we'd worried about tatty old cameras and taken our steering wheel with us when we left Homer for short periods of time. The dogs' arrival into our world, in addition to our significantly-reduced attachment to the clutter of our lives, made it seem such a silly thing to have done. People mattered. Animals mattered. Being kind mattered. But a few electronic devices really didn't matter at all any more.

Still, we arrived unscathed, proving that worrying really doesn't achieve anything. We walked away this time instead of watching them get our motorhome off the flatbed, only returning after it was parked safe and sound in the cavernous garage. It was only nine in the morning and already the day was well on the way to painfully hot.

The friendly manager of the garage, who spoke a little English, told us there was a park nearby where we could sit and wait with the dogs while they investigated the issue. So that's what we did, passing our morning by sitting in the shade, stroking dogs and not thinking about what might happen to us next. Our hope was that it would be something trivial, that they'd have the required part in stock and that we'd be on our way by teatime. Sadly, it wasn't to be.

"You need a new clutch" the manager told via the magic of Google Translate. "We don't have the part you need and can't get it until at least tomorrow. Then it's a full day for a mechanic to fit, so probably two or three days at best. Sorry."

A calm and relaxed Max collected us, wonderfully true to her word, just an hour later. Climbing into the oven-like interior of her little car with our dogs and two overflowing IKEA bags of stuff, she drove all seven of us back to Chiavenna where she veered off up a side street towards a terrace that overlooked the city.

"Here we are" she said. "That's us up there" as she pointed to a huge three-storey house on one side of the road, "and this will be you".

Crossing the street, she unlocked a small gate and took us down a little flight of stairs to a smart front door. This wasn't something we would have ever imagined when we heard the phrase 'granny flat'. This was a house. There was no other word for it. And not just any house, but a delightfully picturesque house with three storeys and two bedrooms overlooking the extensive flood plain that stretched away south. Beneath us we could see the car park that had been our home, the riverside beach where we'd met Max, countless rooftops, church spires and fields.

"Are you really happy with us staying here? Even with the dogs?" we kept asking incredulously.

"Honestly, it's just sat here doing nothing. And don't worry about being in the way. We have work and things to be getting on with. You just do your own thing and we'll do ours. Stay as long as you like and if you want any fresh veg', we have loads in the garden up top. Come up any time and help yourselves."

"Oh, watch out for scorpions too" she added as she closed the door behind her.

We ended up staying for a week, evicting several bulbous and translucent scorpions while we bathed in the warm glow of gratitude at how taken care of we'd been. Our new clutch arrived slowly and, in the relentless heatwave that was still battering the region, the poor mechanic Sergio tasked with doing the work almost melted. I knew, because they called me after three days to say that the work was finished only to change their minds when I got there. I couldn't be annoyed though, not when I saw Sergio's dejected, grease and sweat-stained face as he started mournfully at our uncooperative engine.

As we whiled away our days overlooking the fertile valley plain and the haphazard rooftops of Chiavenna, we couldn't think of a single thing we could have done to plan a better outcome than this.

Walking Through Paradise

No matter how many times fate intervenes, or how many times plans are made redundant by unforeseen events, it's hard to stop the brain from still planning and processing in the background. Similarly, no matter how mindful a moment can feel, it doesn't mean that the next moment won't be full of racing thoughts and daydreams of elsewhere. That's just the way we're wired. The only factor we can work on is how much attention we pay to that constantly passing traffic.

As the spring of 2019 drew to a close, two complete years had now sailed by with five dogs sharing our motorhome. The adventures we'd all enjoyed had been varied, largely unplanned and wholly rewarding. We'd certainly found that 'feeling' we'd sought out. We knew because we'd seen it in their eyes as much as we had in each other's. Far from hindering our freedom, they'd helped us to appreciate it more. They'd intensified the happiness, not diminished it, a fact we felt grateful for every day.

Still, there had been moments when we'd caught our brains wondering how things might have turned out differently if we'd been able to rehome the pups? Or if Leela hadn't been pregnant? Or even if Esther's dad hadn't insisted on ordering that toastie?

It's incredible how the most innocuous choices and accidents can sometimes have such a huge and lasting impact, even when apparently momentous events often fizzle quickly into obscurity.

Mostly we'd observed such thoughts and then moved on. There are few mental speedbumps that aren't flattened by the sight of a wagging tail. But that didn't mean we couldn't still make changes, if we wanted to. It didn't mean we had to ignore our urge to fly solely in human-tandem again, at least for a while.

That's why, as a new summer loomed once more on life's hazy horizon, we'd come to the conclusion that a few weeks of dog-free time would be rather nice, if we could get it. A month, perhaps, or maybe even a little longer? After two and a half years without a single night away from the team, years that had been filled with dog lead-juggling, bum-fur trimming, six-times-a-day sweeping and nocturnal toilet trips (who could forget the five-dog-diarrhoea incident in Liege), we'd be able to go camping in the mountains again, just as we'd done around Mont Blanc the summer before Leela wagged her way towards us.

As usual, Esther made the practical arrangements while I did the driving. It was incredible to think another winter had flown by already, almost as though the longer we spent as nomads the faster time travelled as well.

After Chiavenna there'd been more Swiss passes, more cycles and more playing with dogs in remote, wild places. Autumn had then faded past among the rolling hills of southern France. The impending reality of Brexit had driven us to seriously consider if it wouldn't be wise for us to legally settle outside of the UK more permanently. Although we'd been moving around for more than five years at that point, our administrative lives remained back in Britain. Perhaps, we wondered, it's time to change that in order to avoid a sudden removal of our freedom to roam.

To settle in France, we quickly learned, would basically require us to rent a house long term and initiate a raft of paperwork and bureaucracy, almost certainly stopping us touring around for the foreseeable future. I could go into a lot more detail but the key point is this: ultimately we decided against it. It was a gut instinct more than anything else.

Giving up our freedom to roam voluntarily, in the moment, to avoid the 'possibility' of losing it in the future just didn't feel right to us. Once upon a time it would have done, making us feel in control of our future. However, time and again our travels had reminded us that things change all the time and that we just couldn't take the future for granted in that way. It was a personal decision for us.

Of course, that decision might still turn out to be non-optimal in hindsight. I'm writing this at a time when nobody knows what the details of Brexit will be, but whatever hindsight might have to say about the issue in a year's time (or longer if the dates change again), it can't change the adventures we've had since deciding not to settle down.

After another Spanish winter we dropped off Bella and Rose with friends close to Perpignan, the same couple who had helped us to find Teddy a home with their son, and continued towards the UK to drop Leela, Pati and George off for a holiday with Esther's parents. Then we legged it quickly south back towards the Swiss mountains.

We'd chosen to start hiking from our beloved Val d'Anniviers partly because we felt comfortable leaving our motorhome there for an indefinite length of time, but mostly because we just knew we'd love whatever happened next. We'd seen enough of Switzerland by now to know what we liked, and what we liked were soaring peaks smothered in glaciers and permanent snowfields. With hundreds of miles of trails threading across the valleys and mountain flanks in all directions, we couldn't think of a better place to start walking. We were right.

Four days later we found ourselves racing a thunderstorm as it blew towards us along the vastness of the Mattertal, the beautiful valley named for its most famous peak, the iconic Matterhorn. Already, since leaving the Val d'Anniviers, we'd camped and hiked higher than we ever had before, getting close to 4000 metres in a world defined by unforgiving ice and stone. Bedding down beside mountain streams at close to 3000 metres altitude after spending our days striding along quiet, lofty trails set against a backdrop of some of Europe's highest summits had felt like a reawakening. With each step the scenery and the challenges had evolved, the terrain demanding that we stay focused only on what we were doing. Food, water and shelter were all that mattered up here, a scenario we adored.

Stumbling through the growing drizzle as the dark clouds swooped ever closer, we chanced upon what appeared to be an abandoned cow shed on a long grassy mound. In itself this was nothing special. We were still over 2000 metres altitude and a thousand metres above the valley floor, staring straight down the barrel of a wet and treacherous descent now that the rain had begun. Half an hour ago we'd been able to see peaks, clouds and blue sky. Now all we could see was a wall of thundering wetness that was slowly eating up everything in its path.

We huddled against each other in the doorway of the building as the first short shower passed through, using a brief dry spell to have a look around. On second thoughts, this definitely wasn't a cow shed. It looked more like a private cabin or storehouse of some kind. Not that it mattered very much since it was also locked.

"I really think we should try the door again" said Esther, just before we gave up and started running downhill. "It just doesn't look like someone's holiday home and there isn't a keyhole. There must be a way of getting inside."

So we looked, armed with a bagful of prestigious university degrees as we tried to work out how to open a knotted wooden door. It took us ten minutes, during which we came up with all sorts of ingenious ideas, some involving trapdoors and hidden ladders. Then we noticed the long stick jutting out of the centre of the door, a stick that had been holding the door shut the whole time.

We pulled it out and stepped inside, discovering the unexpected treasure of a basic, unmanned shelter complete with wooden bunks, foam mattresses and blankets stored in the rafters. There was also a table, a wood-burning stove and a plentiful supply of timber with a sharp axe standing next to it. We'd seen such places in France before, stone or log huts in the wilderness where wanderers can take shelter, but we had no idea that they existed in Switzerland too.

With the next band of dense rain imminent, this was like a dream come true in more ways than one. Many years earlier, even as far back as the first few months of our relationship (seventeen years beforehand!), Esther and I had daydreamed of one day living in a log cabin together in the wilderness. Something small and simple is what we'd imagined, possibly on the edge of a forest or alongside a river. It was a dream that had never been wholly forgotten and, although we'd camped in many such places over the years and even stayed in mountain refuges with other people, we'd never had the luxury of our own little cabin, even just for one night.

"Do you think we can just stay here?" we questioned each other. "It might just be for local shepherds or something?" Around us we could see evidence that the place was often used, with candles, matches, pots and pans, and even some photos pinned to the wall.

"It's a shelter on a mountain at over 2000 metres and there's bad weather coming. Even if someone comes, it's not like we're doing anything 'wrong' by sheltering. That's what these places exist for" I reasoned. "I really hope they don't though."

Manfully lighting the wood burning stove, we discovered a ten year old bag of rice at the back of a cupboard (a relief as we'd run out of food) and set about creating a home for the night. Esther did some stretching in the doorway while I chopped wood and fed the warmth-giving flames. For the next twelve hours we existed inside of our storm-hammered dream come true. Safely protected by the thick wooden walls as lightning flashed and thunder bounced between the cliffs above us, we watched the storm through the windows and then gazed in candlelit wonder at the carvings around us. Chiselled into the fabric of the building were initials and dates spanning the decades, many of them going right back to the 1930's. As darkness fell and a dense mist completely enveloped the cabin, the world outside simply faded away. It was the kind of memory that lasts forever, built on a moment that's over before you know it.

Although we obviously weren't aware of it at the time, for the next month we managed to keep stumbling into entirely different but equally magical moments. Two days after finding the cabin, for example, we sat atop a sharply pointed pinnacle known as the Platthorn at 3345 metres.

I can't even begin to list the countless peaks, glaciers and valleys arrayed before us in that vast world of ice, snow and stone. The entire head of the Mattertal and much more beyond was spread out both above and beneath us. We could see everything from the vapour trails of passing aeroplanes to the wisps of smoke emerging from farmhouse chimneys far below. We could see the glacier we'd just been slipping around on to reach this point and the rockfall at the end of it. We could see the famous Matterhorn, of course, and Monte Rosa, in addition to pretty much every other 3000 metre plus summit on our map.

Being here, so high and removed from the mostly-invisible human busyness far below, was an opportunity to appreciate the entirety of the natural engine that had crafted this amazing, wild landscape. The rain, the snow, the glaciers and the rivers, each had done their part, all existing in their own narrow band of mountainside before transforming into the next.

The fact we also had everything we needed to stay alive slung across our backs made us feel totally free, almost like kings of nowhere, with the earth as a combined throne, feasting table and bed chamber. We were utterly contented. Again, part of us didn't want it to end, but experience had taught us that something else would soon come up to fill our hearts. It might be a smile, a sheep, an outlook, an overheard song, or one of the continued acts of generosity that kept crossing our path. From kindly campsite managers to caring shop owners and motherly refuge managers, it was always the people we encountered who had the capacity to move us the most.

In the weeks ahead we'd scramble across the slopes of the Matterhorn, listen to mountain folk tales, hitchhike for the first time, cross the world's longest pedestrian suspension bridge, take our first ever nude communal sauna, smile at countless marmots and ibex, risk hypothermia crossing into Italy, walk over glaciers, straddle metre-wide ridgelines, and fall ill and recover, always in the shadow of snow-capped mountains.

By the time we'd been trekking for four weeks, we'd hiked for more than three hundred kilometres and ascended close to 25000 metres. We were close to completing a giant loop around the Matterhorn, Monte Rosa and dozens of other peaks in this white-coated summit paradise. It had been an astounding adventure and now we only had a single climb standing in front of us.

The final few hundred metres of height gain required to reach the Cabane de Bertol at 3311 metres involved a long, clawing ascent up a steep and stone-studded glacial ice flow. Strapping on some rented crampons, we scratched and chiselled our way upwards, feeling the unfamiliar but reassuring bite of the points beneath us as we continued to steadily gain height. In front of us the ice rose up close to our faces as we leaned into the climb, but behind us the ground dropped away sharply into a gigantic void of clear Alpine air. We hadn't seen a single other hiker all day long, not even on the dusty lower tracks that had bought us to the foot of this untamed frozen river.

The final challenge came in the form of a series of metal ladders and cables hammered into a fifty metre vertical rock wall. With no safety gear, it would have probably been a sensible choice to turn back at this point. But we didn't. After gaining 1300 metres in height already, we were so close that we could practically taste the view that was surely waiting for us just beyond the pointed ridge above our heads.

Esther went first. Gripping the solid metal rungs and climbing steadily away from the rubble at the foot of the ladder. I started a minute later, pleased to feel the firm solidity of the metal clenched in my gloved hands. Holding my body close to the rungs, I used my legs to step upwards, always keeping three points of contact as I moved.

Ten metres from the ground and I could already feel my legs and arms aching from the effort of the climb. At the same time, I was increasingly aware of my pack pulling me gently but incessantly away from the rock. Fifteen metres up and I suddenly became aware of a new sensation. I was scared. Doing what you're not supposed to do, I looked down, and while part of me thought "this is brilliant, how cool is this?", another part simply said "fucking hell, don't fall!"

I couldn't remember getting vertigo on a mountainside before. I'd seen Esther get it and I'd heard it described by others as an uncontrollable loss of coordination and focus. Not just a fear of heights but a dizziness and weakness that overrides motor control, with very little you can do to stop it. I'd never actually experienced it before, until now. My knees were feeling wobbly, as were my arms. Alarmingly, I found myself helpless as the tingling spread through the rest of my body.

I steeled myself to keep moving, focusing on gripping as tightly with my hands as I could until I arrived at the halfway platform with relief. Esther was already tackling the second, slightly less vertical ladder and I watched her with deep admiration. I'd always been the sure-footed one before. The one who didn't mind heights and could walk next to a yawning chasm as though I was skipping along a pavement in a town centre.

"You're amazing" I called out. "Looking good. Doing great". I didn't mention that I'd got the willies just now. What good would it have done? I'd tell her later, probably.

A few minutes later and it was over. A final series of short metal staircases led away from the top of the ladders, ascending past shuttered windows on the side of the refuge that was our destination. We climbed them together and arrived into a frozen world.

Standing on a square-mesh platform outside of the uppermost floor of the refuge, we could now look straight down between our feet to the surface of a glacier more than a hundred metres directly below us. Allowing our gaze to rise slowly, the ice simply continued and expanded in every single direction until it grew into a sight like nothing we'd ever seen.

With the overcast sky seeming to mirror the scene below, what we were looking at was like an expanse of frozen sea, rising, falling, splitting and merging in one powerful mass of blue-white enormity that completely filled our vision. Our map gave various names for the different sections flowing down from the peaks we could see, but to us it was all one. It totally stopped us in our tracks and, before we could even think of going inside the refuge or looking around the other side, we literally fell back onto a wooden bench and stared open-mouthed at it all.

It took us a while to recover our wits. It was hard to believe how the day was turning out. We'd just climbed a glacier, worn crampons for the first time, scaled a vertical, laddered cliff and now we were, quite literally, hovering above what looked like a mini ice age. I'd sometimes tried to imagine what it must have been like when the many glaciers we'd visited over the years had been a thousand times larger than they remain today. What it would have looked like when they literally filled the valleys that they carved and only intermittent stone spires emerged from the ice. Well, now I'd seen it. Ice that filled the world. Only the tallest peaks were visible above it, including the distant Matterhorn which poked out on the eastern horizon.

It was a moment worthy of being a glorious ending, a final ascent that put the cherry on top of an already marvellous hiking summer, an odyssey of togetherness, wilderness and kindness. We did still have to get back to our motorhome over another smaller pass, but this was this felt like the crescendo of our adventure. Then again, the laws of narrative clearly don't know Esther as well as I do.

Her lust for the great outdoors knows no limit, at least not one we've ever discovered. Just five short, aching days after crossing back into the Val d'Anniviers and hugging our motorhome in a combination of relief and sadness, we set out again. Our second, shorter trek was supposed to be a comparatively peaceful tour. We'd already pushed our boundaries in numerous unexpected and often frightening ways for a month. Now, we told ourselves, it was time to slow down and take things easy with the remainder of our time without the dogs.

That's why the original plan was to follow a guidebook version of the tour of the Vanoise National Park in France. It was only an 11 day route that suggested just 4 – 5 hours of trekking a day, not to mention a lot less altitude variation than we'd just tackled.

What actually happened, as you might expect by now, is that we got carried away. Modifying the route, hopping across the border into Italy and tagging on a high-altitude loop of the adjacent Gran Paradiso National Park, our 'straightforward' little walk turned into an epic fifteen days without a rest. With even more glacier crossings, blizzards, near-endless fields of house-sized boulders, countless ibex and the unexpected company of excellent friends for part of the way, our additional 'easier' jaunt ended up taking us further and higher each day than our month around the Matterhorn had. We covered another 250 kilometres with 15,000 metres of ascent. And spent a night sleeping on the floor of a treehouse.

Yet while I might have grumbled and groaned from time to time, rubbing my bruised hips and collar bones in long-suffering faux-stoicism, the truth was that our six weeks of outdoor exploits was all part of the spell that bought and then held us together for so long. It always had been, ever since we'd first flown into Salzburg with an Interrail ticket, a few hundred pounds of student loan left in the bank and a pair of cheap lilos to sleep on. Travel had always been our connection. That's probably why, when we'd gotten the push, we'd turned travel into our lives, even though we'd never stopped to think about it that way.

When our bruised and battered feet reached our motorhome for the second (and final) time that summer, just days before we were due to collect the dogs from their respective holidays, we had to make a decision. Either we could drive constantly for the next four days, side-by-side in a mad attempt to be in two places at once, or we could split up temporarily.

Initially, when Esther suggested taking her hiking gear on the bus to Perpignan, close to where Bella and Rose were staying, I thought she was stoned on high-altitude mountain air. I couldn't imagine walking another step, especially not on my own with two dogs in tow. But we'd made an agreement a couple of years earlier to be a critical friend for each other. To challenge but also support, and so when Esther turned to me and said "I hear your concerns, but I want to do this. I don't know why but I do. Please support me" I did exactly that.

I dropped Esther off at the bus station in Lyon at 7 a.m. on a sleepy Sunday morning, which was good because driving a motorhome through the centre of Lyon at any other time would have given me an aneurysm. If I'd known we weren't going to see each other for an entire month I might have said something profound. Instead, I said "get out quick before the traffic lights change."

Ahead of me was three thousand kilometres of driving, family visits in the UK and three ginger dogs waiting to be collected (though they didn't know that yet). Ahead of Esther was a six hour bus ride and two more ginger dogs in the south of France.

She ended up trekking solo for a whole extra month, covering 360 kilometres with 20 thousand metres of height gain as she moved across the Pyrenean wilderness with Bella and Rose chasing butterflies alongside her.

Physically it was a new challenge and terrain to explore, but it was mentally where the real new experiences occurred. This was the longest time we'd spent physically apart for years and, especially coming off the back of several intense years with young dogs to care for, finding herself alone in the wild was a significant step change.

Esther likes to say that it was our many experiences walking together that gave her the confidence and ability to do what she did. Personally, I think she always had the confidence and ability, she just forgot sometimes. We always knew that the idea to try a solo adventure lived within her, a 'seed' that had been slowly watered over the years whenever we'd encountered women travelling alone, either in campervans or trekking in the hills. The dog collection requirements and the vast distances we needed to cover now provided a long-awaited opportunity. And, if there's one thing I'd always known, Esther's not one to let an opportunity slip by.

With years of dreams at her back, plus the exceedingly kind support she got from Paul and Caroline who'd been looking after Bella and Rose all summer, just a few days after our hasty goodbye in Lyon Esther was putting her feet on the GR10 trail.

266

"Just start stepping" said Paul, who had been a keen Camino pilgrim many times, "the way will provide what you need". It was a lesson that, in a sense, characterised so many of our travels together, but this was the first time Esther was going to have to take that leap of faith into the unknown by herself (and with two excitable dogs to care for at the same time). And so she started stepping.

Although we couldn't possibly have known it when we parted ways temporarily, we had each ended up in exactly the right place at the right time. Just after I landed in Dover and was about to start driving to Esther's parents, I got a call to say my nana was in hospital. If we'd been rushing to collect dogs at opposite ends of Europe I couldn't have so easily changed my plans and gone up to be with my family, but with Bella and Rose already collected and Esther's parents able to wait a bit longer, that's exactly what I did.

I ended up being in the UK for almost three weeks, lending (and receiving) a helping hand in all sorts of unplanned, unforeseeable ways. Esther, for her part, was crossing the mountains in a constant string of fortuitous, uplifting and generosity-laden encounters. Like a trio of Canterbury Pilgrims, it wasn't so much the mountains but the people she met who defined her time alone with the essentials of survival strapped to her back.

Sticking to our now standard approach of having no plan and no certainty, every time she started to get comfortable, life seemed to add a new difficulty level to overcome. And she did, asking for help and trusting to the people who kept popping up as she hiked.

From hitchhiking in search of resupply shops, being gifted food by passing groups of trekkers, or dancing beneath the stars with families, couples and other solo walkers, she was meeting and engaging with people from all over the world, each with their own inspirational stories to share. They, in turn, told Esther she was an inspiration herself. I knew that already of course, but I'm not sure Esther had ever believed me.

For their part the dogs faced every gradient, rock and butterfly with their usual indomitable spirit. Watching them enjoy and be excited by every curve in the trail and every rustle of the leaves made Esther feel she was walking through a children's story, renewing her own appreciation of the details of nature through their eyes. It was actually getting them to rest that was the bigger challenge.

Some nights Esther slept in the tent on the hillside, though she was mostly able to stay in unmanned refuges, often alone and sometimes with others. Together the 'Terrific Trio' crossed the 2785 metre Pic du Canigou, negotiated boulder fields, rode buses and trains, hitchhiked and stayed in everything from spider-encrusted bunkhouses to smart hotels (where Rose managed to throw up all over the bed!) Through it all Esther faced every challenge with optimism and trust that it would all work out, somehow. And, as a result, it always did.

Choosing Winter

In the end it was the changing weather that bought us back together. With rain hammering down hard in the Pyrenees for the week ahead, Esther completed a mammoth 200 kilometre hitchhike-bus-hitchhike combination that carried her right to the doorstep of the place that we'd arranged to meet.

Reuniting with each other and the dogs after so many weeks in dispersed units was a wonderful moment. Our explorations without the dogs, and even briefly without each other, had been exciting, insightful and inspiring in all manner of ways. Mostly, however, they'd made us appreciate the reunion all the more deeply. In the same way that Esther's favourite colour is 'multicolour', we now knew beyond a shadow of a doubt that our favourite lifestyle was 'varied'. Whether we laid our heads in a tent beneath the stars, a king-size bed in a luxury hotel, or a moving mattress in the back of a motorhome, each base would eventually become tiresome in the end. It was keeping things simple, which subsequently allowed flexibility, that we'd fallen in love with, not one particular way of life.

If that flexibility demanded a reduction in possessions, material comforts, personal space, income security, or even the knowledge of what tomorrow would look like, then so be it. Simplicity was a price we were willing to pay to wake up each day interested in discovering what the hours ahead had in store.

Perhaps that's also why, after five winters traversing the beaches and warm places of Spain and Portugal, we decided to make a different choice this time around. Like many couples, Esther and I have never experienced temperature in remotely the same way. I've always rather liked chilly days, because you can always put more clothes on but there's only so many you can decently take off. Esther, in contrast, is essentially solar powered. Point her at a mountain beneath a hot sun and she can march all day on water and happy thoughts (and maybe a slice of melon).

During the summers that we'd spent in a motorhome, especially since the dogs had joined us, on the many afternoons when it had gotten super-hot, I'd often hidden inside with all of the blinds shut trying not to melt. Esther had always wanted to stay outside and keep exploring. Cycling, running, or even strolling outdoors I could just about cope with, to a point, but too much heat had always overwhelmed me and my ginger genes.

As our sixth nomadic winter approached, we decided it was time to try a new form of variety. Honouring my obviously Eskimo heritage, we decided not to drift south towards the beaches for a change. On reflection, we'd seen sun for perhaps 95% of the past five and a half years and, while that sounds delightful on the face of it, you can have too much of a good thing. Perhaps it's an inbuilt British trigger, but even after so long as nomads we still find it hard to sit still when the sun shines. Bad weather is one of the few (and the best) ways to get us to physically rest, something that was definitely at the forefront of our minds after so much hiking and driving in the past three months.

The idea of resting and reflecting on the previously busy months, instead of continuing to move around, was also partly down to an increasing awareness of the importance of respecting the seasons. Although I was still a reluctant and very infrequent visitor to the yoga mat, Esther had kept up a near-daily practice for almost three years now and was slowly immersing herself in the ancient wisdom teachings that underpin the physical asanas. Working with the cycles of the body and the year was a big part of that, including, as winter approached, taking some time to be a little more introspective.

So, that's what we did, casting around for house-sitting gigs in the south of France. As we soon discovered, there were a handful to be found, all seeking to trade various practical to-do lists and homecare requirements for the rewards of a sturdy roof and a pre-agreed heating budget. Unfortunately, there was nothing that called to us. What we really wanted was to curl up in a nest, draw the curtains and light a fire. We also had ideas for books we wanted to write in addition to some other charity and awareness projects that we'd dreamed up among the Alpine pastures.

Torn between preserving our bank balance and retreating to the beaches after all, or following through on our dream of a quiet winter, we eventually decided to treat ourselves. Investing in our future is how we saw it, respecting what we knew we needed in the knowledge that we'd hit the road more refreshed and invigorated by the new year.

Negotiating a good rental deal on a remote, converted farmhouse about an hour north of the Pyrenees, our emotional reunion took place in the sanctuary of the enclosed front garden. Running towards each other, the tanned, lithe athlete in front of me seemed to exude a whole level of confidence that was infectious, leaving both of us laughing loudly as I spun her around on the grass in front of our new temporary home. Around us, four dogs chased like they'd never been separated.

George, was no longer with us. Not because anything bad had happened to him I hasten to add, quite the opposite in fact. After looking after Leela, Pati and George for almost two months, Esther's parents had asked if he could stay with them for a while longer. It was the exact outcome we'd wanted almost three years earlier, but which for various painful reasons simply hadn't been possible back then.

We'd always thought that George would be a perfect companion for them, with his small size and cheeky but generally docile nature, but as the months had flowed and then Sam had passed away, they'd told us they were too heartbroken to ever consider risking such pain again. However, during the weeks the dogs had been with them, there'd been an uplifting effect. They still missed Sam deeply but having dogs back in their lives had changed their minds. Three was a full-time job for them, but George on his own was perfect.

Driving away from their house without him on board was hard though everyone agreed it was the right decision. George was growing up and going to spread his happiness to a new family, just as Jess and Teddy had done. The fact he was going to live with immediate family helped. It didn't feel like he was really 'going' in the full sense of the word.

After the cleaner arrived to let us in officially, we discovered that the house we'd rented absolutely lived up to the photographs we'd seen. It was a smart and spacious three-bedroom house with high ceilings and a very grand open fireplace in the main room downstairs. Out front, the walled-in garden was the size of a tennis court while out back it opened directly onto fields and abandoned orchards. If it sounds opulent, it was. We'd just spent most of the summer in a tent and so we didn't have especially grand requirements, but this place far exceeded our expectations. Thank goodness for low season prices and the friendly property market in rural France.

On our first night back together we took the dogs out the back to romp across the unfamiliar fields, discovering a landscape that was overflowing with tall corn stalks ripe for harvesting. Standing alongside the rustling plantations beneath a fading red sky, we cinched our jackets up against the chilly breeze and waited for the stars to emerge. Already we knew that we'd done the right thing. Holding hands and listening to birdsong, miles away from anything resembling a big city, we could just feel it.

In the increasingly cold and wet weeks ahead we settled into an entirely new routine, one that suited autumnal French life. Every morning we woke up and steeled ourselves to creep out from beneath the blankets, giving up the nest-like warmth in favour of the bracing cold. Depending on how heavily it was (or had been) raining, we'd wrap up against the near-zero temperatures and set out to jog along the slick trails that wound around the immediate area. As had happened so many times before, with no planning or foreknowledge, we'd stumbled upon an ideal location crammed full of traffic-free walking trails that led basically from our door. Usually with all of the four dogs in tow, we'd shuffle or quickly walk through the sloshing puddles as the pack charged through the woods and copses that hemmed us in. Quite what they were chasing we never knew. I'm not even sure they did.

In the afternoons and evenings we both worked on writing projects, lighting candles to chip away at the blank pages as the nights drew in, with varying degrees of success until, eventually, we'd rekindle the fire. As the logs crackled and spat out their friendly heat, the dogs would curl up around us having now shed the worst of the mud caked into them. Sometimes we'd listen to music or watch a movie. Mostly, however, we just watched the flames.

Once or twice we took longer road trips. In early December, when the sun put in a brief appearance, we drove back down to the Pyrenees for a day. Our specific destination was the Cirque de Gavarnie, a natural colosseum of rock straddling the French-Spanish border within the heart of the Pyrenees National Park. With just a few trails heading in and out, this prodigious 1700 metre tall, 14 kilometre wide wall towers like a giant, geological tsunami. Across the top are a string of giant summits, including Mont Perdu (3352m), Pic du Marboré (3248m) and Taillon

(3144m), all of which stand witness to one of Europe's highest waterfalls, a 413 metre free fall. Or at least they do in summer.

When we arrived, thanks to the recent bad weather, the snow was a foot-deep on the ground and the waterfall was totally replaced by columns of giant icicles. The clear blue skies belied the still sub-zero temperatures up here at over 1000 metres and, as our boots crunched along the ice-bound track towards the foot of the wall, we could feel our noses freezing and the blood racing away from our fingers and toes. It was awesome.

We'd been caught in some bad weather in summer, so we'd been cold, but never in such a delightfully idyllic way. It had been a very long time since we'd seen tree branches bowed with the weight of powder snow. It was like walking in Narnia.

As Christmas approached we hunkered down even further to mirror the quickly shortening days, drawing into ourselves and each other to celebrate together in our own simple way. With the fire burning as our only source of heat, we made gifts for each other, something we hadn't done for years, writing poems and drawing pictures. We weren't exactly cut off from society, but as the days slipped quietly by in the same repetitive pattern of gentle industry, moments of laughter and companionship punctuated the short days and long cold nights. It was easy to imagine this was how the world might have been in another era.

As we'd seen many times in the past six years, provided we were warm, fed and felt safe, everything else was largely decorative. The less we had, the more at peace we felt, that's what our experience of a remote winter was underlining. We'd arranged to stay until early February, but after a while the weeks began to flow together and we largely lost track of the date. The only real sense of time we had was the rising and setting of the sun combined with the appearance (or disappearance) of crops in the fields around us.

To be honest, that was enough. This might have been the first real winter we'd chosen in some time, but it was definitely satisfying a deep urge within us. An urge to sit still, recharge and replenish ourselves. It was rebalancing the scales so that we could more fully appreciate and enjoy whatever was to come next.

Lockdown

"Damn it's cold" I said, jumping up and down on the spot to keep warm as the last of the other cars in the car park vanished.

At 1794 metres on the Col du Pourtalet, the February afternoon sun had been surprisingly powerful, but now it was eleven o'clock at night and the temperature had gone sub-zero. After a day of snow-showing in the remnants of a relatively mild winter's snowfall, it was time for us to pack up and head down the mountain into Spain. Unfortunately, for the first time in six years, we'd also managed to lock ourselves outside in the dark.

We'd already spent over an hour trying to jiggle a bent piece of metal around our habitation door to flick the door latch. I'd waggled the metal around and Esther had called out instructions from her position looking through the window, but even though I'd managed to tickle the latch several times, we were still locked out.

We'd then spent a frustrating half an hour trying to get one of the dogs to press the door release button on the dashboard. I'd lost count of the number of times we'd come home to find our hazard lights flashing (and George asleep on top of the steering wheel), so we knew they could do it by accident. Surely, if we could just get them excited enough, one of them would press the right button for us. Sadly, on this cold, dark night in the mountains, they only looked at us tapping on the window and then went back to sleep.

In the end we had to break in. It was worryingly easy. Two snapped window clips and one flexible lady was all it took to get Esther posted through the bathroom window. The dogs still didn't bother getting up.

Our reasons for heading south were simple. After four deliberate months of long nights and frosty mornings, we were now fully ready for some springtime warmth to thaw out our chilled limbs. We had no particular aim or direction, just a vague intention to pootle past Madrid and maybe revisit Granada. Perhaps we'd go east after that, or west. Or maybe straight back up north. The only timing we had in the backs of our minds was to probably get back to the Pyrenees by April, or May.

Moving back into the motorhome after a summer under canvas and a winter enclosed in bricks was marvellous. The compact simplicity of the space felt new all over again, just like Homer had six years earlier. Everything had a place and there was a place for everything, including our four loving sidekicks and their own handful of worldly possessions.

As per usual, if the dogs even noticed a change it was hard to tell. All winter long, whenever we'd opened the door of the motorhome to fetch something, they'd hopped inside and flopped straight onto their usual chairs. To them, the motorhome and us were their primary constants. It was still their home, even if we occasionally put their baskets elsewhere.

It made us happy to see, but it also highlighted a shift in ourselves. Increasingly of late, even the concept of home was growing vague. Once upon a time the idea of 'home' had been simple. First there had been the family home, then there was the home we'd made together. When that changed from bricks and mortar to plastic, rubber and a diesel engine, home had still remained a 'place', albeit one we could move around.

As the expression goes, 'home is where you hang your hat'. Yet now, six years after starting to release attachments to both places and things, we couldn't think of any object or location that we felt overly attached to. We had happy memories linked to hundreds of places, some of which stood out, but there was no all-star showstopper at the top of the list. Home, to us, if we had to define it, was

277

our bodies and the connections we felt with others. 'Going home' was a feeling available to us anywhere. It was to smile, to hold hands, or to fuss the dogs. Everything else was superficial.

Not that I mean to imply some sort of blissful state of constant contentment. We were still human. Having so little structure and so many options still presented challenges, even after so many years. Our usual pitfall was feeling uncertain and unsettled because our minds began scanning for ways we could tweak our situation, either by moving or changing some other physical aspect of our lives. Pondering like this can be useful, to a point, but much of the time it's a distraction away from the business of enjoying the moment. It was (and always will be) a constant practice to catch such wandering thoughts.

Had it really been six years? As we crossed the Pyrenees again we pointed out familiar landmarks that we remembered from previous crossings. To be honest, they probably didn't even count as landmarks, they were just views and places that had stuck in our minds. A swooping road, a particular cliff-face that resembled a frog, or even a layby where we'd once let a tumble of puppies out to pee. We were driving south along memory motorway.

We were visiting some friends near Velez-Rubio, just outside of the Sierra de María-Los Vélez Natural Park, when the Spanish government announced a raft of lockdown measures. Spain was the second European country after Italy to restrict movement in an attempt to slow the transmission of COVID-19. We'd deliberately stayed offline in the weeks since leaving our winter base, so had only the vaguest notion that a 'worrying virus' had been identified on the other side of the world. It was sad news, of course, but it felt very remote. Then we found out that in less than twelve hours' time Spain was going into lockdown.

Our initial reaction was to say "Oh well, it's only for a fortnight, we'll just stay parked where we are. We can take bike rides, go jogging, walk the dogs and do some more writing. Aren't we lucky that we're in such a nice place?"

But as we read the rules our hearts sank. According to the official guidelines, we'd basically be stuck inside of our motorhome full-time, only allowed outside to walk the dogs within fifty metres. Just because we were enjoying being back in the motorhome didn't mean we wanted to spend twenty-three and a half hours a day inside of it. I mean, who would? We might have grown more relaxed and mindful over the years but we were still human.

Of course, we couldn't know whether or not the local police would enforce the rules vigorously but we decided not to take the risk. We started driving at 4 p.m. on a Sunday afternoon and re-crossed the Pyrenees at 2 a.m. on Monday morning. When we'd crossed the Col du Pourtalet heading southbound the roads were totally clear. Coming back via the same pass less than a month later and we found ourselves crawling through a blizzard in the middle of the night, creeping between three-metre tall snowdrifts that smothered half of the tarmac. Coming at the end of a ten-hour drive, it wasn't the most tranquil crossing.

The following day the French government announced similar measures to those in Spain. All foreign nationals were being advised to go back to their home nation and isolate in their homes if they could.

So where did that leave us? We were foreign nationals in France without a house back in the UK, at least not one we could live in (as it was rented out). At the same time, none of our immediate family or closest friends could take us in since they didn't have the space or were listed in the high risk categories. With the rain lashing against our plastic windows, we sat in the foothills of the French

Pyrenees and wondered where we might ride out this global storm.

Two days later we rolled up that welcoming green driveway tunnel into 'French Heaven' once more. We'd emailed both Gordon and the owner of the farmhouse where we'd once watched the puppies shed their baby-coats and transform into young dogs, asking hopefully if we might ride out the lockdown there for a time. Thankfully, the owner had said yes, telling us where to find a locally held key and asking only that we leave the house clean, do any required DIY and cover the cost of any utilities we used.

Rolling back into the overgrown but familiar garden where the seed of our travelling family had become a sapling, as far as we knew the house had stood empty ever since the previous summer. Parking up on the driveway, the dogs burst forth with all the signs that they knew precisely where they were. As hundreds of millions of people in every continent fought to make their way home across the seas and the skies, we looked out on our new world and wondered, what now? What next?

There had been a time in the middle of winter when we'd mused on what our next summer adventure might be. Our preferred option, provided we could arrange dog holidays again, was a cycle tour of some kind. We'd even quickly sketched out a long route that skirted around the fringes of Europe, but then we'd stopped ourselves. I can't say exactly why but the process of working out any of the details at all didn't feel necessary yet. Something inside of us said "wait a while, don't pour your energy into planning just yet. It's too far off." So we hadn't, instead publishing two travel books and drafting a couple of other manuscripts from our winter nest.

I won't even try and claim that we foresaw a worldwide lockdown that would have scuppered any detailed travel plans. We definitely didn't. I think the best explanation is that we'd experienced enough of both our own and the world's inconsistency by now to know that our lifestyle just didn't seem to cope with long-term arrangements very well. Just as with Brexit, our experience was that planning was okay to a point, but not to the extent it diminished the enjoyment of the moment. We'd been enjoying resting and writing beside the fire, so we'd immersed ourselves more fully in that instead.

It was mid-March when we returned to the rural surroundings of the Gers, two months earlier in the year than we had on our first visit. Accordingly the hedgerows and trees were still almost totally bare, opening up the rolling landscape to reveal brown, ploughed fields and spindly, empty vines still awaiting the first buds of spring. Three years earlier we'd arrived to find a region full of green and fertile abundance. This time around we'd get to watch that world emerge from the rapidly loosening grip of winter.

France's lockdown restrictions dictated, as in most European countries, that all non-essential trips and inter-household socialising cease, that most shops closed and that nearly all outdoor exercise was forbidden. Specifically, we were allowed to be outdoors for just an hour per day, and even then we had to stay within 1 – 2 kilometres of the house. We couldn't go out cycling, for example. We also had to take a paper declaration with us stating which of the permitted activities we were doing in case the police stopped us to ask.

For us, in one of the least densely populated regions of France and with our nearest neighbour hundreds of metres away, social distancing came as standard. It was never going to be worth a gendarme's time to crack down on the scattered farmhouses and muddy trails that ran alongside the undulating vineyards. We still basically stayed within the rules though, seeing it as our social duty. We felt very grateful that we had such a large garden around us and that we could take slightly longer walks without seeing any other people.

It was only on our weekly shopping trips that we were really exposed to any changes, and even then they were minor. Apart from quieter roads and some people wearing masks and gloves, the world around us remained unaltered. We certainly never saw any shortages or panic buying. When we looked online we saw constant and worrying updates about spiking infection rates, food shortage fears and overwhelmed hospitals. When we looked out of the window, however, we just saw nature unfolding at its usual pace. Like so many times before, we seemed to have landed on our feet through very little involvement of our own. As our daily routine quickly reverted to something like our winter agenda, the only big difference were worries about family and vulnerable loved ones. As with so many others, we found the clash between wanting to go and help while simultaneously knowing that we had to stay away (no matter what) to be unsettling.

The other slightly peculiar thing that happened to us was that we acquired a lockdown buddy. Pat walked up the driveway just two days after we arrived, crying tears of gratitude that she'd "made it" and expressing profuse thanks that we could help her out. It was baffling to us as we hadn't a clue who she was at the time.

To cut a long story short, Pat was a retired British lady who'd been living in Australia but had just come back to Europe to tour around in a motorhome. She'd only just started out when the lockdown began, finding herself trapped behind a roadblock in Spain. With no home in the UK to return to, she'd heard about us and the house we were in via a circuitous chain of friends that involved Gordon somewhere.

So she moved onto the driveway, discreetly tucking in by the house and largely keeping to herself in our unexpected little commune. She had a dog, Scrappy-Doo, a

282

happy-faced black-and-white little chap just a bit bigger than our pack members. Within a few days Scrappy was an honorary member of their gang. It was easy to see why he'd won several 'waggiest tail' prizes in his time. At a time when many people were pulling together around the world, we were happy that Pat felt safer staying with us and that we could form a little unit for a time. Just as the owner had extended his generosity to us (despite never having met us in person), his agreement to let Pat in underlined the sense of unity.

As spring continued to slowly gear up as March faded into April, one day the countryside seemed to explode in a sudden flash of blossom and opening buds that turned huge bare trees and thorny hedgelines into soft, green clouds wherever we turned. In the space of less than a week the outlook from the house went from distant and barren to short and lush. All of a sudden nature seemed in a hurry to wake up and get going, right at a time when the human world was still grinding along on life support, literally in many tragic cases.

Surprisingly, six years of nomadic life had prepared us quite well for the most obvious challenges of lockdown life. Spending so much time together, often in a confined space was largely par for the course for us. And it helped having projects (like this very book in fact) to work on as the days blurred together, their passing marked primarily by the emptying of the fridge. Every Saturday we'd restock our grocery clock and start again.

Like many of the friends we spoke to in the first few weeks, with no sense of how long the restrictions could last, everything felt on pause in the early days. We watched a few movies, baked some cakes and reconnected with various people we hadn't spoken to in more than a decade. It was fun, in a sense. Basically, when we first returned to France we put our feet up and waited to see what would happen next. Starting a project or making any sort of plans

283

seemed pointless with no idea how long we might be stationary for, so we watched and waited.

But then, as longer timelines were confirmed and it became clear we were looking at several months of isolated living, we threw ourselves into other things. This book, for example, was written during the lockdown, as were various articles and other manuscripts. Generally speaking, we felt happy getting on, though saddened whenever we were reminded of the cause.

That was our main irritant in lockdown, a feeling of helplessness. We knew that we'd caught a lucky break in ending up back in the Gers, a safe and beautiful place to be isolated and there was some guilt attached to that. Intellectually we knew that staying home was the best way we could help, but there was still the nagging feeling that if we weren't quite so isolated we could do something more, either for vulnerable family members or at hospitals etc.

That's why, in mid-April, inspired by professional cyclist Geraint Thomas, Esther spontaneously decided to take on her own fundraiser for NHS Charities Together. You already know a little of the deep and lasting impact that the NHS has made on our lives. Everyone's entitled to their opinion on the NHS when it comes to waiting times, bureaucracy and inefficiency regarding non-critical care, but in an emergency our experience has been that they (the nurses and doctors on the front line) are amazing.

It was on a Saturday evening that I read an article about Geraint raising three hundred and fifty thousand pounds after riding his stationary bike for 12 hours a day, three days in a row, matching a nurse's shift patterns. Just like her idea to walk across the Pyrenees, Esther told me that she didn't know why she wanted to do the same challenge, but she just had a feeling. After her solo trek she'd become more confident not to question such instincts and just act, so before she could talk herself out of it she asked me to set up the bike ready for the next day.

The very next morning, at half past seven, Esther climbed onto the saddle of her own bike mounted on our turbo trainer to do exactly the same thing.

Apart from a handful of sub-60 second comfort breaks, she pedalled right through until half past seven that evening without stopping, maintaining a robust and steady heart rate of around 130 the whole way through. She did the same thing again the next day and again the day after that. A total of 36 hours of riding on the turbo trainer completed in just 60 hours. There had been no prior planning or worrying, she just did it. She was amazing.

Right from the outset support started coming in from online. Despite a flaky internet connection and dubious social media awareness, I managed to get a live feed on Facebook so that friends and family could tune in and say hello. Then it started to spread. On the morning of the third and final day, Esther was interviewed on BBC Radio Tees. A few hours later Team RH, a North-East fitness company run by the effervescent Richie and Rachael, pledged £1000 if the feed was shared 1000 times. That's when the sparks really started to fly.

Esther raised just under £5000 by the end of the challenge. I was so proud of her I could have cried. All day long she pedalled and smiled, waving at the people watching and answering their questions. It was in the evenings, when the session ended and I cut the live feed, that I saw the pain. At the end of the second day she could hardly walk and had bleeding blisters in places where blisters should never be. But she did it, something I know I could never do. She told me that her most motivating thought was the fact that healthcare workers couldn't stop working just because their backs and feet hurt, and nor could those people suffering in hospital beds get up and walk away. That's what inspired her to keep going, in addition to seeing so many people coming together for a greater cause.

In a bizarre way, after a few months of lockdown life, we began to find our lack of immediate options freeing. There was initial resistance, naturally, we're only human. But as the scent of blossom filled the air, the skies emptied of planes and we watched bees flitting between the flowers, we realised that we rarely took this amount of time to just watch. Sure, we'd become more mindful in recent years and were better at not resisting the unexpected than we used to, but we could still see plenty of elements of our lives that were 'non-essential'. Apart from the few weeks we'd spent in Spain, with our winter stay combined with the open-ended lockdown, we realised this was basically the longest time we'd stayed in the same area for six years.

And, like everyone else, we hadn't a clue how long it would last for.

Epilogue

The easing of lockdown restrictions slammed into our isolated little world like a tidal wave, welcome and frightening in equal measure. The blessed simplicity of having options removed, once we'd relaxed into it, had been comforting in its way. Our days had been filled with creative projects, exercise, yoga, dogs, the practicalities of life and the incessant march of summer. Temperatures had climbed, DIY work had been done and at least half a dozen semi-completed projects were floating around our laptops. And then the world started to re-open.

In theory the lockdown measures were eased gradually, but the reality on the ground looked like a switch had been thrown. "Stay Home, Stay Safe" had been unequivocal, while "Be Careful" left the door open for all manner of interpretations. As the economic world rushed to reactivate spending and the media painted a dividing line in society between those who thought it reckless to reopen and those who believed that continued restrictions were the actions of a police state, we still looked out on a physical world that was unchanged. By now the cherries had been and gone, the mulberries were just turning ripe and the sunflowers were getting taller every day.

Not that we were immune to the confusion. The sudden change threw us out as well, leaving us with half-finished projects and decisions to make, decisions that hadn't existed the previous week. Our old friends 'Where', 'When' and 'How' had abruptly re-emerged into our lives and, to be honest, it took us a while to adjust to their return. Then we realised that we'd just have to do what we'd been doing for the past six years, one thing at a time and let whatever came next take care of itself.

Truth is, as I finish this book, I don't have a clue what we're going to do next. In just a few days' time it looks like restrictions will ease further and we'll be able to start touring again. Where we'll go, I don't know? Whether we'll hike or cycle, I can't say? Whether there'll be another lockdown that turns the world upside down again in the next few months, who knows? Perhaps you do know because you're reading this years later, in which case, I hope it all turned out well. Uncertainty is simply an unavoidable part of life, even though we used to like pretending it wasn't.

Speaking of uncertainty and life, I suppose this is the part of the book where I summarise a bunch of life lessons drawn out of our travels and offer them up as a takeaway message. But I don't really want to do that.

Partly I don't want to since any life lessons we've experienced regarding living simply, decluttering, letting go of expectations and not planning too far ahead are (I hope) already fairly obvious by now. Mostly, however, I don't want to do it because everyone is different. Just because we did something doesn't make it an option for everybody else. It might be, but it might not. Everybody walks their own path. My deepest wish is that everyone finds a way of filling their path with love and smiles, and that they can share those gifts with the world.

For the past few weeks I've sat in an attic room overlooking an increasingly green garden hitting a keyboard, trying to work out which of our stories to tell you and which ones there just isn't space for. There's so much that's fallen by the wayside, so much richness and life that hasn't quite made the cut. As you might imagine, it's been hard to sift through our thousands of both happy and challenging memories.

But now, I hope and believe, these words at least capture something of the essence our travels, for that's all a story can ever really capture. Life is written one moment at a time, by people who are constantly changing in a world that doesn't stand still. Truth is, we're not the same people who bought Homer. We're not the same people who adopted Leela. I'm not the same man who started this book. I'm not the same man who was rushed into a hospital to be cut open without anaesthetic. And I'm definitely not the same young man who once threw a pear off a roof, which is where this story began if you can remember that far back.

In short, change happens, all the time, everywhere. And yet, being in control of one's destiny, job, or future finances is a nearly unquestionable ambition in Western society. The popular phrase "take control of your life" even sounds grown-up and spiritual. It's the fundamental message of thousands of self-help books and millions of internet memes.

And why not? For practical matters it's good to know when bills need paying, when shops close and how much detergent to put in the washing machine. These are things we can (usually) control. But on a broader level, we're clearly not in control, as the recent pandemic has shown many people. Our destinies and the destinies of those we love are actually tied up with everybody else's, which are further enmeshed with an infinite number of intangibles that simply can't be predicted. We might know when to catch a bus, but we can't know exactly when a recession will happen, when we might get sick or when a volcano's going to erupt. Hindsight sometimes makes it look like we're better at predicting such occurrences than we really are.

I realise that I'm just stating the obvious right now, but I'm doing it for a reason. Increasingly I find myself looking back across the years at the man I was and remembering how he faced these sorts of worries and challenges. As far as I recall, he faced them by worrying even more. He faced them by trying to exert even more control over the future, usually by limiting his life choices and by always expecting the worst, both of the world and of other people. He faced fear by being fearful. By clinging to what he knew and closing his mind to the unfamiliar.

As you might imagine, I no longer consider that to be an effective strategy for a happy life. It's far better to wake up with an open mind and ask "What adventures shall we have today?" It's a constant practice to embrace the uncertainty of each new morning with an open mind. In many ways, the emotional and mental journey we're on has grown to be even more exciting and important than the physical one.

Nor is it a journey that will ever be completed.

Thank You

Wow! Thank you so much for staying with us right until the end. You've crossed mountains, swum in the sea, tunnelled into pyramids, raised puppies and crash-landed hot air balloons with us, not to mention a bunch of other unexpected activities as well. I really hope that you've enjoyed this journey as much as we did.

If you have, please take a moment to review this book on Amazon. Reviews like yours are the absolute best way for independent authors (like me) to reach new readers. Without your support the chance of this book reaching new readers is massively reduced.

Thank you so much for your time.

Finally, if you want to find out what we did next or where we are now, you can find us in one of these places.

Happy adventures.

www.estheranddan.com

www.instagram.com/estheranddan

www.facebook.com/estheranddan

Acknowledgements

The process of writing a book is an uncertain process. Getting from a blank page to a finished manuscript involves many steps, few of which are clear at the outset. What will I say? What should I include? What shouldn't I include? And, most uncertain of all, how long will it take?

I may have been cocooned in a room by myself for the past couple of months, banging letters like a crazy monkey in an attempt to put them in some sort of order, but the business of life didn't stop in the background.

Just because these words are written in my voice, with the many mistakes and peculiarities that entails (all of which are my fault, despite my friend Richard's best efforts at pointing out my frequent typos), if it wasn't for Esther then this book simply couldn't have been written. Not a word of it.

It takes a lot of love to work on a project like this with a life partner. Not only did Esther look after pretty much every other aspect of our lives while I hid behind a laptop, her memory, reflections, edits, suggestions and constant creative input have made this text far more than it otherwise would have been. In every way that counts, this book is a joint production from the two of us.

Thank you, I love you.

Dan Colegate – June 2020

Photos

1 – Homer and us on a Durham driveway, minutes before we drove south for the first time.

2 – Looking over the Moiry Glacier in the Val d'Anniviers

3 – Obligatory summit photo on the Cime de la Bonette (2802 metres) with our heavy townbikes, the highest point ever crossed by the Tour de France.

4 – Looking out of the Mediterranean Sea from Playa de Monsul, Cabo de Gata Natural Park (this beach was a filming location in Indiana Jones and the Last Crusade)

5 – Ceillac's festival of everything that flies flies "in the air and in the wind" – not sure how this chap made the cut?

6 – Farming!

7 – Homer on top of the world – Grimselpass, Switzerland.

8 – Esther, a dusty old relic, and a pyramid.

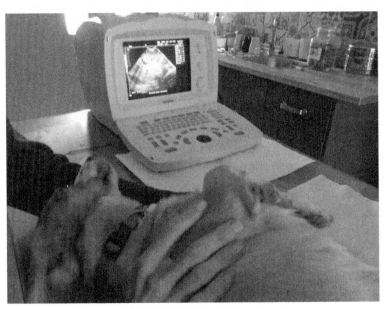

9 – Uh-oh.

10 – Trekking around the Matterhorn

11 – Life, as we know it, has changed.

12 – Touring with the team on board.

13 – Everything that matters is in that box.

14 – In the end, I suppose there's only one destination.

These are just a few images from many (many) thousands. For more photos from our adventures, visit our website at **www.estheranddan.com** or our Instagram page **www.instagram.com/estheranddan**

Also By The Author

Turn Left At Mont Blanc: Hiking The TMB

Book one in the Alpine Thru-hiking series is a hiking story that makes you want to dust off your boots and head straight to the nearest mountains.

From one stunning viewpoint to another, from valley to col, from acts of random kindness to moments of unbelievable fortune, this was an adventure that pushed them to the limits of their bodies, their relationship and forced them to face up to some of their deepest fears.

Written in a light-hearted but direct manner, this is a funny, inspiring and brutally honest account of what it was like to head into the mountains unprepared, under-planned and over-geared and come out on the other side with a whole new outlook on life.

Available on Amazon now.

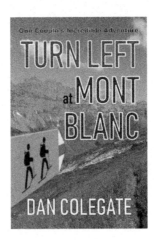

Just Around The Matterhorn

Book two in the Alpine thru-hiking series. Lose yourself in the heart of the Alps, in the shadow of Europe's most iconic mountain.

Starting in the beautiful heart of the high Swiss Alps, Dan & Esther decide to try the Tour of the Matterhorn, a loop around Europe's most iconic mountain. But with no fixed itinerary or timeframe, they find themselves taking a somewhat different route as they hike and camp higher than they've ever been before.

Having started out determined to "take it easy", they instead find themselves pushing their boundaries across glaciers, precipitous ridges and vertical laddered cliffs while also battling illness and at times being hardly able to eat. Yet through the kindness of strangers, the inspirational people they meet and by leaning on each other when the going gets tough, a challenge that could have been a step too far instead becomes the adventure of a lifetime.

Available on Amazon now.

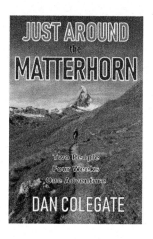

Walking Through Paradise

Book three in the Alpine thru-hiking series takes you on a magnificent journey through Western Europe's largest nature reserve.

Just five days after their demanding four-week adventure around the Matterhorn, Esther and Dan set out into the wilderness once again. Their goal is simple, to enjoy a peaceful walking holiday in the Alps. However, as usual, the moment their shoes hit the trail their plans go straight out of the window and the adventure takes on a life of its own.

Driven by an inexplicable thirst to always look beyond the next summit, their initially sedate hike from refuge-to-refuge soon becomes an expedition across blizzard-ridden 3000-metre passes, tumultuous boulder fields and snow-packed glaciers, turning each day into a unique pilgrimage through some of the most remote and stunning Alpine scenery they've ever seen.

A perfect book for anyone who wants to experience the awe-inspiring magic of Europe's most beautiful wilderness.

Available on Amazon now.

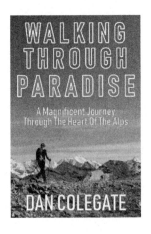

Love, Fluff & Chasing Butterflies

Illustrated dog poems inspired by an amazing true story.

Love, Fluff & Chasing Butterflies is a glorious celebration of an amazing true story that underlines the special bond which can exist between dogs and their humans.

It was while touring through Europe in a motorhome that Dan & Esther decided to adopt Leela, an abandoned dog on the south coast of Spain. What they never expected was that just two weeks later Leela would give birth to six puppies!

What came next was a story of love triumphing over circumstance as they turned their lives upside down to care for the pups, ultimately taking to the road with five dogs in a motorhome.

Love, Fluff & Chasing Butterflies is a collection of uplifting, insightful and honest poems inspired by their experiences together.

Available on Amazon now.

dog poems inspired by an amazing true story

love,
fluff &
chasing
butterflies
DAN COLEGATE

Where Are We Now

Poems For When You're Feeling Lost

Perfect words to create a quiet moment, wherever you are. Inspired by six years of nomadic adventures through Europe, this collection of 49 poems focuses on the 'little' things that affect us all, such as life, love, death, telling the truth, and what are we all doing here in the first place?

If you've ever felt lost, these poems are intended to help steer you back.

Available on Amazon now.

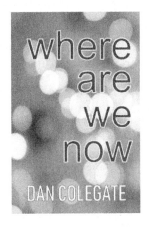

Printed in Great Britain
by Amazon

51813021R00180